About Pfeiffer

Pfeiffer serves the professional development and hands-on resource needs of training and human resource practitioners and gives them products to do their jobs better. We deliver proven ideas and solutions from experts in HR development and HR management, and we offer effective and customizable tools to improve workplace performance. From novice to seasoned professional, Pfeiffer is the source you can trust to make yourself and your organization more successful.

Essential Knowledge Pfeiffer produces insightful, practical, and comprehensive materials on topics that matter the most to training and HR professionals. Our Essential Knowledge resources translate the expertise of seasoned professionals into practical, how-to guidance on critical workplace issues and problems. These resources are supported by case studies, worksheets, and job aids and are frequently supplemented with CD-ROMs, websites, and other means of making the content easier to read, understand, and use.

Essential Tools Pfeiffer's Essential Tools resources save time and expense by offering proven, ready-to-use materials—including exercises, activities, games, instruments, and assessments—for use during a training or team-learning event. These resources are frequently offered in looseleaf or CD-ROM format to facilitate copying and customization of the material.

Pfeiffer also recognizes the remarkable power of new technologies in expanding the reach and effectiveness of training. While e-hype has often created whizbang solutions in search of a problem, we are dedicated to bringing convenience and enhancements to proven training solutions. All our e-tools comply with rigorous functionality standards. The most appropriate technology wrapped around essential content yields the perfect solution for today's on-the-go trainers and human resource professionals.

Pfeiffer
www.pfeiffer.com   *Essential resources for training and HR professionals*

For Shane and Thad,
thanks for energizing me.

—Elaine Biech

Trainer's Warehouse Book of Games

Fun and Energizing Ways to Enhance Learning

Elaine Biech

Editor

Pfeiffer
A Wiley Imprint
www.pfeiffer.com

Published by Pfeiffer
An Imprint of Wiley
989 Market Street, San Francisco, CA 94103-1741
www.pfeiffer.com

For additional copies/bulk purchases of this book in the U.S. please contact 800-274-4434.

Pfeiffer books and products are available through most bookstores. To contact Pfeiffer directly call our Customer Care Department within the U.S. at 800-274-4434, outside the U.S. at 317-572-3985, fax 317-572-4002, or visit www.pfeiffer.com.

Pfeiffer also publishes its books in a variety of electronic formats. Some content that appears in print may not be available in electronic books.

Library of Congress Cataloging-in-Publication Data

Trainer's Warehouse book of games : fun and energizing ways to enhance learning / Elaine Biech, editor.
　　 p.　cm.
　　Includes bibliographical references.
　　ISBN 978-0-7879-9092-3 (pbk.)
　　　　 1. Employees—Training of.　 2. Organizational learning.　 3. Experiential learning.　 4. Educational games.　 5. Group games.　 I. Biech, Elaine.　 II. Trainer's Warehouse (Firm)
　　HF5549.5.T7T6636 2008
　　658.3'124—dc22

　　　　　　　　　　　　　　　　　　　　　　　　　　　　　　　　　　　　 2007049560

Acquiring Editor: Martin Delahoussaye
Director of Development: Kathleen Dolan Davies
Development Editor: Susan Rachmeler
Production Editor: Dawn Kilgore

Editor: Rebecca Taff
Editorial Assistant: Marisa Kelley
Manufacturing Supervisor: Becky Morgan

Printed in the United States of America

Printing　10 9 8 7 6 5 4 3 2 1

Contents

Contents   **ix**

Contents   **xiii**

Preface

Who'd have thought that a father-daughter team, a Williams College physicist and a Yale graduate, would manage a catalog company that strives to bring fun and inspiration to trainers, facilitators, educators, and presenters? Trainer's Warehouse's mission is to be a full resource of hard-to-find and innovative products that do just that.

In 1994, Michael Doctoroff left a secure job and began making picture frames in his basement, and Office Images, Inc., was born. Orders for one to twenty-five frames for office cubicles arrived weekly. One day, two orders arrived, each requesting over five hundred frames. To his surprise, Mike learned that both buyers intended to use the frames for training certificates. Within months, Mike renamed the company Trainer's Warehouse and committed to finding and creating products that enabled trainers to do their jobs better.

Susan Doctoroff Landay joined the company in 1997. Her experience in training and marketing and as a Ringling clown provides a solid background for the Trainer's Warehouse strategy. The company's first twelve-page two-color catalog featured thirty items. Today, the full-color catalog has multiplied in size and offers over 350 products, including more than one hundred exclusive items.

Many trainers, educators, consultants, and presenters depend on Trainer's Warehouse to supply them with creative as well as practical, exciting as well as useful tools, props, materials, and, yes, toys to "entertrain" their participants.

This book features learning activities used by many of the company's satisfied customers. Here's what you'll find in the book's three sections.

- Section One serves as an introduction to the activities. One chapter shares some insight into activities and learning offering some great debriefing questions for any game or learning activity. The second chapter sets the stage and creates an environment of fun and experiential learning.
- Section Two focuses on Training Techniques. Every trainer and educator who has a need for a new and different icebreaker or energizer, searches for better ways to ensure participation and retention, and wants creative ways to review material and close sessions, will find ideas here.
- Section Three provides a collection of activities geared toward specific workshop topics using the many items found in the Trainer's Warehouse catalog. Topics are in alphabetical order and range from Change Management to Teamwork and Team Building.

Already own a number of Trainer's Warehouse items? Looking for new ways to use them? The Trainer's Warehouse Materials list at the end of the book will lead you to other techniques to use with the same items. Additionally, at the back of the book, there is a grid of Primary and Alternative Uses for Activities, so you can see how some of your favorites might be applied to other topical areas.

Like the Trainer's Warehouse mission, this book will bring ideas, fun, and inspiration to trainers, facilitators, educators, and presenters. Enjoy!

Appreciation

Thanks to the contributors who have added substance and functionality. Your constructive contributions have produced a work that will be appreciated by your colleagues.

Susan Landay and Michael Doctoroff, thank you for entrusting me with your resource-rich catalog and loyal customers. Here's another product for your creative catalog.

Martin Delahoussaye, editor, thank you for another inspirational idea for the profession.

Lorraine Kohart, ebb associates inc, this is more your book than mine. Thanks for your extraordinary effort, persistent prodding, and your fresh focus.

Dan Greene, thanks for your steady support.

Susan Rachmeler, developmental editor, thank you for your practical ideas and your uncommonly common sense.

Section 1

What's Ahead

This section introduces Trainer's Warehouse and presents the purpose of this book.

The section helps you set the stage and create an environment conducive to experiential learning and introduces the concept of using fun when learning.

It also offers several key background tips so that you can be successful in introducing, conducting, and debriefing an exercise.

Chapter 1

Experiencing Learning: The Whys and Hows of Involving Participants

Training and developing others is one of the most exciting and rewarding jobs anyone can have. You can affect the lives and work of many people, and influence individuals abilities to be successful, while at the same time have a significant role in increasing your company's bottom line.

This chapter introduces you to a couple of concepts that will ensure your success as a trainer. It acquaints you with the concept of experiential learning activities, sometimes called ELAs. It also provides several tactics for working with participants who believe they are "too serious" to have fun while they are learning.

Using Experiential Learning Activities

Experiential learning happens when a learner participates in an activity, processes the activity, identifies useful skills or knowledge, and transfers the learning to the workplace or life in general. ELAs attempt to imitate daily life experiences. Participants "experience" what they learn before processing or discussing the activity.

To be successful, ELAs must have all of the following characteristics:

- Have a structure, including specific steps and a process that will lead to anticipated results
- Focus on a specific goal
- Incorporate a high level of participation

- Provide concepts, information, and data for participants to review and analyze
- Require processing or debriefing so that participants can uncover the learning that occurred

The Experiential Learning Cycle (*Reference Guide,* 1999) identifies five required steps of experiential learning activities: experiencing, publishing, processing, generalizing, and applying.

Step 1, Experiencing. Participants complete a defined task, often using props, toys, and materials such as those from Trainer's Warehouse. The activity may be associated with a game or fun. If the process ends here, learning is left to chance. Therefore the trainer or facilitator leads the participants through a series of questions.

Step 2, Publishing. Participants share their observations of what happened during the activity. Generally the trainer or facilitator guides the discussion with carefully crafted questions. Participants have an opportunity to share what they observed and experienced and how it felt. The trainer usually begins with a broad question such as, "What happened?" and then focuses on the more specific questions that lead participants to the learning outcome for the specific activity.

Give participants an opportunity to share observations. You may begin with broad questions and then focus on more specific concepts. Here are some examples:

- What happened?
- What did you observe?
- What helped or hindered the process?
- What results did you see?
- Did anything surprise you? What and why?
- How do you feel about what happened?

Step 3, Processing. Participants have an opportunity to discuss the dynamics and results of the activity. In some cases observers may also be used to help define what occurred. This step helps participants interpret why something happened.

The key here is to allow participants to discover this for themselves, avoiding your desire to "tell" them why. Ask questions such as these:

- Why do you suppose that occurred?
- What did you learn about yourself? About others?
- What can you glean from this activity?
- What principles might be true based on your experience?

Step 4, Generalizing. This step helps participants connect what they learned to real life. It uses questions to help participants identify why what they are learning is important. It uncovers the "so what" related to the activity. The following questions may be used to help participants connect their experiences to real-life situations:

- How does this relate to your situation?
- What does this suggest to you?
- What patterns and similarities come to mind? Are there exceptions?
- How does this experience help you understand others like it?
- What if . . .?

Step 5, Applying. To be most effective, an ELA must allow participants to plan effective change based on what they learned during the activity. This step requires that participants move from "so what?" to "now what?" Trainers assist learners to apply what they learned to real-life situations at work or in their personal lives. Participants may establish goals, contract for change, make promises, identify potential workplace changes, or initiate other actions that result from their experience.

By this point, participants will have a greater understanding of the purpose of the activity. Facilitate a discussion about how they will apply their learning back at the workplace or in their personal lives. This application step brings closure to the activity. Questions such as these will get at the answer to the question "now what?"

- What will you do differently as a result of this experience?
- How will you transfer your knowledge and skills to the workplace?
- How and when will you apply your learning?
- How will this help you be more effective in the future?
- What support would make this change easier to implement?
- What's next?

Your role is to help participants discover the learning from what they have completed. Remember that your task is not to tell them, not to assign your learning on them, but—through a series of questions—to help them uncover the lesson themselves. The lesson they need to learn may not be the lesson you want to teach. This is called experiential learning.

Note: As you gather the group's feedback, record the answers on a flip chart so you can refer to them or perhaps even distribute important learning points later.

Every trainer should be skilled in using experiential learning activities. It is a powerful tool that turns fun into action, games into skills. All of the activities in this book are not formal ELAs. However, it is important to note that the activities that qualify as ELAs will likely require more attention and processing than others.

Working with Serious Participants

Many trainers, consultants, facilitators, teachers, and others in the field of workplace learning and performance fully embrace the concepts of fun and interactive training to accelerate the learning process. Others pass up the opportunity to use props and toys such as those found in the Trainer's Warehouse catalog and lament, "I wish I could use your 'toys,' but I teach engineers (or accountants or bankers or doctors) and they're too serious for that."

This comment heard by Trainer's Warehouse, was so prevalent that they wondered whether new teaching theory was required for these serious-type learners or whether trainers and facilitators simply needed new language and tools to sell the concept of playful learning to these serious learners, while still maintaining their credibility and professionalism. At the same time, Trainer's Warehouse had heard hundreds of testimonials about how using reinforcement games, fiddles, and other playful toys creates positive energy in the classroom, improves retention within the learning environment, and translates into greater productivity outside the classroom. So the question was, how to help all trainers to experience the same success, whether their participants were "serious" or not.

Susan Doctoroff Landay, company president, uses an approach developed by Roger Fisher, author of *Getting to Yes,* to help trainers and facilitators be more successful. She has identified several tactics that can help you convert serious and skeptical students to active and laughing learners. These tips might prove helpful to gain buy-in from skeptical learners.

Tactic 1: Be Open About Your Interests and Theirs Right from the start

Don't wait until the end of an exercise to address participants' concerns and goals. Instead, lead your group into an activity by articulating both their concerns and your interests. You might say, for instance, "I understand you may be a bit skeptical about my crazy games and toys. In fact, if you're like others I've taught, here are some of the thoughts that might be in your head." Read from the column of Participant's Interests and Concerns in Table 1.1. Then ask, "Before I go on, do you have other thoughts you'd like to share with the class and me?"

It is important to start with *the participants'* perspective. Once they feel heard and understood, they'll be more likely to listen to an alternative perspective. After they have expressed their concerns, list some of your interests and concerns.

Table 1.1. Interests and Concerns

Participant's Interests and Concerns	Trainer's Interests and Concerns
This is a waste of time.	Need to prove success to managers
I don't want to embarrass myself.	Learning needs to be fun to be successful.
This is beneath me.	I don't want to look stupid.
I'm smart; just tell me what I need to know and I'll remember it. I don't need stupid games.	They're smart. . . . I don't have all the answers, but I can help them share their learning.
I have other, more important things to do.	The organization has spent a lot just to get people into training—it has a purpose.
I won't learn anything. This trainer has never done my job, so what can she add?	When people experience emotion, the learning is memorable.
I won't learn anything new.	If all I do is lecture, nobody will remember anything.

Tactic 2: Allow Participants to Experience Control

Allow participants to feel some control and involvement in selecting the teaching method. This doesn't mean that you will need to redesign the training session. When offered options, chances are high that the group will select the same things you did. Their participation in the selection process means they'll more readily buy into the creative teaching methods, without you having to "sell" the idea.

You might say something like this: "I've given a lot of thought to the format of the session, but think that input from a group like you could be extremely valuable. Let me share some of the components, then you can add to the list. Let's brainstorm a list first and then decide what to do. If we take five minutes to get a solid start, it will make the entire session more successful. Here are some options I've thought of:

- Lecture
- Role play
- Simulation games
- Q&A sessions
- Working in small groups"

At this point, invite the group to continue adding to the list, with suggestions such as:

- Senior employees help junior employees
- Junior employees help senior employees
- Use magic tricks
- Tell content-related jokes
- Play some music

Tactic 3: Use External Standards or Criteria to Choose Among the Options

Identify third-party assistance or some "blue book" standard to add support to the decision. You may wish to share some of these data points with participants and invite them to supplement with their own experiences.

- Retention can increase up to 800 percent if humor is used when presenting (Ziv, 1984).
- Students using lots of visuals did 12 percent better on short-term recall and 26 percent better on long-term retention (Meier, 2000).
- Standing speeds up information processing 5 to 20 percent, compared to sitting down (Jensen, 1996, p. 150).
- Four-member teams rewarded based on the group's average scores performed significantly better than trainees rewarded on individual scores only (Hagman & Hayes, 1985).
- Data shows that tasks that are interrupted mid-process are more memorable (Allen, 2001, p. 13).
- Each of us might be a different type of learner. Some are visual (they need to see something to remember it). Some are auditory (they need to hear something to remember it). Some are physical (they need to do it to learn it). And some are kinesthetic (doing something with their hands helps them to remember) (Russell, 1999).
- Data shows that the presence of "happy chemicals" in the brain, like serotonin, stimulates memory. Serotonin is naturally produced in response to music, laughter, and physical activity (Jensen & Cabney, 2000).
- Sixty percent of what is presented in training is forgotten if it's not used immediately. Seventy-five percent is lost with six months, and 85 percent within one year of training (Broad & Newstrom, 1992).

Together, choose among the options. Given the brainstorm of options and data shared, ask the group members which learning formats they most want to use in the session. When polling the participants, mark down their responses so they feel heard. Let them know that you'll adjust your session accordingly.

Tactic 4: Communicate the Training Process

Although most of your training time will be utilized in talking about the content, it's always okay to take a break and explain the process. The "process" is:

- The method by which you're teaching
- The pace at which you're teaching
- Topics that will be covered next
- Questions that remain unanswered
- Agenda for the remainder of the session

Tactic 5: Build a Relationship with Your Learners

Relationships are built on mutual respect. Remind participants that you, too, have lots to learn. Invite them to share their knowledge with you and to approach you at a break with important feedback, questions, or comments.

Whether you're teaching doctors, accountants, engineers, software developers, scientists, bankers, or financial analysts, remind yourself of the old cliché, "everybody's different." No two individuals and no two learners are alike—each has a different familiarity with your topic, sense of humor, ability to communicate, and so on. Don't make assumptions about your participants without checking in with them. You might surprise each other!

These five tactics will help you create support for using activities, props, and toys to teach skills and knowledge in your sessions.

Whether you are looking for a process to ensure learning occurs or tactics that prepare participants for the learning they are about to experience, Trainer's Warehouse can provide the materials, and this book offers over one hundred ways to use them.

References

Allen, R. (2001). *Train smart: Perfect training every time*. San Diego, CA: The Brain Store, Inc.

Biech, E. (2005). *Training for dummies*. Hoboken, NJ: John Wiley & Sons.

Broad, M., & Newstrom, J. (1992). *Transfer of training*. New York: Perseus.

Hagman, J.D., & Hayes, J.F. (1985). Cooperative learning: Effects of task, reward & group size on individual achievement. Unpublished technical report, U.S. Army Research Institute for the Behavioral and Social Sciences, Alexandria, Virginia.

Jensen, E. (1996). *Brain-based learning*. San Diego, CA: Turning Point Publishers.

Jensen, E., & Cabney, M. (2000). *Learning smarter: The new science of teaching*. San Diego, CA: The Brain Store, Inc.

Meier, D. (2000). *The accelerated learning handbook*. New York: McGraw-Hill.

Reference guide to handbooks and annuals. (1999). San Francisco, CA: Pfeiffer.

Russell, L. (1999). *The accelerated learning fieldbook: Making the instructional process fast, flexible and fun*. San Francisco, CA: Pfeiffer.

Ziv, A. (1984). The influence of humorous atmosphere on divergent thinking. *Contemporary Educational Psychology, 8*, 68–75.

Setting the Stage for Playful Learning

Trainers committed to incorporating experiential learning activities into their session plans can do a lot to create a total room environment, or ambience, that is conducive to laughter, play, and enhanced learning. What we call "playful learning" goes by lots of names, all of which sound a bit serious and scary—but they are not. You may have heard a few of these terms:

- Accelerated learning
- Right-brain, left-brain learning
- Kinesthetic learning
- Whole body learning

All of them refer to the trainer's need to facilitate learning for all kinds of people—those who learn by hearing, by doing, by seeing, by experiences, and by feeling. Why? Because, as many who write on these topics remind us, we all learn more when all of our senses are engaged. That is, when we are feeling good; when we have positive emotional experiences; when our hands are occupied; when our surroundings are pleasant; and when we're happy.

Establishing a climate conducive to learning is key to every successful training event. You can set the stage for having fun and creating an atmosphere of playful learning right from the start. Welcome your participants to a room that is colorful and exciting, that has tactile items on the table and posters on the wall, that meets participants with music and tempts with toys. A room that shouts "fun" is the perfect setting. Once the session starts, your opening activities will set the tempo and the tone for the session. An interactive and playful icebreaker, for example, tells participants that it is safe to have fun.

As a trainer, you are the key to setting the stage for playful learning. Trainer traits that encourage playful learning include:

- Demonstrating a sense of humor
- Being open to new ideas
- Encouraging participation
- Showing that you are people-oriented and approachable
- Building trust with participants and among participants
- Displaying subtle competence
- Exhibiting sincerity
- Using tools and toys to support your training design and playful learning climate

Trainer's Warehouse offers a range of tools, gadgets, and goodies to create a classroom that makes learners feel welcome and invites them to relax and get ready to learn. These include:

- Using fiddles for tactile learners
- Playing music to set the stage
- Posting signs to create a theme, provide reminders, and deliver messages
- Providing welcome items to create an inviting climate
- Using balls and other throwables
- Taking frequent breaks

Fiddle While You Work

Every trainer and facilitator has been faced with the dilemma of providing tactile experiences for those participants who prefer a kinesthetic learning style. "Fiddle" is a term used to refer to any small toy that participants can manipulate in their hands or "fiddle" with. Although fiddles may look like toys to the untrained eye, they can be serious learning tools," states Sharon Bowman, author of *Presenting with Pizazz*. Fiddles can enhance for learning environment by:

- Promoting a relaxed, playful mindset—setting a creative-friendly tone in your session.
- Improving focus—kinesthetic learners will focus better and absorb material more quickly if they have something to do with their hands.
- Relieving stress—playing with toys and hand-held manipulatives is believed to relieve stress.
- Engaging the whole brain—discussions are left-brained; toys tap into the creative right brain.

How can you use fiddles?

1. Leave a pile of fiddles in a basket in the front of the room or on each table.
2. Invite learners to take one. If it makes you feel more comfortable, you can explain some of the benefits of having "toys" in class. However, it may create a more experiential opportunity if you wait to explain until after the learners have had some time with them.
3. Proceed with your lesson or learning point while students handle the fiddles.
4. At the end of a session, engage your group in a discussion about the effect of having the fiddles on the tables. You may wish to ask questions, such as:
   - Who used a fiddle?
   - Did some of you tend to use them more or less than others?
   - What was the perceived value to those of you individuals who used them?
   - Were some of the fiddles preferable to others? If so, why?
   - Can you identify other ways that people fiddle when not given an "official" fiddle? (e.g., doodling, twirling pencils, tapping the table, playing with rings or hair)
   - Did "fiddling" enhance learning or interfere with listening?

Your debrief may teach learners about themselves and their own learning styles, sensitize them to different ways that others learn, and introduce learners to the value of making kinesthetic learning tools available in their own meetings.

The Trainer's Warehouse collection of fiddles or kinesthetic learning tools have been "specially selected for quiet mindless 'fiddlebility.'"

Play Music to Set the Right Mood

Lenn Millbower and others have written extensively about the use of music in the training room to energize, relax, and engage learners. Experts match the "beats per minute" (BPM) to the learning goal. For instance, 120 to 165 BPM songs are known to activate the production of adrenaline and increase heart rates if you want learners to get going, speed it up, move quickly into groups. 60 to 70 BPM songs stimulate the production of serotonin, a common neurotransmitter that helps us feel pleasant and cheerful. These songs are best to play when you'd like to reduce stress, but encourage productivity. Finally, 40 to 55 BPM (just below the resting rate) songs will slow the pace of learners' heart rates and help them de-stress, unwind, and slow down.

In addition to mood-setting music, Trainer's Warehouse recommends using songs with humorous lyrics to introduce breaks, bring people back from breaks, encourage out-of-the box thinking, request that cell phones be turned off, etc.

With the right songs, music is a wonderful way to send an important message in a non-threatening way. As such, Trainer's Warehouse developed a CD entitled "Laughable Lyrics," which promises just that—funny songs for training and other meeting events.

Another Trainer's Warehouse product is a musical tool called a Boomwhacker. Boomwhackers provide you with a host of training applications. You may use them to develop group spirit; build employee rapport; introduce participants; learn effective team planning; experience the satisfaction of achieving an objective; appreciate the interdependence of group members; focus on the importance of communication skills; enjoy making music together; and simply have fun.

Use Boomwhackers in teams of (ideally) eight players—with each person holding one of the eight Boomwhacker tubes. The eight Boomwhackers in each set are perfectly tuned to play eight different musical notes when "whacked" against a table, wall, or floor. The notes are clearly marked on the tubes. Assign a challenge to your groups and have them perform their creations for the rest of the class. You may wish to incorporate several of these challenges into your exercise.

- Create a rhythmic pattern in a specified time-frame (2 to 10 minutes)
- Play a familiar song
- Make up a new song
- Repeat the exercise, requiring the groups to work without speaking

Whether you play a CD, use Boomwhackers, or produce music in some other way, remember that it helps to tap into the playful aspect of learning.

Post Signs

You can also engineer a positive environment for learning with signs. Signs can be used to send playful yet serious messages. Trainer's Warehouse has a line of traffic signs that tactfully request that students turn off cell phones, be quiet, listen to others, ask lots of questions, and more. While those signs may be already made, you can also make up your own signs or look for other humorous ways to convey information. For instance, Delta Song Airline put a whole new spin on the traditional safety presentation at the beginning of each flight by delivering it as if it were a New Age relaxation experience.

Signs can also be used to welcome participants to the session. By posting a session sign outside the door, you can ensure that participants will know that they are in the correct location. Signs that present quotes can motivate and stimulate participants. And finally, signs may have graphics or pictures that add color to the training room.

Welcome Participants

Participants should feel the positive energy right from the start. That is why it is important for you to be prepared to greet even the earliest participant's arrival. Tables and chairs should be arranged, equipment tested and ready to roll, materials organized on the tables, participants' places arranged, music set to the right tunes and at the correct sound level, posters hung, flip charts prepared, and refreshments set out. When all these things have been completed ahead of time, you can be relaxed and ready to great your participants.

Ensure that your participants feel welcomed to the training room. Plan ahead so that they walk into a relaxed atmosphere and an environment that sings "fun." The room says you took the time to get ready for them and that you care about their learning needs. If you have prepared ahead, you have time to greet them and welcome them to a great training session. Trainer's Warehouse offers several products that can help you establish a welcoming environment.

The Welcome Kit is intended to inspire participation, open-mindedness, and fun. It includes things such as a slinky, a noisemaker, a foam question mark, and other toys that represent metaphors of important learning messages. Wouldn't your participants be surprised to see a carryout box packed with these items sitting at their places? You can delight your participants with other items as well, such as fiddles mentioned earlier, Koosh® balls or other throwables, crayons, colorful paper, neon bright Post-it® Notes, or two-sided index cards.

Investing in your welcome sets the stage right from the start and tells your participants that this learning experience is going to be worth their while and also a playful experience.

Play Ball![1]

Once the stage is set, you will want to continue to create an environment of playful learning. What better tool to use than balls?

Balls are playful by nature. Since childhood, we have been taught to have fun with balls—playing catch, dodge ball, 4-square, SPUD, kickball, soccer, and more.

---

[1]This discussion about balls was written by Steve Sugar for Trainer's Warehouse.

They are also terrific teaching and learning tools. Trainer's warehouse believes that the best balls used in training should be S.A.F.E.:

Soft: They shouldn't hurt (people or things) when thrown hard.
Aesthetically pleasing: They should look fun!
Feel: They should be pleasant to touch.
Easy: They should be easy to catch.

Using balls in the classroom provides many benefits. Balls can:

- Create a relaxed playful mindset.
- Engage the whole brain, since discussions are left-brained and toys tap into the creative right side.
- Provide versatility when used for stress relief, games, team selection, and reinforcement.
- Encourage participation, since many people can't resist playing with them!

Listed here are a few general ways you can use balls in learning activities:

Tactile learner prop or stress relief. Leave a few balls on learners' tables so they can pick them up and occupy their hands.

Icebreaker. At the start of a session, introduce yourself, what you do, something you like about your job, something you don't like, and a favorite pastime, for example. Then toss the ball to another person and ask that person to introduce him- or herself in a similar manner. Keep the ball moving around the room until everyone has been introduced.

Lesson reinforcement and discussion summary. At the close of a discussion or session, tell the group you're going to throw the ball out to someone and ask that person to share a learning point or other relevant comment with the rest of the group. That person then passes the ball to someone else. Continue until everyone has had a turn.

Team selection. Have an assortment of different kinds (or colors) of balls. Have every participant pull a ball out of a bag or box. When all have been distributed, ask participants to find all the people who have similar balls. At the end of the game or exercise, let players take their balls as parting gifts.

Role play. Role playing can be anxiety-producing for participants. Use balls to make the exercise more fun and less scary. Give the person in the "hot seat" three balls. When that person gets stuck and needs a suggestion for what to say (or do) next, invite him or her to throw a ball to someone for help.

Brainstorming. Toss a ball from person to person (quickly). Whenever someone catches the ball, he or she needs to state a brainstorming idea. Remember, don't mix creation of ideas with evaluation of ideas—the goal is to put as many ideas on paper as possible, and at this pace you might identify a few funny suggestions. There will be plenty of time to weed through them later.

Play "What If?" The goal is to have your group dream up a success story. The holder of the ball makes up an opening sentence of the story, then passes the ball to another person. The recipient adds a sentence to the story, building on what's been said, then passes the ball to someone else. Play continues until the story comes to a close. Follow up the exercise with a discussion of the story that was woven together by the group.

Teach juggling. Introducing a physical challenge is often a useful way to balance the mental challenge that learners experience in class. Frequently, it also results in role reversal—the "pro" is not necessarily the boss or supervisor. This can be incredibly refreshing for individuals who are better at something than their "superiors."

Assign roles. Divide the group into teams of three or four. Give each team a ball. Ask the teams to play "Hot Potato" or "One Potato" to pick a leader, an observer, or a person to "go first."

- *One Potato:* Have the group pass the ball from player to player while chanting, "one potato, two potato, three potato, four, five potato, six potato, seven potato, more." Whoever has the ball at the end of the chant is "it."
- *Hot Potato:* Play music for 7 to 10 seconds while the ball is tossed from player to player. When the music stops, the person with the ball is "it."

Energizer. Play catch. That's right! When you take a break, ask your group to go outside and play catch.

Take More Breaks

More than eighty years ago, Bluma Zeigarnik, a Russian psychologist, studied the consequences that occur when tasks or learning are left undone. When out to lunch one day, Zeigarnik noticed that a waiter had better recollections of still unpaid orders than of those that were paid. This led her research into a Gestalt phenomenon that demonstrates that tasks which are interrupted seem to be most memorable. Today we find the effect is widely used as a plot device in TV series and movies for maintaining viewer interest by using cliffhangers.

This same Gestalt psychology, the Zeigarnik effect, has been used to demonstrate why learners remember material better when they leave learning unfinished. In addition, researchers at the Massachusetts Institute of Technology say regular breaks are key to forming memories. David Foster and his colleagues say that when rats take a break while exploring an unfamiliar area, their brains instantly replay the information they have just experienced. This occurs in the human brain as well, in a place called the hippocampus that plays a key role in memory. Foster learned that when the rats took a break after running a track, the cells fired in reverse order, replaying multiple times, but up to twenty times faster.

Findings such as these suggest that if you want participants to remember the content of your training session, at times it may be better to leave learning unfinished before breaks and to take breaks more frequently.

Summary

Have these ideas and products from Trainer's Warehouse piqued your interest? Ready for more? The rest of this book presents over one hundred activity ideas for using these and other products from Trainer's Warehouse. Try them as written or adapt them to address your content and your participants' needs.

Once you become familiar with the products available from Trainer's Warehouse, create your own activities. Susan and Mike would be delighted to hear from you about how you use their products.

References
Millbower, L. (2004, March). *ASTD Info-Line: Music as a training tool*. Alexandria, VA: ASTD.

Zeigarnik and Foster's research is available at http://en.wikipedia.org/wiki/Zeigarnik_ effect.

Section 2

Training Tools and Techniques

This section presents training tools used in all types of training scenarios, whether e-learning, classroom, one-on-one, or on the job. The chapters are presented in roughly the same order as they would be used in a learning event: openings, icebreakers, energizers, participation encouragement, comprehension and retention, time and people management, training techniques, rewards and recognition, review of knowledge and skills, and closings.

Chapter 3

Openings

First contacts create lasting impressions. Designing and delivering a good opening is one of the most important aspects of the entire training session. Catching and holding participants' attention right from the start is a talent you can learn. The American Society for Training and Development (ASTD) offers a Training Certificate Program. One of the objectives of the program is to teach trainers how to open their training sessions with PUNCH:

- **P**romote interest and enthusiasm for the content. Participants will desire more after an opening that incorporates an element of surprise, uses props, or uses a creative activity.
- **U**nderstand participants' needs, both from a content as well as a personal perspective. The trainer may learn something about participants' experience and expertise, where they work, or the problems they face.
- **N**ote the ground rules. This allows participants to have many of their concerns quelled, such as, "What time is lunch?" and "Where's the restrooms?"
- **C**larify expectations by discussing the agenda and the learning objectives. The opening also identifies other expectations participants brought with them.
- **H**elp everyone get to know one another through the use of icebreakers, discussions, or other activities.

The four activities in this chapter present several ideas to accomplish PUNCH.

Getting to Know You Differently

Objectives
- To share knowledge about self, based on the perception of others.
- To identify and clarify expectations.

Audience
10 to 15 individuals; especially useful for intact teams working on team building, communication styles, or diversity and inclusion.

Time

20 to 25 minutes.

Materials and Equipment

- Koosh® ball (medium).
- Mr. Sketch® scented markers.
- Easy-Snap™ Easel and flip-chart pad.

Area Setup

Round tables are best, but any training setting will work.

Process

1. Write the following information on the flip chart:
   - Title: Introductions.
   - Hi, my name is . . . and I prefer to be called . . .
   - My role/function is . . .
   - I've been with (name of company/organization) for (time).
   - Four words that others might use to describe me are . . .
   - My expectations/hopes for this session are . . .

2. Tell participants that you're going to throw the Koosh ball to someone at random and ask that person to introduce him- or herself, using the prompts on the flip chart. When the person is done, he or she should then throw the Koosh ball to someone else.
3. Ask them to continue the process until *everyone* has been introduced.
4. Debrief the activity with the following questions:
   - What did you learn about individuals in the session?
   - What are some common expectations you all hope to have met during the session?
5. Capture the expectations/hopes on the flip chart.
6. Post the expectations/hopes flip-chart page on the wall.
7. Point out to participants which of their expectations you will or will not cover during the session.
8. Tell participants that they will be responsible for making sure their expectations are met by actively participating in the session.

Insider's Tips

- Start by introducing yourself and sharing your four descriptive words.
- Before starting the activity, communicate the two "Koosh Ball Rules." Rule 1: If there are drinks on the table, please protect them during the exercise. Rule 2: Keep your eyes on the ball because it may be coming your way!
- Don't be surprised if people find out for the first time what their teammates preferred to be called.

Submitted by Marcia A. Chambers, Ed.D.

Marcia A. Chambers is president and CEO of Chambers Consulting Services, Inc., a firm that works with organizations on leadership, team, and individual effectiveness. Marcia has been in the consulting and training field for twenty years. She is a certified coach, providing both personal and executive coaching, and works with both management teams who want to move their organizations forward and individuals who want to maximize their full potential. She has worked with organizations and individuals in the areas of team building, conflict management, gender and communication, and diversity and inclusions.

You're a Superhero

Objectives
- To provide an opportunity for participants to learn about one another.
- To provide a transition to the session topic.

Audience
Any group size. This is useful for networking groups or teams. This activity is particularly well received by the Gen-X age group.

Time
15 to 30 minutes (depending on the number of participants).

Materials and Equipment
- A write-on wipe-off (or Dry Erase) reusable Tent Card for each participant.
- A Whiteboard on a Stick for each participant.
- Several different color Dry Erase markers for each participant.

Area Setup
Any classroom configuration with tables and chairs.

Process
1. Use this activity as an icebreaker at the beginning of a session.
2. Distribute name cards, Whiteboards on a Stick, and markers to each person.
3. Ask participants to imagine what they would be like if they were superheroes. Spark imagination by asking the following questions:
    - What would your superhero name be?
    - What special powers would you have?
    - What would your costume look like?
    - What would your battle cry be?
    - Would you have a sidekick?
4. Ask participants to write their superhero name on one side of their name card and their first name on the other.
5. Encourage them to draw a sketch of their superhero costume on the whiteboard stick.
6. Have participants explain their superhero personas to the class and show their drawings.
7. Tie this theme into the class topic by using a statement like, "You don't have to be a superhero to write a SMART objective. We are going to learn how in this class."

Insider's Tips

- Have your own superhero persona prepared in advance to use as an example.
- If the group size is over 20, consider having the participants share their creations in smaller groups rather than with the entire class.

Submitted by Amy Drennen

Amy Drennen has been an instructional designer and trainer at Yazaki North America Inc. since 2000. She enjoys applying adult learning principles to make learning more effective by creating fun experiences that reach all types of learners. She feels her biggest accomplishment in the training world was helping to create a shift in her corporation's learning culture through her innovative designs and constant striving to educate class participants about learning styles. This shift can be seen by comparing participants scoffing at kinesthetic toys at the beginning of her career to a recent complaint that there weren't enough toys to go around.

Fun Caps Versus Boring Tent Cards

Objectives
- To add an element of fun right from the beginning of a training session.
- To afford participants an opportunity to express their creativity.

Audience
Any training seminar group on virtually any subject—especially effective if one is addressing a paint company or the local Association of Professional Painters!

Time
Attendees can start by simply printing their first names on the bill of the cap or anywhere else it will be legible. They can then work on it to further adorn and improve it during the training session.

Materials and Equipment

- Painter's hats, enough for each participant to have his/her own.
- Mr. Sketch® markers, a complete set for each table.
- Tent cards, enough for each participant to have his/her own.
- Stickers (optional for additional decoration).

Area Setup

Place the caps on a table along with tent cards. Displaying a few creative, previously decorated samples tends to encourage others to select the hat rather than the card. Markers should be on the tables where participants sit.

Process

1. Tell participants that they have a choice to write their names on tent cards as usual or to use a cap to express who they are. Encourage participants to be adventuresome and take the hat as opposed to the "boring and ordinary" tent card. Who wants to be "ordinary." Reassure them that they will not need to wear the hats.
2. If participants are from different cities, departments, branch offices, etc., encourage them to work together to come up with a theme for their group.
3. If the group will later be arranged in teams for breakout activities, the team can then create a unique style or design.
4. Another suggestion is to draw something that illustrates individuals' favorite food, pastimes, city, movie, etc.
5. Awards can be given at the end of the training session for the most colorful, most creative, most interesting, etc.

Insider's Tip

My experience is that about 60 percent of a group will select the traditional tent card initially. Later some will ask for a hat because they see what others have done. We recommend they save the hats to place in their offices as a memento of their exhilarating training experience. Many assume they will have to wear the hat—on learning that is not required, they choose the hat.

Submitted by Bruce Graham, CCDS

Bruce Graham has been a licensed realtor in Somerset County, New Jersey, for thirty-three years. His agency is the second-largest independently owned real estate company in the state with twenty-five offices serving twelve counties and eastern Pennsylvania. He prepares and presents new agent training and specialized courses for Prudential New Jersey Properties' 650 sales professionals at their corporate training center in Somerset, New Jersey.

Topic Walk

Objectives
- To understand participants' perceptions of the main topic of the program.
- To obtain varying perspectives on the program topic.
- To evolve a consensus on the objectives of the program.

Audience
Any size group attending a training program.

Time
15 to 30 minutes (varies with the size of the audience).

Material and Equipment
- A flip-chart sheet for each participant.
- Two flip-chart sheets for the facilitator—one for his/her own definition and one for the group's consensus definition.

- Mr. Sketch® markers.
- Masking tape or Tac on Strips to attach pages to the wall.
- Optional: White Boards on a Stick and Dry Erase markers.

Area Setup
Room with sufficient space for a gallery walk.

Process
1. Ask each participant to define the program topic (e.g., empowerment) as they perceive it in their own words.
2. Provide each participant with a flip-chart sheet and one Mr. Sketch marker. Ask them to write their definitions and names on the page and then attach the page to the wall.
3. Attach your (facilitator's) definition also along with the participants.'
4. Request that participants take a gallery walk, reading each definition and asking for clarification from the author. *Note:* if you use White Boards on a Stick, have participants carry their sticks and walk around reading others' definitions.
5. Facilitate a discussion among the participants to arrive at a consensus definition.
6. Record the consensus definition on another flip-chart sheet and post that sheet on the wall after removing the other sheets.

nsider's Tips

- The definition could be the central theme/focus for the program.
- Since the definitions may not vary much, a good trainer could easily make necessary modifications to the original definition.
- The participants are more likely to accept ownership for the program if they are involved it its definition and focus.
- The facilitator may get a glimpse on the preparedness and understanding of the participants on the topic and thus will be better able to deliver the program at the appropriate level.

Submitted by Mohandas Nair

Mohandas Nair is a management educator. He teaches, trains, facilitates, mentors, and coaches management students and corporate executives. He has a graduate degree in mechanical engineering and has wide experiences spanning more than thirty years in industrial engineering and human resources development in industry, consultancy, and education. His vision: "To make a positive impact on every individual I meet and 'touch' and help them to understand their true potential."

Chapter 4

Icebreakers

An icebreaker is an activity conducted at the beginning of a training program that introduces participants to each other. It may also introduce content and in general helps participants ease into the program.

Training sessions are more effective when they start out with an icebreaker. Participants get to know each other and feel more at ease about participating early in the session. Think about these guidelines from *Training for Dummies:*

- Never ask anyone to do anything you would not want to do.
- Select icebreakers based on the type of group you're training.
- Relate the icebreaker to the content.
- Use icebreakers to set the tone and to demonstrate the level of participation you expect.
- Observe the group during the icebreaker to learn something about the group and the individuals.
- Watch the time during an icebreaker.

You are sure to find a perfect icebreaker among the eight presented in this chapter.

Shake It Icebreaker

Objectives

- To enable participants to become better acquainted with two or three other people in the room.
- To reduce initial shyness and create a sense of fun.

Audience

Any group; especially useful for participants who don't yet know each other well but who must work together.

Time

15 to 25 minutes.

Materials and Equipment

- One Collection of Shakers for each participant. Each container includes two each of seven different shakers; you'll need three to four of each type of shaker to compose groups of three to four people.
- Optional: Prepared flip chart or slide with small group questions.

Area Setup

Space to move around.

Process

1. Prior to participants' arrival, randomly place one shaker on the table in front of each place or beneath each person's seat. Another option is to give a shaker to each person as she/he enters the room.

2. Near the beginning of the session, tell people that they'll be participating in a short activity to help them get better acquainted with some fellow participants.

3. Ask everyone to stand and begin making noise with their shakers. Tell them to locate the two or three other people in the room who have a shaker identical to their own. Tell them to form their "shaker" groups and remain standing as they get acquainted (based on your instructions) for 10 minutes.

4. Explain that each person should share three pieces of information about him/herself that the other two or three people do not know. Alternatively, the facilitator can write a few specific questions on a flip chart (or slide) that people will individually respond to within their small groups. These questions can directly relate to the training or meeting topic.

5. Ask the groups to rattle their shakers in unison when they have finished their discussion, or signal the end of the activity by using one of the shakers yourself.

nsider's Tip

- You might have participants use the shakers throughout the training or meeting. For instance, people could be asked to respond to group polls by raising or rattling their shakers.

Submitted by Sunny Bradford, Ph.D.

Sunny Bradford, Ph.D., is principal of Bradford Consulting Associates, a training and organization development firm founded in 1990. Sunny has worked extensively with non-profit, government, and Fortune 500 companies. She specializes in leadership development, team effectiveness, culture assessment, workforce diversity, and large-scale change. She has served as feedback specialist with the Center for Creative Leadership and is a certified workplace mediator and Achieve Global trainer. Sunny has given presentations for the American Management Association, National OD Network, and various ASTD chapters. She is also an adjunct faculty in the Master's in Organization Leadership Program at Antioch University New England Graduate School.

Red Light, Green Light

Objectives
- To serve as an icebreaker.
- To expand awareness of interests and skills of other participants.

Audience
Twenty or more.

Time
10 to 25 minutes at start of the session or as a break activity of the same time duration.

Material and Equipment

- Classroom Cop (a tri-colored light box with one remote that controls the duration of time.)
- Chime, Tingsha, or other noise-maker.

Area Setup

Classroom Cop set at the head of the classroom, either on a table or hung on the wall.

Process

1. Assign a topic to each of the three colors of the Classroom Cop. For example, the green might represent "hobbies," the yellow represent "job responsibilities," and the red represent "information about your company or department."
2. Give participants 2 or 3 minutes to collect their thoughts about the chosen topics. Explain that they will converse on the topic represented by the lighted light until the light begins to blink and you sound the chime.
3. When the light begins blinking, they should begin walking around randomly until the blinking stops. *Note:* you will probably need to use a chime or other noise-maker to signal when the light has changed, because the group will be noisily involved in conversation.
4. When the flashing light stops, the dialogue should resume with the person in closest proximity to them.
5. The subject of their conversation should be in conformance with the light that is lit. As such, when the light changes color, so must the topic of their discussion.

nsider's Tips

- Select your topics according to your training needs. They might include things like pet peeves, big problems, proud achievements, likes, dislikes, next presentation subject, etc. You might assign the topics to each color light or begin your session by having the group assign the topics.
- The light should stay uniform for 2 or 3 minutes so people can have short but substantive discussions. The blinking light duration should only be 10 or 15 seconds. Much longer blinking might result in uncomfortable encounters for

the participants. Of course, adjust the time segments to correspond to your own group dynamics.

- If a particular topic seems to work well, there is nothing wrong with staying on that topic for a few sequences.

Submitted by Mike Doctoroff

Founder and Chairman of Trainer's Warehouse, Mike Doctoroff has 50+ years experience as an entrepreneur, physicist, and inventor. At Trainer's Warehouse, he is always hunting for new products to help trainers do their job better and have more fun in the process. Some of Mike's expertise about learning comes from his lifelong dedication to self-improvement. Always looking to challenge his brain (and improve his communication with his Assembly Team at Trainer's Warehouse) Mike's recent success is learning Conversational Spanish. Indeed, you CAN teach an old dog new tricks! He brings his expertise in teaching and training to the Greater Boston ASTD as a member, presenter, and Board Member. Mike holds his undergraduate degree from Williams College and his MBA from Rochester Institute of Technology.

Tents Tell All—Myriad Uses for Table Tents

Objectives
- To break the ice at the beginning of an event.
- To facilitate the gathering and grouping of individuals in a large group meeting.
- To allow self-disclosure in a non-threatening way.

Audience
Any size group.

Time
15 to 30 minutes (depending on size of group).

Materials and Equipment
- Tent Cards—one per participant.
- Table numbers or table tents with colors on them—one per table.
- Mr. Sketch Markers® (several per table).

Area Setup
Tables ready for assignment, with a number or color in the middle of each and seating for five to eight.

Process
1. Prepare a tent card for each participant, pre-assigned with a colored dot or number to correspond to his/her table assignment. Any other instructions for reorganizing the group later can be symbolized on the inside of the tent card (e.g., *, #, +, $).
2. As participants enter the room, have a reception table where they sign in and pick up a tent card, which tells them where to go.
3. Once the event is convened, have each person take a marker and write in the name he or she wishes to be called during the training session. Tell them to complete both sides of the tent card, so that all can see.
4. For warm-up introductions, have participants write or draw any of the following on their cards:
   - Nickname.
   - Favorite year.
   - Something they are most proud of.
   - A miniature map of the country or globe, portraying where they have lived.
   - One goal for the event.
   - A hobby.
   - A symbol that best describes them.
5. Ask for a round of introductions at each table, with participants explaining the personal data on the tent cards they created.
6. When all have finished, the tent cards should travel with the participants as they move through the training session. Breakout group assignments can be written inside the tent cards, or the facilitator can ask that all cards be thrown in a pile and withdrawn, as in a lottery, to assign pairs, triads, breakout groups, or new table groupings.
7. If there are no formal evaluations at the end of the experience, ask participants to turn over the tent cards and use the right sides for feedback on "did wells" and the left sides for "could improves."

Insider's Tips

- The list of descriptors for the tent cards is endless, as long as they are not too personal or take too long to portray to the group.
- People become attached to their tent cards when they bear personal information. Do not attempt to take one away if the individual objects.

Source

Inspired by Lois B. Hart.

Submitted by M.K. Key, Ph.D.

A licensed clinical-community psychologist, M. K. has over thirty years of experience in organizational quality. She teaches, consults, and speaks on topics such as leadership, customer value management, tools for change (improvement and innovation), corporate culture, team development and facilitation, mediation of conflict, and creativity. Prior to forming Key Associates in 1997, she was vice president of the Center for Continuous Improvement with Quorum Health Resources, Inc. Her doctoral, master's, and bachelor of arts degrees, Phi Beta Kappa, *cum laude,* and honors in psychology, have all been with Vanderbilt University. She has served for years as adjunct associate professor of Human and Organization Development at George Peabody College of Vanderbilt. She has authored several books, including *Managing Change in Healthcare: Innovative Solutions for People-Based Organizations*, and *Corporate Celebration: Play, Purpose, and Profit at Work*, with Terry Deal.

The Hats We Wear

Objectives

- To identify the different roles team members play within and outside the organization.
- To make participants aware of the importance of relationship building.

Audience

Ten to twenty participants.

Time

30 to 45 minutes.

Materials and Equipment

- One Painter's Hat for each participant.
- Markers.
- One Painter's Hat prepared in advance by facilitator.

Area Setup

Any room arrangement.

Process

1. Introduce the activity as an icebreaker. State that the more we know about each other, the more we are able to identify and empathize with each other, thus building relationships that lead to a more cohesive team. By knowing each other's interests, we are able to communicate more easily, share new ideas, and solve problems faster.

2. Distribute the hats and markers. Tell participants they have 5 or 6 minutes to identify three different roles they play in life and to draw a representation of each on their hats. State that they will want to identify one role they play on the job and two roles they play outside their jobs. Explain that they may draw pictures, use words, be creative, and have fun. Share an example that you have completed before the session.

3. Once time is up, ask for a volunteer or share your own roles first. For example, you may draw a stick figure with an easel board to identify yourself as a trainer. Then you may draw a soccer ball with the word "Mom" beside it to identify yourself as a "soccer mom." Finally, you may draw a church, identifying yourself as an active member.

4. Go around the room until each participant has had time to share his or her roles. Participants may wear their hats or simply hold them up for others to see. Allow time for others to admire their talents and their artwork!

 nsider's Tips

- As a variation, you may have participants guess each other's vocations based on their hats.
- This makes a great "takeaway" for your training session.

Submitted by Lorraine Kohart

Lorraine Kohart has been in the training field for eighteen years. She has worn myriad hats as she relishes life, motherhood, and growth opportunities. Lorraine holds a BS in financial management, has owned an orchid business, and currently is joyfully employed with ebb associates inc.

Toys Are Us

Objectives
- To introduce participants to each other in a fun and non-threatening way.
- To gain insight into participants' roles in relation to the topic.

Audience
Any group; maximum of fifteen.

Time
15 to 30 minutes, depending on size of group.

Materials and Equipment
- Assortment of Fiddles and Classroom Prize Pack items. Make sure there are more items than participants and no duplicates.
- Table large enough to display an assortment of items.

Area Setup

Classroom setup of your choice and a table at the front or back of the room.

Process

1. Place the assortment of toys on the display table.
2. Explain that on your signal, participants are to get up, go to the table, select a toy, and return to their seats.
3. When they return, tell them that they have 2 minutes to study their toys and think about how the toy they selected represents them. (Alternatively, you may ask how it represents the topic, their organization(s), or their roles in relation to the topic.)
4. Ask for a volunteer to share his or her insight with the rest of the group. Continue soliciting volunteers until everyone has had an opportunity to participate.
5. Debrief the activity by asking the following questions:
   - What was your reaction to using a toy to represent yourself?
   - What was the value of using a toy rather than simply asking you to talk about who you are?
   - What did you learn about yourself?
   - What did you learn about others?
   - How can these insights be helpful as we explore the topic?

 nsider's Tips

- This activity can be used as an icebreaker at the beginning of a session or within the session to introduce a particular subtopic or segment.
- A variation of the activity would be to use the fiddles in a sales training or influencing program. You could ask the participants to describe the features and benefits of the toy or to try to "sell" the toy to the rest of the group.

Source

This is adapted from an activity in the *Train-the-Trainer Facilitator's Guide* by Karen Lawson, published by Pfeiffer, 1998.

Submitted by Karen Lawson

Karen Lawson, international consultant, speaker, trainer, author, and executive coach, is president of Lawson Consulting Group, Inc., a firm that helps organizations cultivate outstanding leaders. She has published ten books on the subjects of influencing, coaching, communications, and training, as well as dozens of articles in professional journals and anthologies. She is one of only four hundred people worldwide to have earned the Certified Speaking Professional designation awarded by the National Speakers Association. She has received numerous awards for her outstanding contribution to the training and speaking professions and was also named one of Pennsylvania's "Best 50 Women in Business."

Who's on My Team?

Objectives
- To allow team members an opportunity to get acquainted with each other on a more personal level.
- To allow participants to share their perspectives and expectations regarding effective teams and team members.

Audience
Any natural team. Recommend a group of no more than ten.

Time
Will vary depending on the group size, but will probably be no more than 30 minutes.

Materials and Equipment
- An index card and a pencil for each participant.
- Tunes for Trainers music playing in the background as the members first enter the room and when they are completing their cards. This tends to create a relaxing environment.
- Flip chart prepared with questions. (See Step 1.)

Area Setup

U-shaped or tables with three to four individuals at a table.

Process

1. Post the following questions on a flip chart:
   - List one thing that probably no one in this room knows about you (unique or humorous) that you do not mind sharing.
   - Name your favorite music, band, or movie.
   - Name your favorite vacation spot or place you would like to visit.
   - If you could start your career again, what would you be doing?
   - What do you like to do when you are not at work?
2. Provide each person with an index card and a pencil.
3. Have everyone think about the posted questions and write their answers on their cards.
4. For a less threatening approach, begin by sharing your own information, then ask the participants to share their information.
5. An optional and more effective approach is to collect the cards and pass them back out, ensuring no one has his or her own card. Then have each individual read the card he or she has and have the person and/or the team guess who it might belong to. Once they have guessed, have the real card owner acknowledge the card and add any clarity he or she may want to add. If you use this option, make sure individuals write in a legible manner.
6. Debrief the activity by asking whether there were any surprises about the information shared and why it is surprising.

Insider's Tips

- This activity is a good warm-up for a team-building or initial activity when a group comes together for the first time to work on a project. It should be used as an opening activity. It may also be used as an energizer.
- You can use all of the questions above, just some, or create some of your own that might be better suited for your particular group, organization, or industry.

Submitted by Edwin Mourino, Ph.D.

Edwin Mourino has spent over twenty-five years in the HRD field in a variety of organizations and capacities. His broad industry experience includes the Air Force, retail, utility, hospital, and aero defense. Edwin has expertise in leadership development, learning and development, and diversity. He has been published in various professional magazines and has presented at numerous industry conferences. He has been both a chapter president and National Advisor Committee member with the American Society of Training and Development (ASTD). Edwin's experience includes internal management and external consulting. He has also taught in the university setting, both in undergraduate and graduate levels. Presently Edwin works as an internal organization development professional for Lockheed Martin.

Press Conference

Objectives

- To serve as a lively way to introduce new team members or group participants by randomly selecting an introductory statement.
- To demonstrate the unexpected and random requests that may occur when meeting with the news media, stockholders, or employees.

Audience

Twelve or more participants, any level.

Time

15 to 30 minutes.

Materials and Equipment

- Twelve favorite items statements (see Preparation section).
- One Turn 'n Learn Game Wheel, mounted on easel or flip chart.

Area Setup

Need room to set up wheel where all participants can see it.

Preparation

1. Write favorite items statements on the game wheel. Some examples follow:
   - Movie star and why you selected this star.
   - Means of transportation and why you selected this vehicle.
   - City and why you selected this city.
   - World leader (living) and why you selected this leader.
   - Animal and why you selected this animal.
   - Television show and why you selected this show.
   - Movie and why you selected this movie.
   - Business leader and why you selected this leader.
   - Singing star and why you selected this singer.
   - Food and why you selected this food.
   - Holiday and why you selected this holiday.
   - Vacation spot and why you selected this spot.
   - Public (concert or athletic) event and why you selected this event.
   - Color and why you selected this color.
   - Article of clothing and why you selected this article.
   - Number and why you select this number.
   - Letter and why you selected this letter.

- Country and why you selected this country.
- Continent and why you selected this continent.
- River and why you selected this river.
- Lake and why you selected this lake.
- Language and why you selected this language.
- Historical (deceased) person and why you selected this historical person.
- Season of the year and why you selected this season of the year.
- Cartoon character and why you selected this character.

2. Set up game wheel on a wallboard or flip-chart easel, making sure that the wheel turns freely.

Process

1. Ask for a volunteer to introduce him- or herself.
2. Spin the game wheel.
3. Have the participants introduce themselves—their names and then the names of their favorite items—as selected on the game wheel.
4. Continue this selection process until all participants have introduced themselves.

 nsider's Tip

- If the wheel duplicates a selection too often, you may wish to spin again.

Submitted by Linda M. Raudenbush, Ed.D., and Steve Sugar

Linda M. Raudenbush holds a BA in mathematics and secondary education from St. Joseph College, an M.S. in applied behavioral science from Johns Hopkins University, and an Ed.D. in human resource development from George Washington University. Linda has more than twenty-five years' experience in training, organization development, and leadership coaching in both private and public sectors. Linda holds an ACC in leadership coaching granted by International Coaching Federation. She has been adjunct professor at National-Louis University and Strayer University, and is in her eighteenth year of part-time teaching at the University of Maryland, Baltimore. She is currently employed as an internal HRD/OD consultant and leadership coach at the U.S. Department of Agriculture. Linda is an active volunteer in her community, having been nominated as the

Maryland Volunteer of the Year for 2003 and 2004, and was awarded Volunteer of the Year in 2005 for Faith-Based Initiatives.

Steve Sugar writes "fun with a purpose" activities that have helped thousands of learners to experience classroom topics in a more meaningful way. Steve holds an A.B. in economics from Bucknell University and an M.B.A. in economics, statistics, and management from George Washington University. Steve served two tours as a Deck Watch Officer in Vietnam for the U.S. Coast Guard. Steve currently teaches business and education courses for the University of Maryland Baltimore County (UMBC). Steve is the author or co-author of *Training Games* (an ASTD Info-line), *More Great Games, Games That Teach, Games That Teach Teams, Games That Boost Performance,* and *Primary Games*. Steve has developed three game systems featured by Langevin Learning Services—the Management 2000/ Learn It board game, the QUIZO game system, and the X-O Cise dice game.

This Treasure Is Me

Objective

- To facilitate introductions in a new group.

Audience

Twenty-five is probably maximum (contingent on time available). Can be used for a group of strangers or people who do not know each other well, or teams that have not worked much together.

Time

20 to 40 minutes.

Materials and Equipment

- Treasure Chest (could substitute fiddles but pairs must have different toys).
- Paper and pencil/pen to take notes.
- Flip chart and markers.

Area Setup

Enough space so that people can spread out to talk to their partners. Keep the toys hidden until ready to use.

Process

1. If you're going to use this activity, do not have participants introduce themselves prior to conducting it.
2. Prior to the session, write three of the following on a flip chart. Your choices will depend on your goals for the day or anything else that is relevant:
   - How does this toy represent you in the workplace?
   - How does this treasure represent your goals in life?
   - How does this treasure portray your sense of humor?
   - How does this treasure represent you?
   - How does this treasure represent your connection to this team?
   - How does this treasure represent today's subject matter?
3. When you are ready to begin, explain to the participants that they are going to complete a nontraditional introduction of themselves.
4. Unveil the Fiddles and explain that whatever treasure participants select will ultimately be used to introduce themselves to the group and that they can keep it afterward.
5. Ask them to each select one treasure.
6. Ask the participants to form pairs with someone who has a different treasure.
7. Explain that each pair should answer the questions listed on the flip chart verbally to one another and that then they will each introduce the other to the group. Allow 10 minutes for participants to obtain information from each other and to prepare for the introductions.
8. Have them return to their chairs and allow partners to voluntarily decide when to stand up and introduce each other.

Insider's Tips

- This activity does not need to be done at the beginning of the session, but you should be no more than 25 percent through the session when you use it.
- Partners may be selected in one of two ways:
  - Find someone you don't know well and who has a different treasure than you have.

- If 90 percent of the people have different treasures, count off 1, 2, 1, 2, etc., and all 1's find a 2 for a partner—chaotic, but fun. Facilitator needs to ensure that partners all have different treasures.
- Although duplicates among the whole group will not be detrimental to the process, I would not have more than three duplicates of any treasure.
- This activity usually works better with people who do not know each other well.

Submitted by Harriet Rifkin

Harriet Rifkin has twenty-five years' experience in human resource management, training and development, particularly in leadership development. Her skill as a facilitator and executive coach to many organizations has proven consistently successful. Her leadership roles have included an office of employee relations and communication in the financial industry and corporate director of human resources for an architecture and engineering firm. She has published on writing employee handbooks and human resource policy manuals, and she has received several leadership awards. Harriet has been an external resource to organizations for several years, giving her clients the tools they need to be effective leaders and therefore engaging their most important asset—their people!

Chapter 5

Energizers

E nergizers are brief activities that provide relief during a long session, a lengthy or difficult and cerebral topic, or the afternoon doldrums. Energizers are sometimes called motivators and can have a number of other outcomes besides "energizing." According to Edie West, author of *201 Icebreakers,* energizers can also:

- Stimulate positive interaction and creative thinking among participants.
- Re-generate interest and excitement about the subject.
- Improve communication and build trust.
- Boost problem-solving skills.
- Reduce fears.
- Increase participation and involvement.

This chapter presents several energizers you can use as relaxers after a tense discussion, to remove the cobwebs during a difficult topic, or when the group's energy is ebbing.

Non-Trash Trash Can

Objectives
- To reward participants for insightful comments, questions, and participation.
- To encourage a fun, light, and creative environment.

Audience
Any group size or type.

Time
A minute or two at various times throughout the training session.

Materials and Equipment
- Classroom Prize Pack, small toys, candies, etc.
- Medium-sized colorful plastic trash can with movable, swinging lid or small kitchen or bathroom trash can with swinging lid.

Area Setup

Have the trash can visible in the room at the beginning of the session to raise participant curiosity.

Process

1. Put prizes in a medium-sized colorful plastic trash can with a movable/swinging lid.
2. During the training session, when a participant contributes something to the group by asking a significant question, offering an insight, answering a question, sharing with the full group, presenting a summary from a small group, etc., invite the person to make a trip to the Non-Trash Trash Can. Everyone loves reaching in and taking a prize and seeing what others receive.

 nsider's Tips

- At breaks, allow participants to trade prizes.
- This can be a great "energy pick up" during group reporting, which may at times become long.

Submitted by Kathy Cleveland Bull

Kathy Cleveland Bull is a professional speaker, trainer, and consultant. Her company, N~Compass Consulting, helps clients "navigate the art and science of change." Kathy presented a two-day seminar on change for African business leaders in Nairobi, Kenya, and appeared with Dr. Phil and Deepak Chopra at The Power Within Live Event in cities across North America. Kathy is one of three professional speakers recommended by Dr. Spencer Johnson to provide training built on his book, *Who Moved My Cheese?* She has trained more than 75,000 people to successfully manage change in their work and lives using the "cheese" metaphor. Prior to forming her own firm in 2001, Kathy was the director of training and organization development for over two thousand Student Affairs employees at Ohio State University.

Call Me Princess Java

Objective
- To stimulate, energize, and prepare for creative work.

Audience
Any group; especially useful when between transitioning topics.

Time
5 to 10 minutes.

Materials and Equipment
- Dry Erase Name Cards, one per participant.
- Dry Erase markers, assorted colors, one per participant.

Area Setup
Anywhere.

Process

1. Provide each participant one Dry Erase Name Card and one Dry Erase marker.
2. Tell participants that they are going to create a new, fun name for themselves.
3. Ask participants to shout out the names of their favorite pets (e.g., Princess, Daisy, Spot, Bangles, Tuxedo). Inform them that these will be their new first names. Instruct them to write their new first names on their tent cards. Remind them to leave room for their new last names.
4. Ask participants to shout out the name of a street where they previously lived (e.g., Java, Avocado, Walnut, Seaside, Jamboree). Inform them that these will be their new last names. Instruct them to write their new last names on their tent cards.
5. Have all participants re-introduce themselves to the group, using their new, fun names.

nsider's Tips

- Always allow participants to substitute pet or street names if they aren't comfortable with the first one chosen.
- This activity is great after lunch to energize participants for the afternoon.
- This activity can be repeated for multi-day sessions. Just ask participants to pick new pet and street names each day.

Submitted by Holly M. O'Neill

Holly M. O'Neill is president of Talking Business, a marketing consultancy that specializes in focus groups, branding, and brainstorming. Her insights and strategies have helped clients launch new products, create influential brands, and develop powerful advertising. Recognized as an expert at bringing innovation to marketing and marketing research, Holly has advised such clients as GlaxoSmithKline, Experian, and Nestle. A popular speaker and author, Holly's credits include co-authoring the brainstorming book, *101 More Great Games & Activities*; contributing to *Orchestrating Collaboration at Work*; teaching branding and marketing research at UC Irvine; publishing in *Quirks* and *American Marketing Association (AMA) News*; and presenting at the AMA, the Qualitative Research Consultants Association (QRCA), and the Harvard's Entrepreneurs Conference. Holly is the producer and host of the cable TV show "Talking Business."

Surprise Info

Objectives

- To energize a team by having new and surprising areas to explore.
- To allow team members to get to know one another better.

Audience

An intact team of no more than fifteen members.

Time

10 to 15 minutes for initial set up and then 5 minutes throughout the day at low-energy points.

Materials and Equipment

- Slim Line Answer Boards, one for each participant.
- Dry Erase markers, one for each participant.

Area Setup

No special setup.

Process

1. Provide each person with a Slim Line Answer Board and a marker and ask everyone to write their names at the top of the boards.
2. Have everyone write in two facts, either personal or professional, about themselves that have not been told to anyone on the team (e.g., "I took ballet lessons in college," "I won the award for best employee of the month at my last company," or "I had purple hair for a party").
3. Have everyone turn in their boards to the facilitator.
4. Facilitator chooses an item from the entries submitted and reads one fact aloud. The team has to guess who submitted the item. Select one or two more to read, but save others for later in the day.
5. Read a few more at various points in the day when the energy is low.

 nsider's Tips

- This is a great exercise for reenergizing the group at slow points.
- Everyone looks forward to guessing who did what throughout the day, so read only a few in the beginning.
- Keep the content side hidden from everyone's view so that you can use it during the day without anyone knowing what is on the boards.

Submitted by Jan M. Schmuckler, Ph.D.

Jan M. Schmuckler, organizational psychologist and leadership coach, works with executives and managers to achieve outstanding business results. Her more than twenty-five years of experience with leading companies in the high technology, biotechnology, and financial sectors around the world brings unique perspectives for competing more effectively. Currently, Jan is the director of the Coaching Certificate Program for John F. Kennedy University as well as heading her own consulting firm. She received her Ph.D. in organizational psychology from the Wright Institute. She has written several articles for the Pfeiffer Training and Consulting *Annuals*.

Everybody Dance

Objectives
- To build up energy at the beginning of a training session or during a break.
- To use in the middle of a session that is dry or when participants are unresponsive.

Audience
Any size group.

Time
- 1 or 2 minutes for a break.
- 5 to 15 minutes as people are entering room.

Materials and Equipment
- Everybody Dance CD.
- CD player.

Area Setup
Nothing special.

Process

1. For beginning of session: Have CD playing when people enter to create energy. Turn off when you are ready to begin talking.
2. For a break: When you take a break, put on CD, but low enough that people can still talk to each other.
3. When training is dry or people are unresponsive, say, "Okay, everybody up! Everybody dance now!" and turn on the CD. Have everyone dance at their seats, just to create movement and energy. People will be able to stretch and laugh and will be more responsive when you restart the session. Do this for just a minute or two.

Insider's Tip

- Have CD player ready and working so music can play without interruption.

Submitted by Sion Segal

Sion Segal is a founding partner of The Protea Group, a provider of organizational assessment and consulting, corporate training, and team development services. He has over twenty years of experience working with individuals, groups, and organizations in both corporate and non-profit settings. His mission is to provide cost-effective training and consultation with proven effectiveness to help organizations develop and grow. His quick intellect, dynamic personality, and pragmatic approach are key to his success in empowering organizations to fully actualize their potential.

Chapter 6

Participation Encouragement

John Newstrom, co-author of the *Games Trainers Play* series, says that "learning is not a spectator sport!" To ensure maximum participation, a trainer must be well prepared. Participation requires the trainer to create and maintain a safe learning environment, be flexible enough to accommodate a range of needs and preferences, and appeal to all learning styles. A trainer can manage how much participation occurs in a session.

The book *Training for Dummies* lists a number of ways to increase participation, including these:

- Set an expectation of participation right from the start.
- Build in participation activities early in your session.
- Share the role of trainer with the participants.
- Get participants up and moving around.
- Invite participants to share in small groups before requiring them to speak in front of the entire group.
- Practice speaking less and listening more.
- Ensure that the environment is safe enough for even the shyest to speak up.
- Encourage participation all the way to the end.

This chapter presents five ways to build more participation into your training sessions.

I'm No Chicken Award

Objectives
- To encourage introverts to share their thoughts and ideas.
- To celebrate when students participate.

Audience
Any training session, any size.

Time

5 minutes the first time, and then a few minutes each additional time throughout the session.

Materials and Equipment

- One rubber chicken.
- Camera.

Area Setup

Nothing special.

Process

1. Give the rubber chicken to the first quiet student who answers a question, asks a question, or in some way participates. Provide an explanation of why he or she was chosen.
2. Explain that this person will pass the chicken on to someone else that he or she thinks shows courage during the session and who has stepped up to share his or her thoughts and ideas. The chicken is passed on to new participants throughout the time together—over the course of the day or multiple days.
3. The person passing it must share with the group why he or she thinks the person receiving the chicken deserves the award.
4. Take a photo of the presentation(s). Post pictures of the awardees in a slide presentation on the last day of the session.

Insider's Tips

- Model the first presentation very clearly. Vocalize compliments to the person receiving the chicken.
- Lead the clapping and celebration of the group.
- If someone takes home the chicken overnight, he or she may need a reminder to bring it back to the next day's session.

Source

Encouraged by Carolyn Warman.

Submitted by Dawn Brenner

Dawn Brenner is the Future Leaders Program Coordinator at Leadership York, an organization dedicated to encouraging students and adults to take on leadership roles in the community since 1978. Staff members work with curriculum committees and colleagues to fine-tune new activities. Dawn was an educator for thirty-six years and has received many awards, including Outstanding Teacher Award from Shippensburg University, Junior Achievement of South Central PA Teacher of the Year, and Teacher Who Made a Difference from CHADD. Dawn serves on the York County Junior Miss Board and the Junior League of York advisory board and is an active member of Delta Kappa Gamma.

Share, Scratch, and Win

Objectives
- To make class time fun and interactive.
- To encourage participation and monitor comprehension of material.

Audience
Any group size will work.

Time
Activity continues throughout training session.

Materials and Equipment
- Scratch and See tickets.
- Corporate gifts, such as coffee mugs, pens, mouse pads, etc., or an assortment of Fiddles or a package of prizes.
- One big winner gift valued at $25 or more.
- Treasure Chest or decorated box to hold giveaways. (Decorate it with the theme of your session or make it look like a crazy box from a game show.)

Area Setup
Conducive to any arrangement.

Process
1. Have Scratch and See tickets pre-printed with the following: "You win from the box," "Try Again," and one card that says, "You're today's Big Winner." Pre-determine how many tickets you will need, based on the length of your session, the number of participants, and how many tickets you expect to award per hour. You may wish to consider having at least three per participant or set some other goal.
2. Have a decorated box full of inexpensive corporate giveaways set up at the front of the room.
3. Inform group members that their participation will be rewarded with a scratch ticket. Each time a participant answers a question correctly or gives input during class, he or she will receive one scratch ticket.
4. Participants must wait until the end of the session to scratch off their tickets. Everyone does it together. It keeps the excitement and participation building because you never know who has the big prize of the day.
5. Participants with "You win from the box" tickets can select the gift(s) of their choice from the box.
6. The big winner ticket is awarded the large prize. To ensure this ticket has been awarded, you will have to be sure to give away all tickets before the end of the session.

Insider's Tips

- Remember to reiterate that the tickets must be held until the end of the session to scratch off.
- To add levity, reward participants for their "art" work. Have little party Play-Doh® at every seat, along with colored pencils. It keeps that creative side of the brain entertained while the logical side has to work on technical issues. You wouldn't believe the Play-Doh sculptures and doodled art that are created.

Submitted by Beth Ducker

Beth Ducker is the National Education and Performance Manager for Hartford Steam Boiler (HSB). During her nineteen-year tenure, she has worked in both underwriting and marketing roles. Currently she is managing continuing education and corporate training, for which she designs and instructs courses for HSB's internal and external customers. Beth is a certified instructor in numerous states and is one of HSB's national keynote speakers.

High Five

Objectives
- To acknowledge participation.
- To recognize good ideas.

Audience
Any size group.

Time
A few seconds for each acknowledgment.

Materials and Equipment
- Reward Coins, known in this exercise as "High Five Coins."
- A prize.

Area Setup

Nothing special.

Process

1. Announce at the beginning of the session that every time a participant offers an idea or suggestion, you will give the person a High Five Coin. You may also wish to do this for correct answers during the review process.
2. Every time someone offers an idea or suggestion or gives a correct answer, give him or her a High Five Coin. The person at the end of the training with the most High Five Coins receives a prize.

 nsider's Tips

- When a High Five Coin is given out, everyone must "high five" each other.
- Start off giving every participant a pile of coins. Have them "high five" each other when they have a good idea or useful feedback from a team member.

Submitted by Sion Segal

Sion Segal is a founding partner of The Protea Group, a provider of organizational assessment and consulting, corporate training, and team development services. He has over twenty years of experience working with individuals, groups, and organizations in both corporate and non-profit settings. His mission is to provide cost-effective training and consultation with proven effectiveness to help organizations develop and grow.

Rapid-Fire Review

Objectives
- To promote and encourage full class participation.
- To check for understanding during a review session.

Audience
Any size class.

Time
Variable.

Materials and Equipment
- A Whiteboard on a Stick and a Dry Erase marker for each participant.
- Prepared questions related to the topic being reviewed.
- Optional prizes.

Area Setup

Standard classroom setup.

Process

1. Distribute a Whiteboard on a Stick and a marker to each participant, or, if desired, break the class into subgroups and provide a whiteboard and marker to each subgroup.
2. Ask questions based on the topic being reviewed.
3. Instruct the participants (or subgroups) to write their answer on the whiteboards and hold them up.
4. Then discuss the correct answer.
5. As an option, you may wish to track individual or subgroup correct answers with a simple tally. Award prizes at the end of the day or the session to those with the most correct answers.

Insider's Tips

- I find that some people do not feel comfortable answering questions out loud. Whiteboards on a Stick allow you to see who understands and who does not.
- Participants don't have to worry about the "know it all" shouting out the answer.

Submitted by Nicole Walton

Nicole Walton is a payroll specialist trainer at Paychex, Inc., and has been with the company for ten years. She has held several positions in the company, including branch mentor and trainer as well as branch supervisor. She currently conducts a training program that runs about every two weeks with about thirty-two specialists per session.

Pick It Up!

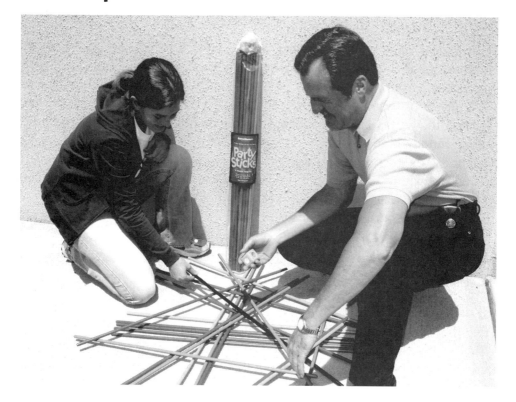

Objectives
- To reinforce and reward desired behaviors.
- To build teamwork.
- To maintain high energy throughout a training program.

Audience
Any size group, sitting in teams.

Time
This activity is designed to be woven throughout a workshop or training. Short segments of 3 to 5 minutes are integrated into a longer session.

Materials and Equipment

- One set of Jumbo Pick-Up Sticks per team of two to five (21 sticks plus one die in each set).
- One Giant Die.
- A large chart at the front of the room reading: Yellow = 5, Red = 10, Blue = 15, Green = 20, Black = 25.
- Prizes for one winning team.

Area Setup

Participants sit in distinct teams. Enough space at the front of the room for a pile of Jumbo Pick-Up Sticks. Because the game will be played throughout the training session, the playing space should be situated within the main classroom.

Process

1. At the beginning of the training session, solicit two volunteers to come to the front of the class. Hand one a set of ten Jumbo Pick-Up Sticks; give the other eleven sticks. Tell them to hold the sticks approximately one foot above the ground and to cross their two groups of sticks, forming an X. Invite the rest of the class to count in unison "1, 2, 3," at which point the two volunteers drop the sticks in a jumble on the floor.

2. Explain that teams will have opportunities throughout the training program to roll the Giant Die and attempt to pick up a stick of the matching color. Reference the chart to show various point accumulation for different stick colors. The more chances to roll the die, the more chances to earn points. At the conclusion of the training, the team with the most points wins a prize.

3. Throughout the training, when a participant on a team displays a behavior you would like to reinforce (i.e., volunteering, correctly answering questions, insightful comments, etc.), bring a team member forward to roll the die. The participant then attempts to pull out a stick matching the color rolled without moving any other stick. If the color white is rolled, any stick can be selected. If the color rolled does not have any matching sticks left, the die can be re-rolled once. If again there are no matching sticks of that color left, the participant can select a stick of any color. If another stick is disrupted, the turn is over with no point accumulation. Rotate which team members have the opportunity to come forward, regardless of which team member "earned" the right to roll the die. Teams can bring sticks won back to their table groups.

4. When the black stick is extracted, it can be used to help withdraw other sticks in future turns (just like the rules in regular-sized Pick-Up Sticks) by the team that extracted it successfully. If they move other sticks in the process, all teams will have access to using the black stick.

5. At the conclusion of the training program, ask teams to total their points—although most teams keep careful track of point accumulation along the way! Even if sticks remain in the front pile, the game can end at any time.

Insider's Tips

- Be consistent! Participants can take the rules surprisingly seriously.
- Jumbo Pick-Up Sticks can be integrated into trainings on virtually any topic. This activity works best in training programs ranging from one to four days in length. Shorter sessions do not have enough time to complete the game, and longer sessions spread out the challenge too long.
- The facilitator can make an optional chart at the front of the class keeping track of teams' point accumulation next to the Point Distribution Chart.
- The winning team can be presented with a single prize to share (e.g., a large bag of candy, a group privilege, or outing) or a set of matching individual prizes.
- You may use this as a team-building activity. If you do, you may wish to lead a group discussion, with questions such as:
  - Who did you define as your team? Was this a competition? What was the impact of the boundaries your team created? (e.g., Did the team with the black stick lend it out to other teams?)
  - What change in rules would make the group more collaborative? How could the group have been more collaborative within the confines of the current structure?
  - Did your team improve over time, even if different members were extracting sticks? Why?
  - What lesson from this activity can you apply to future teamwork?

Submitted by Devora Zack

Devora Zack is president of OCC, a leadership development firm with more than seventy-five clients, including Deloitte, America Online, DHS, OPM, Ann Taylor, SAIC, USDA, and the U.S. Treasury. OCC provides seminars, coaching, and consulting in leadership, change, communications, and team building. Devora is visiting faculty for Cornell University and program director for the presidential management fellows orientation. Her articles have been featured in Pfeiffer *Annuals* for three years. She has an MBA from Cornell, a BA from The University of Pennsylvania, and certification in neurolinguistic programming and MBTI. She is a member of MENSA and Phi Beta Kappa and has U.S. secret clearance.

Chapter 7

Comprehension and Retention

Participants must understand, retain, and be able to implement the content in order for a training session to be truly successful. Mel Silberman, author of *Active Training,* believes that there are at least three ways trainers can maximize understanding and retention:

- Provide memory aids by reducing the key points and critical concepts to headlines.
- Use analogies and examples of real-life situations. Then use these examples to link the content to the knowledge and experience of the participants.
- Use visuals and demonstrations to enable participants to see as well as hear the content discussion.

Mel also suggests that trainers can ensure comprehension and retention by allowing participants to review the material throughout the session. This chapter presents a couple of creative ways to ensure comprehension and retention.

The Organic Quiz Show

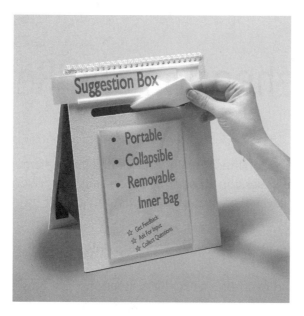

Objectives
- To enhance learner comprehension and retention of technical or voluminous reading material.
- To create a more interesting context for an in-class reading segment.

Audience
Any group, especially good for a collection of small groups. Not recommended for more than six small groups of three to six. Can also be played as an individual game if there are six or fewer participants.

Time
Varies based on the amount of time it takes to read the material to be covered, typically 15 to 20 minutes. Then allow 25 additional minutes. Total run time is typically 45 minutes.

Materials and Equipment
- Reading materials or manual.
- 3 × 5 ruled index cards—at least 10 per participant.

- A pen or pencil for each participant.
- Tip Taker (Suggestion Box).
- Optional: prize(s) such as Top Banana, Dilbert Accomplish-Mints, or assorted prizes from the Classroom Prize Pack.

Area Setup
As you wish; small-group tables are best.

Process
1. Have participants individually read and review the reading assignment, and tell them how many minutes they have to complete this task.
2. Hand out blank index cards and pens or pencils. It is best to place a pile in the center of each group table, with at least ten cards per participant.
3. Tell participants that they will generate questions and answers based on the assigned reading and will write them on the index cards (one question and answer per card). This activity is similar to writing a final exam for a course in that they should look for questions that capture the key points of the reading material.
4. On one side of the index card, participants should write one simple question. The questions can be open-ended, multiple-choice, or true/false; however, they should not write trick questions. They should not write the question unless they are sure of the answer.
5. Participants should write the answer to each question on the other side of the index card. If they wrote a true/false question, they must also state why it is true or false in the answer.
6. Participants should repeat this process during the reading time until they have generated five to ten questions.
7. Tell them to include the page number on which the answer appears in the reading assignment text.
8. When time is up, have participants place all of their completed cards inside the "Tip Taker." Ask for a volunteer to assist you. The person will be the "team accountant" to keep track of the scores.
9. Ask participants to divide into teams (table groups with three to six people per team).
10. Have participants coach each other on what they learned about the reading content. In particular, they may mention the questions and answers that each wrote on the index cards. Allow 10 minutes to coach each other on all the sections.

11. While the participants are coaching each other, you and the "team accountant" will gather all the cards from the Tip Taker bag and shuffle them. Review the questions and select some of the best ones. Place the questions in priority order.

12. When the 10-minute coaching session is over, explain the rules and begin the game: read a question aloud and randomly select someone within each group (one group at a time) to try to answer the question. If the selected participant thinks he/she knows the answer, he/she should respond. If the participant answers correctly, his/her group receives 5 points. If he/she is wrong, his/her group loses 5 points.

13. A selected participant will have 10 seconds to provide the correct answer.

14. If the selected participant doesn't feel prepared to answer, his/her group may assist him/her. If the participant who received group input answers correctly, the group receives 2 points. If he/she still answers incorrectly, despite receiving group assistance, the group loses 5 points.

15. Run the game for 10 to 15 minutes, as needed/appropriate, and call time when time's up. Add up all the scores and announce the winner. The team with the most points wins! Optional: Reward the winning team with prizes.

Insider's Tips

- Encourage and offer empathic comments such as "good try," "great job," and/ or other positive reinforcement to keep the group motivated.
- Consider acting like a game show host if you are inspired to take it to the next level of wackiness.

Submitted by Halelly Azulay

Halelly Azulay has over twelve years of professional experience in performance improvement and workplace learning with regulatory, corporate, government, non-profit, and academic clients. Halelly's company, TalentGrow, improves the human side of work by increasing the leadership and interpersonal communication skills of leaders and their teams. TalentGrow provides a variety of services that are geared toward facilitating performance improvement, including learning solutions, team building, performance improvement consulting, and coaching. Halelly has worked with all organizational levels, from C-level and senior leaders to front-line managers and individual contributors. Her focus areas include team building, management and leadership, communication skills, coaching, and change management.

Monster MNEMONIC Maker

Objectives

- To improve memory by mnemonic applications.
- To review the learning during the program to ensure comprehension and retention.

Audience

Any group.

Time

15 to 20 minutes.

Materials and Equipment

- A set of MNEMONIC Monsters.
- An answer board or flip chart for each participant.
- A marker for each participant.

Area Setup
Normal training room setup.

Process
1. At the end of the training session, give a monster to each participant. State that this is a mnemonic monster and that MNEMONOIC stands for Monster Name Equals Memory Of Necessary Information Chunks.
2. Challenge participants to name their monsters with the perfect mnemonic that represents all they want to remember from your session.
3. You may use some of the following examples: You may call your monster "PEPE" to remember: Patience, Energy, Persistence, and Excellence; "VIEW" to remember Visionary, Inspiring, Enthusiastic, and Wise; or "DOT" to remember Decide, Organize, and Try.
4. Ask for volunteers to share their mnemonics for increased information recall.

 nsider's Tips

- You may place individuals in groups to develop mnemonics.
- You may play a follow-up game, giving the mnemonic and having groups or individuals state what they stand for.

Submitted by Susan Doctoroff Landay
Susan Doctoroff Landay is currently the president of Trainer's Warehouse. She joined her father in 1997, in what was then a fledgling business. Prior to that, Sue spent two and half years consulting and training in the field of negotiation and another two years marketing a business history consulting company. She graduated from Yale College (BA in 1986), the Kellogg Graduate School of Management at Northwestern University (MBA in 1992), and Ringling Bros. and Barnum & Bailey Clown College (MFA in 1987). Susan values using humor to enhance presentations.

Continuous Learning Review

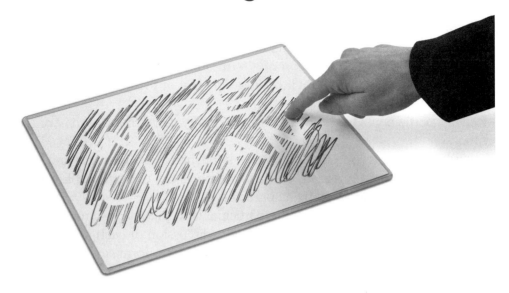

Objectives
- To review the learning during the program to ensure comprehension and retention.
- To encourage participants to be responsible for their learning.
- To understand gaps in learning, enabling prompt action.

Audience
Any group of twenty or fewer participants.

Time
15 to 30 minutes every day of a program.

Materials and Equipment
- An answer board or flip chart for each participant.
- A marker for each participant.

Area Setup
Normal training room setup.

Process

1. Divide the training program into modules.
2. Brief the participants on the importance of summarizing and reviewing the program content.
3. Ask participants to summarize and review each module after completion. Have them each write a question or a term on his/her answer board. Have them take turns holding up their boards. The rest of the group answers the question or defines the term.
4. Request participants to comment on their observations of the summary process.
5. Then have a discussion primarily to check for misperceptions, missing learnings, etc. Elaborate, if needed, on certain aspects not understood. Ensure that the module was understood by all participants.
6. At the end of the program, ask the participants to provide a summary of each of the modules. Ask for volunteers to lead a discussion of each module. If you have more participants than modules, have them form small groups. Ask them to end their discussion with one important question from the module.
7. Fill in the gaps, if any, to conclude the program.

 nsider's Tips

- Encourage the participants to keep the review process brief and to the point.
- Sufficient time should be allotted for this process while designing the program module.
- Participants feel more responsibility to participate and concentrate on the program, ensuring learning.

Submitted by Mohandas Nair

Mohandas Nair is a management educator. He teaches, trains, facilitates, mentors, and coaches management students and corporate executives. He has a graduate degree in mechanical engineering and had wide experiences spanning more than thirty years in industrial engineering and human resources development in industry, consultancy, and education. His vision: "To make a positive impact on every individual I meet and 'touch' and help them to understand their true potential."

Chapter 8

Time and People Management

Trainers want to keep things moving along in the session and at the same time encourage as much participation as possible. Maximizing participation uses more time, although we know it is critical. At times you may have a participant or two in your session whose behavior uses up time. Undesirable behaviors, such as returning from breaks late or allowing cell phones to ring, interrupt the flow of the session, may have a negative effect on the positive climate you are trying to create, and use up time, so you risk the chance that some participants may get out of hand.

The seven methods presented in this chapter offer creative ways to manage both your time and undesirable behaviors.

Money for Trivia

Objectives
- To encourage participants to return from break on time.
- To energize a group.

Audience
Works well for groups from three to twelve people.

Time
Each session takes about 7 minutes.

Materials and Equipment
- Classroom Prize Pack and Dilbert encourage-mints (any one of four available). Some prizes need to be better than others.
- Two containers for the prizes—one to hold the better prizes, one to hold the less expensive prizes.

- Series of prepared, non-relevant, trivia questions, preferably at least a dozen trivia questions for *every* break for *every* class you train. Mix in some class topic-related questions.
- Play money.
- Paper for each participant.
- A pen or pencil for each participant.
- Puzzle Power Software (optional).

Area Setup
No special seating required.

Process
1. Introduce the idea of trivia before each break to encourage participants to come back from break on time.
2. After each break, read six to eight trivia questions to the group, one at a time. Remind the group not to say the answers out loud. Tell them that others might be able to come up with the answer a few questions later after they have thought about it a bit longer.
3. Allow about 30 seconds to think about each question and to write down an answer.
4. Review the answers by asking the class for the correct answers. Each answer is worth $10 in play money.
5. Give each participant money for each correct answer. Give them credit for partial answers (example: Who are Donald Duck's nephews? Huey, Louie, and Dewey. Give part of total amount for knowing two of the three).
6. At the end of session, have them count their money and award the "grand" prize container to the person with the most money. Encourage clapping and congratulations. Have the winner choose one prize from the container.
7. Have the rest of the group choose a "runner up" prize from the second container.

Variations
- As the participants are introducing themselves at the beginning of the session. I have them tell us their favorite pastimes. For the last trivia of the day, have them list each person's name. Then from memory, list each person's favorite pastime. This starts the group moaning and groaning and staring at each other. Again, they receive money for all the correct answers they can come up with. (Give them credit for remembering their own.)

- You could also hand out a customized crossword puzzle in the morning that pertains to the training topic. Present it with the introductions, tell them they will use it as a review at the end of the session, and encourage them to complete it by telling them it will be worth "points." Throughout the session, remind them to be working on their crossword puzzles. At the end of the day when they are counting their money, it gives them another chance to win the grand prize. (For each correct answer they receive $10.) Use Trainer's Warehouse Puzzle Power Software to create the crossword.

Insider's Tips

- You may wish to give them hints during the trivia session.
- You might want to skip the prizes for the rest of the class and just hand out one prize to the winner.
- Internet trivia offers easy adult or easy children sections or Trainer's Warehouse's Pre-presentation Trivia has some great questions ready to use in PowerPoint slides.

Submitted by Patricia Burggraff, CPP, SPHR

Patricia Burggraff, CPP, SPHR, has been employed with ADP for several years as a senior client trainer. She is also an ADP certified payroll specialist. Patricia's background is HR and payroll and she holds a B.S. degree in business administration in human resource development and an AAS degree in accounting.

Wheel of Consequences

Objectives

- To keep a group on track.
- To have a pleasant way to reprimand undesired behavior, such as cell phones ringing during a training session, speaking over the trainer, checking emails, returning late from lunch or breaks, etc.

Audience

Any group size.

Time

The activity can be used throughout the entire training session to keep everyone on track.

Materials and Equipment

- Turn 'n Learn Game Wheel with various consequential activities in each "spoke."
- Hula Hoop®, straw hat, paddle ball, and other fun diversions.

Area Setup

The room may be arranged for the class currently in session.

Process

1. Create the ground rules at the beginning of the workshop. You may have some "starter" ground rules such as "start and end on time" or "breaks every 90 minutes" posted on a flip chart. Ask participants to add to them. Once the list is complete, gain agreement to the ground rules from all and post on a wall. Tell participants that the wheel is the enforcer.
2. If a participant breaks the rules (cell phone rings or returns late from lunch), he or she must spin the wheel.
3. Whatever activity the wheel lands on, the participant must do:
   - Dance around a straw hat.
   - Say the Pledge of Allegiance to the flag.
   - Bring the instructor some water.
   - Use the Hula Hoop.
   - Paddle ball for 60 seconds.
   - Sing the Alphabet Song.

Insider's Tips

- Don't give in when the participant hesitates to do an activity.
- This is a great way to get everyone to come back from lunch and breaks on time and to keep the session on track.

Submitted by Carolyn E. Conway

Carolyn E. Conway has twenty-three years' experience in credit union and bank branches, fifteen of those as a branch manager. She has currently been with CUNA Mutual as a lending specialist/business consultant for eight years, most recently focusing as staff development manager at Georgia Federal CU in Atlanta, Georgia.

Break Time—Roll the Dice!

Objectives
- To involve participants in determining the length of their breaks.
- To add interest and interaction.

Audience
Any training or meeting group.

Time
Less than 2 minutes.

Materials and Equipment
- Two large Dry Erase Cubes.
- Dry Erase markers.

Area Setup
Front of room, visible to audience (table or floor).

Process
1. Prior to the group event, write a single number on each side of both dice cubes.
2. Prior to a break, ask one or two participants to roll the dice in front of the room, then add up their numbers and use that for the length of the group's break time.

Insider's Tips

- To ensure minimum and maximum break times to suit your event, customize the dice by selecting numbers carefully. For example:

Die 1	Die 2
Two	Five
Three	Six
Four	Seven
Five	Eight
Six	Nine
Seven	Ten

- For larger groups and/or longer desired break times, consider using more than two dice and involving more participants.

Submitted by Amy Henderson

Amy Henderson has been involved in all facets of training and development for over eighteen years. She has thousands of classroom hours facilitating training and has designed and implemented a wide range of programs. Her specialty is customizing every program to the particular needs of each client. She has delivered training to construction foremen in the Arizona desert and insurance executives in Manhattan. Amy does her homework and makes the content of her programs practical and real-world. Coupled with her ability to quickly connect with people, training participants can't help but become involved.

Let's Return

Objectives

- To gain control of a training room in a way that is not disruptive.
- To allow participants to finish their thoughts before coming back together.

Audience

Any group.

Time

5 minutes.

Materials and Equipment

- Tingshas.

Area Setup

A space where everyone can see you.

Process

1. Tell everyone how long the breakout exercise they are working on will take before they start. You will not necessarily end after this amount of time; instead, you will end when 80 percent of the group has finished completely.

2. As the exercise progresses, give the group a 2-minute warning when you see that at least half of the teams are finishing up. This will encourage everyone to finish up.

3. Give a 30-second warning. After about a minute, when people are nearly done, stretch your arms wide apart as if you were measuring something very wide and say in a normal voice "We're going to end in this much time." Begin to walk among the participants.

4. Start to move your hands together, as if what is being measured is getting a bit smaller. Repeat again in a normal voice "We're going to end in this much time." Notice how the participants start to refocus on you and how the room becomes quieter.

5. Continue to walk through the room, repeating moving your hands together a little, and repeating the phrase until the entire room is quiet. Plan to be at the front of the room when your hands finally come together.

6. Pick up the Tingshas from the front table and lightly ring them to get the attention of anyone who is still distracted. At this point, the whole group will be focusing on you.

Insider's Tips

- There is no need to yell, although there will be noise and it will seem as though no one hears you. Eventually they will.
- Be careful not to hit the Tingshas too hard together. They can be very loud and jarring.
- Airport Security will search your bags if you leave these Tingshas in your carry on. Take them out and put them through in a tray.

Source

I learned this technique at an Accelerated Learning Conference, probably from Doug McPhee. I believe he originally used it for kindergarten classes.

Submitted by Lou Russell

Lou Russell is president and CEO of Russell Martin & Associates, a twenty-year-old consulting and training company headquartered in Indianapolis. She is the author of *The Accelerated Learning Fieldbook, Project Management for Trainers, Training Triage, IT Leadership Alchemy, Leadership Training,* and *The 10 Steps to Successful Project Management.* She is a frequent contributor to *Training, Computer World, Cutter Executive Reports,* and *Network World,* among others, and publishes the monthly Learning Flash online newsletter and a column for *Inside Indiana Business.* A popular speaker, Lou addresses national and international conferences such as the ASTD, Training Directors Forum, Project Management Institute, Project World, and LotuSphere. She holds a computer science degree from Purdue University, where she taught database and programming classes, and a master's in instructional technology from Indiana University.

Prize Roulette

Objectives

- To create an energetic way to re-start the session following a break.
- To initiate a dialogue about the use of incentives in the workplace.

Audience

Any number, any level.

Time

5 minutes.

Materials and Equipment

- Several prizes for each spin.
- One Turn 'n Learn Game Wheel, mounted on an easel or flip chart.

Area Setup

- For smaller groups (twelve or fewer), write in each name or initials on the game wheel.
- For larger groups (twelve or more), write the numbers 1 through 12 on the game wheel.
- Set up the game wheel on a wall board or flip-chart easel, making sure that the wheel turns freely.

Process

1. For smaller groups, ensure initials/names match the participants.
2. For larger groups, assign each player a number 1 through 12. (Player 13 is assigned "1," player 14 is assigned "2," etc.)
3. Inform the group that you will spin the wheel immediately following each break, and that the name or number shown receives a prize.
4. Following each break, announce the prize and then spin the game wheel.
5. Determine and then announce the initials/name OR number.
6. Player (or players) with that number are eligible to receive the announced prize. Player(s) must be present to receive the prize.
7. If the winner is not present, he or she does not receive the prize. Spin again.

Variation

Teams may be assigned a color. Spin the wheel and award prizes to each participant of the team assigned the color. All members of the selected team must be present to win.

Insider's Tip

- This activity works best when you announce, "I will award a prize following each break, and the winning participant, or participants, must be present to receive the prize."

Submitted by Linda M. Raudenbush, Ed.D., and Steve Sugar

Linda M. Raudenbush holds a BA in mathematics and secondary education from St. Joseph College, an MS in applied behavioral science from Johns Hopkins University, and an Ed.D. in human resource development from George Washington University. Linda has more than twenty-five years of experience in training, organization development, and leadership coaching in both private and public sectors. Linda holds an ACC in leadership coaching granted by International Coaching Federation. Linda has been adjunct professor at National-Louis University and Strayer University, and is in her eighteenth year of part-time teaching at the University of Maryland, Baltimore. She is currently employed as an internal HRD/OD consultant and leadership coach at the U.S. Department of Agriculture. Linda is an active volunteer in her community, having been nominated as the Maryland Volunteer of the Year for 2003 and 2004, and was awarded Volunteer of the Year in 2005 for Faith-Based Initiatives.

Steve Sugar writes "fun with a purpose" activities that have helped thousands of learners to experience classroom topics in a more meaningful way. Steve holds an A.B. in economics from Bucknell University and an M.B.A. in economics, statistics, and management from George Washington University. Steve served two tours as a Deck Watch Officer in Vietnam for the U.S. Coast Guard. Steve currently teaches business and education courses for the University of Maryland Baltimore County (UMBC). He is the author or co-author of *Training Games* (an ASTD Info-line), *More Great Games, Games That Teach, Games That Teach Teams, Games That Boost Performance,* and *Primary Games.* Steve has developed three game systems featured by Langevin Learning Services—the Management 2000/ Learn It board game, the QUIZO game system, and the X-O Cise dice game.

The Chicken Rules

Objectives
- To give participants an opportunity to structure their learning environment.
- To introduce an element of fun to a group meeting of any kind.

Audience
Any size group. Most useful for groups that meet repeatedly or over a longer period of time.

Time

A few seconds, interjected periodically throughout the meeting.

Materials and Equipment

- Rubber Chicken (Chicken Little or Squawking Rubber Chicken).
- Flip-chart easel and markers.

Area Setup

Nothing special required.

Process

1. Initiate the session with basic ground rules. Present the rubber chicken and explain how the chicken will rule.
2. At each break, the chicken will be tossed from one person to another, or one table to another, so that a new person catches the chicken at each throw.
3. On catching the chicken, the receiver may state a ground rule that the group must follow: for example, "Speak one at a time." The facilitator will add this rule to the others listed on the flip chart.
4. At the next break, when the chicken is tossed again, another rule may be added.
5. At the conclusion or at some interim point, the group should agree to the whole set of ground rules as their "group agreement." If there are any that the group objects to, eliminate those rules.
6. The result is an agreed-on set of cultural guidelines, which can be used repeatedly with the same group.

nsider's Tips

- This process can also be used purely for fun. Chicken-catchers may state playful rules, e.g., everyone must face the back of the room.
- The game can also be used to teach learning points. For example, the subject could be communication. Chicken-catchers would be asked to guide the group in a communication practice, such as "Use non-verbal communication only until the next break."

Source

Inspired by M.K. Key, Ph.D., Key Associates, Nashville TN.

Submitted by Carson Key Whitehead

Carson Key Whitehead is a sophomore, majoring in advertising in the College of Communications, at Appalachian State University in Boone, North Carolina. A Nashville native, she grew up observing and assisting her mother, Dr. M.K. Key, in classroom activities. Her overheads and quips have entertained thousands of students across the years. She is a creative thinker, with a great sense of humor, and is somewhat fearless with her ideas.

Cell Phone Attack

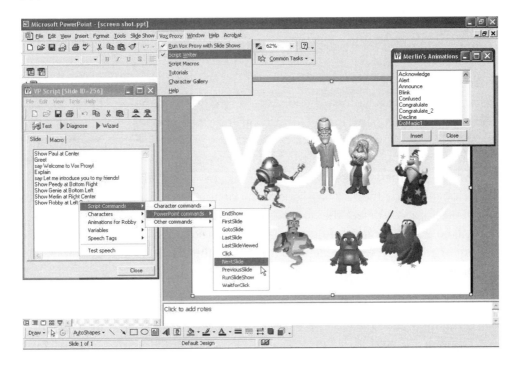

Objective

- To make participants aware of the need to turn off cell phones.

Audience

This probably works best with more playful groups. Think about the kinds of folks who might give you a hard time with cell phones in the first place.

Time

Less than 5 minutes.

Materials and Equipment

- Vox Proxy Software.
- PowerPoint presentation.
- LCD and screen.

- Sound system for the computer.
- "Laughable Lyrics" CD (optional).

Area Setup
Any setup will work as long as participants can see the screen.

Preparation
1. Use the Vox Proxy software you own to create an animated character who occasionally asks participants to turn off their cell phones.
   - Vox Proxy provides a variety of characters, so choose the one that matches the theme of your training the best. For instance, use Merlin for a "King Arthur" themed workshop on leadership or an ogre-like creature for a "Robin Hood" themed workshop on coaching.
   - Make sure you select the "balloons on" option. In this way participants will be able to read *and* hear what the characters say. For better visibility, enlarge the size of the balloons (follow the instructions in the Help section of Vox Proxy to do that).
   - It's very easy to change the words the character says, so customize them for the particular class. For example, you may have the character say something like "Please turn off your cell phones—yes, that includes the group at the back too!" Of course, use your best judgment. You will know what participants will or will not tolerate, and whether people will find this funny or embarrassing. Try changing the characters' warnings to match the training content, participants, or even the time of the year. For example, around Christmas have "Santa Claus" say, "If you don't turn off your cell phones you will get no Christmas presents!"

Process
1. Show the character at key moments during the class, at the beginning of each day, or after lunch.
2. For added fun, use the Cell Phone song from the "Laughable Lyrics" CD.

 nsider's Tip

- You will most likely use this activity only if you already own the Vox Proxy Software.

Submitted by Cris Wildermuth

A native of Rio de Janeiro, Cris Wildermuth is an international executive coach and trainer, traveling extensively throughout Latin America. She is the author of *Diversity Training* (ASTD Press), specializes in personality diversity, and is currently completing her doctorate in leadership at Bowling Green State University. When back home, Cris enjoys developing unforgettable leadership, diversity, and team-building workshops populated by international spies, gourmet chefs, and zoo animals.

Chapter 9

Training Techniques

E very trainer seeks new creative ways to present material. Who hasn't attended a Bob Pike training session or read one of his books looking for his latest, greatest training technique? When looking for the most creative training technique, don't forget the basics of active learning. Ensure that the activity and the methodology are right for your participants. The following will remind you of several basic training guidelines:

- Activities must support the learning objectives.
- If the activity requires props or timers, they must be acceptable to the audience.
- Activities should not offend participants in any way.
- Everyone should be able to participate.
- The time invested should yield a proportionate amount of learning.
- You should be confident that you can implement the technique and that participants will achieve the anticipated results.
- Build in time to process the activity at its conclusion.

Activities are potent learning tools as long as you select then appropriately, take time to prepare, and ensure a successful outcome for your participants. The training techniques you select should support your objectives.

Magic Coloring Book

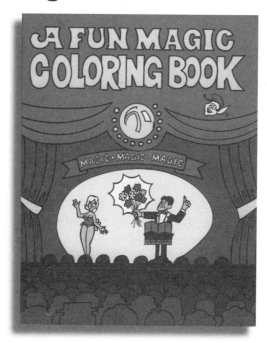

Objectives
- To show the class how they "fill in" and color their presentations with their own stories.
- To bring showmanship into the demonstration of creating a dynamic presentation.

Audience
Any group. Should be a size so that all can see the process.

Time
It can be as little as 3 minutes (quick explanations of each page as it relates to the process) and as long as 8 to 10 minutes (audience participation and lengthier explanations of each step of the process).

Materials and Equipment
- Magic Coloring Book.

Area Setup

The room should be set up in a horseshoe style or fishbone. Make sure every participant can see as you show the magic coloring book.

Preparation

Practice flipping through the coloring book—become familiar as to how it works.

Process

1. Start by showing the group the very bottom of the coloring book—all the blank pages should show no color. Ask the group, "What do you see?"
2. Explain that we all start out with a blank page when we begin designing our presentations (or learning to supervise, or becoming a team member, or whatever you will use this prop to demonstrate).
3. Then flip from the very top. Ask the group, "What do you see?"
4. Explain that once we begin learning content or gaining experience it starts to tell a story. It is still in black and white. So what is missing? Obtain some responses.
5. Flip the pages from the middle. Warning: At this point almost everyone is so amazed at your magic that they don't always hear the final part of the demonstration. They want to know, "How did you do that?"
6. Explain that the "color" portion of the magic coloring book is the color of our personal stories and illustrations in our presentation (or the experiences as a supervisor, or the knowledge of team work).
7. Ask for suggestions of elements that will add color to presentations (or supervision or teamwork, or whatever your topic happens to be).

 **nsider's Tips**

- Practice on family and with different venues for illustrative purposes.
- Because this prop is so simple, it is easy to use in many different situations.
- Teach someone else to use it and have them demonstrate—you'll be a hero.
- Feel free to embellish and enhance the showmanship by tapping the book on a table a few times to "shake the pictures into place," before flipping through the book the second or third time. Alternatively, flex the binding a few times for the same effect.

Source

One of my Dale Carnegie trainers, Earl Taylor, is a master at magic and illustrations. It is because of his excitement that I have, over the years, developed a love for showmanship.

Submitted by Carrie Gendreau

Carrie Gendreau is the owner of The Training Connection, a firm that helps grow people by guiding them in developing powerful and effective leadership training and communication skills. Carrie has been in the training and consulting field for over twenty-seven years. She is a certified Dale Carnegie instructor. She is currently an instructor for Granite State College and calls herself a "tour guide" (not professor). She contributed to, edited, and compiled the book *Wit and Wisdom from the Front Porch*. Carrie was listed in *Who's Who of Entrepreneurs 2002–2003*.

Name Tent Teams

Objective
- To quickly create teams or subgroups.

Audience
Any training or meeting group.

Time
Less than 5 minutes.

Materials and Equipment
- One name card per participant. (Any of the following will work.)
  - Disposable Tent Cards.

- Print & Slide Name Card with holder.
- Upright Reusable Name Card with white stand.
- Sturdy Tent Cards (Reusable).
- Different colored markers (Dry Erase or regular, depending on type of name tent).
- Optional: Different colored stars or stickers.

Area Setup
One table tent in front of each participant.

Process
1. Prior to the group event, determine individuals you wish to have form sub-groups based on who is in the larger group.
2. Assign each subgroup or team a color.
3. Write each participant's name on an individual name tent using the same colored marker for those individuals you want in each subgroup. Do not draw attention to the different colors.
4. During the session event, when you are ready to break into subgroups or teams, simply ask participants to gather with those participants whose names are written in the same color on their name tents.

Insider's Tips

- To speed up the process, assign areas for each color: blue team on the left, red team in the middle, etc., and challenge them to see how quickly they can gather with their new teams.
- To create another subgroup or team, prior to the group event, place colored stars or stickers inside or underneath each name tent and ask participants to find their stickers and see what new group they are part of. Simply ask participants to gather with those who have the same sticker inside their name tents: all blue stars on the left, red stars in the middle, etc.

Submitted by Amy Henderson

Amy Henderson has been involved in all facets of training and development for over eighteen years. She has thousands of classroom hours facilitating training and has designed and implemented a wide range of programs. Her specialty is customizing every program to the particular needs of each client. She has delivered training to construction foremen in the Arizona desert and insurance executives in Manhattan. Amy does her homework and makes the content of her programs practical and real-world. Coupled with her ability to quickly connect with people, training participants can't help but get involved to really learn.

Ticket Mixer to Assign Groups

Objectives
- To promote networking among participants.
- To create small groups, pairs, and trios for classroom activities.

Audience
Works with any size group, including large audiences.

Time
Use this activity multiple times throughout a training session. Each use will last approximately 2 or 3 minutes as participants mix and mingle to find their pairings.

Materials and Equipment
- Raffle tickets, torn in half.

Area Setup
Any room arrangement will work.

Process

1. At the beginning of the training session, give half a ticket to each participant.
2. When a training activity calls for small groups, or partners, or trios, refer to the tickets:
   - When pairs are needed, have participants stand and find their ticket matches. ("Drop This Ticket" and "Keep This Coupon" with the same ticket number.)
   - The next time pairs are needed, use last ticket digit to find partners with an opposite odd or even number (1, 3, 5, 7, 9, find a 2, 4, 6, 8, 0).
   - The third time pairs are needed, use last ticket digit to find the same odd or even number (1, 3, 5, 7, 9 find another 1, 3, 5, 7, 9, and 2, 4, 6, 8, 0 find another 2, 4, 6, 8, 0).
   - The fourth time pairs are needed, have participants find someone who has the same words on his or her ticket: "keep this coupon" or "drop this ticket" (the numbers don't matter for this grouping).
   - The fifth time pairs are needed, tell participants there are two kinds of tickets based on the last ticket digit: low numbers (0 to 4) and high numbers (5 to 9). Have participants find someone else with that same kind of ticket.
   - When trios are needed, have participants find a "two-on-one" group (two "drop this ticket" with one "keep this coupon" or two "keep this coupon" with one "drop this ticket").
   - When small groups are needed, have participants find their common ticket numbers using the last digit (all the 1s together, 2s together, 3s together, etc.).
     - Depending on the size of the group, you could make the groups smaller by segregating the "Keep This Coupon 1s" from the "Drop This Ticket 1s." the "Keep This Coupon 2s" from the "Drop This Ticket 2s", etc.
     - You could also make the groups larger by combining odds and evens or low numbers (0 to 4) and high numbers (5 to 9).
   - The next time small groups are needed, have participants line themselves up by ticket number, lowest to highest. Starting at the beginning of the line, the first five or six people become Group 1, the next five or six people become Group 2, and so on.
3. For longer sessions, or to increase the amount of networking, have participants give their tickets to the persons on their left (or right) and begin the Ticket Mixers again!

Insider's Tips

- Prior to the training session, tear apart the tickets and put them into a bowl. Be sure to count the number of tickets and have an exact number (1 participant = 1 ticket). This will allow each participant to select a ticket from the bowl as he or she enters the room.
- Be creative! Create your own Ticket Mixers to fit the size of your group. For example, instead of using the last ticket digit, use the fourth ticket digit.
- In a large group, or one that might need extra help to network, ask participants to physically move somewhere in the room to designate their tickets, then direct participants to find their pairs, trios, or groups. For example, have all the "keep this coupons" move to the right side of the room and the "drop this tickets" move to the left side of the room.
- Depending on number of participants, facilitator might wish to announce additional rules, such as "the person needs to be at a different table" or "the person needs to be someone you have not yet worked with today."
- If there are an odd number of participants, allow participants to find their pairs/groups. Assist with any leftover participants by forming one trio or asking those participants to act as observers.
- At the end of the session you may wish to select one number to receive a prize.

Submitted by Cindy Huggett

Cindy Huggett is a Certified Professional in Learning and Performance (CPLP) with over fourteen years' experience in organization development, performance management, leadership, program design, classroom facilitation, and adult learning. In addition to her consulting practice, Cindy is a training performance consultant for AchieveGlobal. She has been honored as a Triangle Business Journal 40-Under-40 Award Recipient, and co-founded Triangle Impact, a nonprofit organization that provides volunteer opportunities for busy professionals. She's also the past president of the ASTD Research Triangle Area Chapter and a current member of ASTD's National Advisors to Chapters.

Fiddle While You Learn

Objectives
- To establish an informal, upbeat, fun, exciting learning environment through the use of colorful and unusual learning aids that encourage handling.
- To support different learning styles by acknowledging that your cognitive brain can be actively learning while your hands are occupied with a kinesthetic action.

Audience
Any group of up to fifty adult learners.

Time
For the duration of an entire session.

Materials and Equipment

- Assortment of fiddles, approximately 10 percent more fiddles than participants. (Some of the best fiddles are Bug Eye Bob, Smiley Star, Pufferball 5, Small Koosh®, Tangle, Stress Pad, Bend-eez®, Gumby®, Klixx™, Urchin Ball, Squeeze Star, Iso Flex, Poof, and Kabob.)

Area Setup

Participants should be seated and divided into table groups for the duration of the session.

Process

1. Prior to the session, provide an assortment of fiddles in the middle of each table so that each table has one or two more fiddles than learners.
2. Introduce content of the session as you normally would, including an explanation of the fiddles and statement of their purpose (see Objectives above).
3. Ask participants to fully participate in content lesson while they "fiddle" with an item of their choosing from their tables.
4. At the end of the lesson/session, debrief the activity using two or three appropriate questions from this list:
   - Did you keep your original fiddle? Why/why not?
   - Which fiddle did you select? Why?
   - What did you do with your fiddle?
   - While you were fiddling, how did it impact cognitive learning of the lesson?
   - What did your table group members do with their fiddles?
   - How did you feel about fiddling at the start of this session? At the middle? At the end?
   - What did you learn about how you learn? How others learn?
   - Did you find that fiddling reduced or increased your distractions during training?
   - Where, when, and how can you apply what you learned today about fiddling and learning?

Insider's Tips

- This activity is ancillary/secondary to the primary learning in your lesson/session; position it as such.
- It is better to use this activity part-way through or toward the end of a workshop, not at the beginning, because you would already have established class norms for learning and behavior.
- To ensure that everyone is fiddling, ask about the fiddles during the first session break: "Is everyone comfortable with his or her fiddle?"
- This activity is suitable for all adult learners and all types of jobs, positions, and fields.

Submitted by Linda M. Raudenbush, Ed.D.

Linda M. Raudenbush holds a BA in mathematics and secondary education from St. Joseph College, an MS in applied behavioral science from Johns Hopkins University, an Ed.D. in human resource development from George Washington University, and a certificate in Leadership Coaching from Georgetown University. Linda has twenty-five years' experience in training, organization development, and leadership coaching in both private and public sectors. She has been adjunct professor and has published articles and chapters in *The Adjunct Faculty Handbook, Human Resource Development Quarterly,* Pfeiffer Annuals, *The ASTD Training and Performance Sourcebooks*, and the 2002 McGraw-Hill publication, *Creative New Employee Orientation Programs.* Linda consults in the HRD/OD/coaching fields and is currently employed as an internal HRD/OD consultant and leadership coach at the U.S. Department of Agriculture.

Music Makes the Training Go Round

Objective
- To create a motivating climate through use of various music activities for a full-day or multiple-day program.

Audience
Unlimited.

Time Estimated
Minimal; used during individual/group activities or during/returning from breaks.

Materials and Equipment

- Two or three CD players, depending on how the day is sequenced.
- CDs: "Everybody Dance"; "Tunes for Trainers"; "Best of Mozart"; "Laughable Lyrics for Meetings & Training."
- Enough Boomwhackers so that each participant can have one.

Area Setup

No special arrangement is needed.

Process

1. Create different environments through the use of music. As participants arrive, play "Tunes for Trainers" as background music. Encourage introductions; however, music will also bridge conversation gaps for quiet participants as they settle in.
2. When calling a morning or afternoon break, begin a countdown using "Laughable Lyrics for Meetings and Training." Begin class immediately at end of the countdown.
3. Energize group post-lunch with "Everybody Dance" as they return or during a stretch break.
4. During individual reflection or small and large group work, play quiet selections to stimulate thinking.
5. During a mid-afternoon slump, take 5 minutes and energize the group by having them create a song or rhythm work with the Boomwhackers, adding a chant around a major concept from the content.
6. As participants leave, play appropriate selection from "Laughable Lyrics for Meetings & Training."

nsider's Tips

- Multiple CD players helps avoid fumbling while changing CDs.
- Depending on group size, multiple Boomwhacker sets may be needed so that each person has one.
- Pay attention to participant reaction to too much music to avoid overload.

Submitted by Marjorie Treu

As president of Team Fusion, Marjorie Treu has twenty-three years of adult education experience in the travel, banking, manufacturing, and service industries. Her main focus is on executive and management development, leadership development, sales and sales management, and all aspects of human resources training. Her current emphasis is on organization development with a passion for working with team leadership through all stages of team formation, coaching teams in trouble, and experiential team building. Marjorie holds a bachelor's degree in education from the University of Wisconsin-Milwaukee and a PHR certification. She serves on the board for the Southeastern Wisconsin chapter of ASTD, most recently as president.

Birthday Ball

Objectives
- To create a novel way to introduce a list topic of strategies.
- To model how to add humor and energy to learning.

Audience
Any group.

Time
8 to 10 minutes.

Materials and Equipment
- Flip chart and markers.
- Light-Up Timer Ball.
- A numbered list of strategies pertaining to your topic on a handout for each participant.

Area Setup
Participants may be in any room arrangement.

Process

1. Find out from the audience who had a birthday last month and who has a birthday this month and next month. Take three names. Write the names on a flip-chart sheet.
2. Distribute the strategies handout.
3. Give the ball to the first person in the row or at a table. That person gently throws the ball to the next person, who throws it to the next, and so on. While the participants are throwing the ball, have the group sing "Happy Birthday" to the first person on the list.
4. Whoever has the ball when the song has finished reads a strategy. (Have the strategies numbered and tell them to read the strategy next to a number of their choice.)
5. You then explain the strategy.
6. Repeat two more times using the next two birthday names.

 nsider's Tips

- For large groups, use two balls, with one starting at the front and another in the back.
- A variation of this is to start the light in the ball, keep passing it on, and whoever has it when the light stops reads the strategy.

Submitted by Yvette Zgonc

Yvette Zgonc is a highly sought-after national teacher trainer whose workshops consistently earn her the highest evaluations from workshop participants. She is a veteran classroom teacher, counselor, and mentor teacher. Yvette is Brain-Based Certified with the Jensen Learning Corporation and her love of brain-based teaching is infused in all her workshops. She is the author of the best-selling book, *Sounds in Action: Phonological Awareness Activities and Assessment* and is a contributing author to *Cooperative Discipline*. Teachers say they enjoy her dynamic presentations because they are both motivational and grounded in the realities of today's classrooms.

Chapter 10

Rewards and Recognition

Reward behavior you want repeated: few concepts are as solidly proven as this one. It works with children and adults, family and friends, colleagues and subordinates. And, of course, it also works with participants.

Spontaneous rewards can be implemented in your training session with minimal planning and effort. Check the ideas presented in the activities in this chapter to encourage the kind of behavior you want repeated in your training sessions.

Team Challenge

Objective
- To reward behavior outside a classroom you want repeated.

Audience
Any group; field and office staff.

Time
10 to 15 minutes.

Materials and Equipment
- A copy of the rules for the Team Challenge for each participant.
- Prize Wheel.

- Bulletin board with sheet(s) for tallying points accrued.
- Package of prizes; you could also use movie passes, free tank of gas, gift certificates, Dilbert Encourage-mints, etc.
- Grand prize.

Area Setup

Space for the Prize Wheel and bulletin board to post the team names and points accrued.

Process

1. Create five to ten teams of four to seven employees.
2. Provide each participant with a copy of the rules for winning prizes. For example, I use this activity for safety monitoring and participants receive a copy of the World Safety Cup Rules.
3. Pick the calendar year for competition, for example January 2009 to January 2010.
4. During a regularly scheduled meeting present the Team Challenge or, in our case, "The World Safety Cup." Select a time period for the challenge and to review the team's point total.
5. The team with the least number of points every two months (or whatever time period you choose) will be allowed to spin the Prize Wheel and be awarded a prize.
6. The team with the least number of points at the end of the calendar year wins a grand prize. In our case, the team with the least points as of January 2010 will be the Safety Cup Champions and win the Grand Prize.

Insider's Tips

- This activity can be reviewed in your morning staff meetings (we do it every two months).
- It is a fun, motivating way to that ensure employees practice appropriate behavior. In our case it provides an opportunity to reward employees who practice safety.

Source

Encouraged to submit by Kristen Costa from Connecticut Safety Engineering
Services, LLC.

Submitted by Yara Almodovar

Yara Almodovar is a Norwalk Community College graduate with an associate's
degree in marketing. While in college, she participated in an internship program
that placed her in the company she is currently working for, Two Men And A
Truck®. Yara is certified at various employment training seminars and classes,
locally and at the home office located in Lansing, Michigan.

Team Challenge Example: World Safety Cup Rules

1. If an employee has an accident and/or is injured on the job, the employee's team is charged 1 point.
2. If you are in an accident or hurt in an accident that is not the fault of any fellow (company) employee, your team will not be charged a point.
3. Any accident/injury that is not reported to management within 48 hours will count as 2 points against your team.
4. Any safety procedure violation will result in 4 points for your team.
5. New employees will be added to existing teams on a rotating basis, and no accidents/injuries will count until they have completed training.
6. A team that identifies an unsafe practice that becomes a new safety procedure will have 6 penalty points removed from its accrued total.

You're a Star!

Objective
- To recognize team member strengths and contributions.

Audience
Any size.

Time
10 minutes.

Materials
- A piece of 8.5" × 11" card stock for each participant.
- A pen or marker for each participant.
- A Docu-Pocket for each participant.
- Omni-Tabs for hanging the Docu-Pockets.
- Star Post-it® Notes, enough so that each participant can have five to ten.

Area Setup
Participants should have room to walk around.

Process
1. Ask each person to print his/her name in large letters on 8.5" × 11" card stock, insert it into a Docu-Pocket, and hang the Docu-Pocket in the room using the Omni-Tabs.
2. Give each person a stack of five to ten star Post-it® Notes.
3. Ask participants to look around the room and to identify something that they want to acknowledge about a team member's talent, achievement, or measure of support. Participants write what they appreciate about each of five to ten team members, listing one talent, achievement, or measure of support on each of the five to ten on star Post-it® Notes.
4. Ask participants to then distribute their Post-it® Notes by handing each recipient the Post-It® note that lists the item of talent, achievement, or measure of support, orally telling the recipient what they appreciate about him or her.
5. Have recipients place their Post-it® Notes on their Docu-Pockets.
6. Individuals can walk around the room to view each other's Post-it® Notes.

 nsider's Tip

- You may also have participants place the stars directly on the recipient's Docu-Pocket. Each recipient can read his or her collection of stars to the group.

Submitted by Jan Ferri-Reed, Ph.D.
Jan Ferri-Reed, president of KEYGroup®, has been helping leaders to create productive workplaces that retain talent. She is a frequently featured speaker, guest commentator, and consultant to a variety of industries and organizations of all sizes on leadership, teams, and retention. Representative clients for whom Jan provides services include MBNA America, U.S. Steel Corporation, Liberty Mutual, Volkswagen-Audi-Porsche, Pitney Bowes, MTV Networks, The IAMS Company, and Merrill Lynch. Jan is an active member of the American Society for Training and Development (ASTD), the Human Resources Planning Society (HRPS), and Pittsburgh Human Resources Association (PHRA).

Wanna Deal or Not?

Objectives
- To encourage participation.
- To review key concepts learned.

Audience
Ten to twenty participants.

Time
- Format I: Duration of the session.
- Format II: 30 minutes.

Materials and Equipment
- A Whiteboard on a Stick for each participant.
- Package of prizes and other inexpensive rewards such as Dilbert Encourage-mints or Achievement Pins. (One prize will be needed per participant.)

Area Setup
Classroom or U-shape style.

Process
The name of a prize is written in advance on each whiteboard; each student is issued a whiteboard (face-down) so the text cannot be seen by anyone.

Format I
Participants can be awarded a chance to turn over one of the whiteboards. (Create your own system for determining who receives the chance to flip a board. Perhaps the person volunteered in the session, received 100 percent on a skill check, etc.) The participant can choose which board to reveal. If he or she does not like the prize, he or she can flip one additional board. The first prize is eliminated from the game and the second prize will be given to the participant. *Note:* Once a person has decided he or she does not want the first choice, he or she cannot revert back to it. Subsequent participants can either choose the "eliminated" prize or flip over a new board.

Format II
At the end of the session, divide the group into two teams and conduct a review session. Each team will have the chance to eliminate a board from the other team by answering a question correctly. Continue with the review until there is only one board remaining. The team that still has a board will receive the prize on that final board.

Insider's Tips

- You may have to explain the concept of the "Deal or No Deal" game in more detail for those participants unfamiliar with the TV show.

Submitted by Stacy Lowman
Stacy Lowman is currently a support services training manager at Home Depot Supply, Inc. He started in July of 2002 as a trainer in human resources. Stacy holds a bachelor's degree in communications from the University of North Carolina at Greensboro and is pursuing a master's degree in human resources management. He has worked at Hughes and at Sprint as an educational consultant.

Chapter 11

Review of Knowledge and Skills

Reviewing knowledge and skills presented in a training session is a perfect way to solidify concepts, answer lingering questions, build retention, and clarify any misconceptions. Reviews can occur anytime during a session—not just at the end. A subject review can occur following a critical knowledge area, especially when the upcoming content is dependent on clear understanding of the concepts that were just completed. This allows participants to reflect on what they have learned and to prepare themselves for future content.

As a trainer, identify the areas within your session where content could be reviewed for enhanced understanding. Then use one of the techniques presented in this chapter. The contributors have outdone themselves with eleven creative, lively, and proven review activities.

Koosh® Ball Review

Objectives
- To review training materials.
- To encourage participation.
- To make review fun.

Audience
Any group, any size.

Time
5 to 15 minutes, depending on depth of review.

Materials and Equipment

- Koosh® ball.
- A prepared list of review questions for training content.

Area Setup

Any setup.

Process

1. Prepare a list of review questions from your training session.
2. Start the second day with, "What did we learn yesterday?"
3. Tell participants that you will throw the Koosh ball and ask a question from yesterday's materials. Ask for a volunteer.
4. Throw the Koosh ball to the volunteer and ask a question about the learning from the day before. When the person answers the question, he or she may throw the ball to anyone (his/her choice) in the room. Once someone catches the ball, ask the next question.
5. If someone gets stuck on a question, he or she can ask for help and throw the Koosh ball to his or her "lifeline."
6. The review continues until you run out of questions.

 nsider's Tips

- To encourage the first volunteer, I mention that the questions get harder as the review progresses. I usually have people begging to be first.
- Another option is to have each participant ask a question of the next person. This usually works better after one review has been done as described.
- Although the process shown is for a multi-day session, this technique could also be used in a one-day session. Instead of asking about what was learned the previous day, ask about what was learned in the previous section.

Submitted by Victoria Arellano

Victoria Arellano is a corporate trainer with over twenty years of experience. Her training career started in the U.S. Army, where she was a soldier and trainer for ten years. She has trained classes from military sensitive programs to non-technical corporate training. She is also an organization development specialist with ten years of experience. Her specialty is working with work teams in conflict. She holds a master's degree in conflict mediation and is a volunteer mediator for the City of Vancouver, Washington.

Stick 'em Up Review

Objectives
- To review material after or during a training session.
- To review material from the previous day(s) for sessions held over multiple days.

Audience
Any group.

Time
10 to 20 minutes, depending on how much material is to be reviewed.

Materials and Equipment
- One Whiteboard on a Stick for each participant.
- One Dry Erase marker for each participant (the pen-style markers with eraser work best).

- Erasers or tissues if not using markers that have erasers.
- Paper clips (or some way to keep track of participants' points).
- Prizes, such as those in the Classroom Prize Pack, if desired.

Area Setup
Any setting works.

Process
1. Distribute whiteboards, markers, and erasers/tissues (if needed). Explain the rules of the review.
2. Tell the participants that you will ask a question and that they are to write their answers on their whiteboards. If the participants are all facing the same way, have them show their answers immediately after they finish. Tell them that you will give an extra point to the first person with the correct answer, and you will give points to all with correct answers. Also say that the more difficult questions will be worth more points. If the room is arranged so that participants can see each other's boards, ask them to hide their boards until you say to show them. Award a point to each person with the correct answer.
3. Make the last question a "wager" question. Participants write the number of points they will "wager" on their boards along with their answers. If an answer is correct, the participant receives the extra points. If the answer is incorrect, he or she loses the points.
4. If you have a tie, have an all-or-nothing question to determine the winner.
5. If desired, reward the winner (or several top scores) with a small prize. You may wish to reward everyone with a bag of small wrapped candy.

nsider's Tips

- Include a mix of easy and difficult questions.
- For extra fun, you can designate additional questions (not just the last one) as "wagering" questions.
- I find handing a person a paperclip to keep score is easiest. You may, however, list participants' names on a flip chart and track their points with hash marks.
- Don't be afraid to give hints or act out the answers.
- Have fun!

Submitted by Ruby A. Bohannon

Ruby A. Bohannon began her training career at an early age, when she attempted to teach the family cat to sit up, roll over, and beg. Only "beg" was successful, and then only when he was in the mood. In every job, Ruby was always the person who "acquired" the responsibility to train others; she finally got the hint—that she was good at it and enjoyed it so should do it for a living. Ruby has been a full-time training professional for over ten years and feels blessed to have a job that allows the use of her creativity in a way that benefits others.

Content Relay

Objective
- To review lots of content in an enjoyable way.

Audience
Six to twenty-five participants.

Time
This relay can be tailored to the time you have available. Allow 60 to 90 minutes.

Materials and Equipment
- Lined note cards.
- Pens.
- A copy of the content for each participant.

- Flip chart or whiteboard and appropriate markers for keeping score.
- Timer, clock, or watch with a second hand.

Area Setup

Need enough space at front of room so that up to twelve participants can form two single-file lines.

Preparation

1. Before the session, prepare lined index cards that direct participants to create a question out of specific sections of the material so you can be sure that they cover all the material. For example, I use sixty cards for a twenty-eight-page insurance contract review for twenty-four participants. At the top, note the section they must ask the question from, and at the bottom, put the page number. That way if there's a question, it limits the amount of digging that needs to be done to find the answer. *Note:* You may not use all questions for the game, which is okay. The most important part is the time they spend finding the sections in the content and thinking about it to create the questions.
2. Create a tie-breaker question in case you need it.
3. Divide the cards in two equal stacks.
4. Draw a sample of the card on a flip chart or create a sample card for each table.

Process

1. Divide the participants into two teams. You can either have them choose a team name or name them Team 1 and Team 2.
2. Distribute cards, pens, and a copy of the content to each team.
3. Tell the teams that they are to create questions based on the section of content identified on each card. They should also write the correct answer on the card.
4. Tell the teams they have 30 minutes to complete their questions and answers. Team members can divide the cards up so that they are working on different content.
5. Once time is up (or when all cards are complete), collect all the cards, keeping the two team's separate.
6. Have all of the participants from each team stand up at the front of the room. Have each team form a single-file line. As each person answers a question, that person goes to the end of the line.

7. Explain that, after a question is read, the person at the head of the line will have 30 seconds to answer. If he or she can answer the question correctly without help, the team earns 2 points. If he or she answers correctly with help from the team, the team earns 1 point.

8. Advise that the ruling of the judge (you) is final. Feel free to go back to the printed content if you need to. Also feel free to eliminate a question if it is not worded in a way that allows the other team to answer; remember that they are being written by the participants.

9. Begin by reading one of Team 1's questions to Team 2 and then alternate either until the questions are gone or you run out of time. Try to allow a few minutes at the end to clarify any questions.

10. If you have to use the tie-breaker question, read it to the group. The first person to raise his or her hand can attempt the answer first. A correct answer wins for his or her team.

Insider's Tips

- Have fun with it; the participants will feed off of your energy.
- Walk around as teams are creating questions; most likely they have never created questions before. Encourage their efforts and give a little help if they need it, but resist the urge to create the questions for them.
- Suggest that if they finish creating questions before the allotted time, they could spend some time reviewing the part of the content that they weren't creating questions for, since this might help them in the game.
- This format is really designed for large pieces of content (I used a twenty-eight-page insurance contract). If you use less content, you will have fewer questions and may want to reconsider using the relay format and instead have them ask questions back and forth at their tables.
- In a larger group, you can ask each team to designate a reader. After you collect each team's cards, give them to the other team's reader. The readers will take turns reading questions to their own teams, e.g., you hand Team 1's questions to Team 2's reader, who then reads the questions to his/her own team.

Submitted by Carol A. Dawson, CIC, AIS, CISR

Carol A. Dawson works for Nationwide Insurance in Des Moines, Iowa. She has responsibility for designing and delivering property and casualty insurance training, with a concentration in personal lines insurance. She has been an insurance professional for fifteen years, with roles in customer service, agency production, quality assurance, underwriting and, finally, training. She is currently working on her master's degree in adult learning, performance, and development as well as her CPCU (Chartered Property Casualty Underwriter) designation. She is president of 1100 Toastmasters and is a contributor and content editor for Central Iowa ASTD's Pipeline.

Goal Setter Game

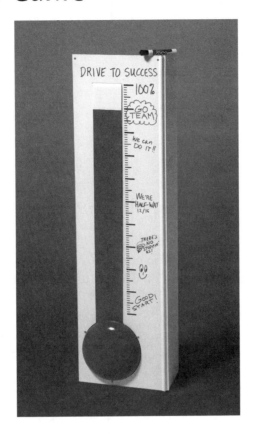

Objective
- To review information or test new material.

Audience
Typical session of twenty to thirty people in two teams.

Time
20 to 60 minutes, depending on need for review.

Material and Equipment
- Portable Goal Getter Thermometer.
- Dry Erase marker.
- Prizes.

Area Setup

The Portable Goal Getter Thermometer is placed at the head of the class, either on a table or mounted to an A-frame easel. Prizes are indicated on the Goal Getter Thermometer with the Dry Erase marker. You identify specific prizes at chosen intervals on the thermometer.

Preparation

Prepare questions for review ahead of time.

Process

1. Divide the group into two teams.
2. Explain the rules for play:
   - The first responder is elected by the toss of a coin or other appropriate means.
   - The facilitator asks the questions.
   - If Team 1 answers the question correctly, they receive another turn.
   - For each correct answer, the goal setter will be moved upward toward the next goal/prize.
   - After five correct responses, the other team automatically receives a turn.
   - If a question is answered incorrectly, the other team receives a turn.
3. Play for a set amount of time or until you have completed the review questions.
4. Distribute prizes as planned.

nsider's Tips

- Questions should increase in difficulty as the "temperature" rises.
- To remove individual tension, create subgroups within a team.
- Rewards need not be expensive. A few of the Trainers Warehouse products might suit this purpose well. Consider Scratch 'n See because you can give each person in the team a scratch card at minimal cost and only have a few big winners. Or you might choose a low-cost prize package.
- You can create more lively interactions by creating more teams.
- Use of a stopwatch will allow you to change teams if a team goes over its allotted time.

Submitted by Mike Doctoroff

Founder and Chairman of Trainer's Warehouse, Mike Doctoroff has 50+ years experience as an entrepreneur, physicist, and inventor. At Trainer's Warehouse, he is always hunting for new products to help trainers do their job better and have more fun in the process. Some of Mike's expertise about learning comes from his lifelong dedication to self-improvement. Always looking to challenge his brain (and improve his communication with his Assembly Team at Trainer's Warehouse) Mike's recent success is learning Conversational Spanish. Indeed, you CAN teach an old dog new tricks! He brings his expertise in teaching and training to the Greater Boston ASTD as a member, presenter, and Board Member. Mike holds his undergraduate degree from Williams College and his MBA from Rochester Institute of Technology.

Alphabet Review

Objectives
- To review content that falls into specific categories.
- To reinforce learning through recall.

Audience
Three or more participants.

Time
30 minutes (more if desired).

Materials and Equipment
- Time Timer or other timing device.
- Create a game kit for each group, including the following:
  - One or two Dry Erase dice, depending on the number of categories in the topic.
  - A Letters Thumball®.
  - Stop watch or other timing device.
  - Note pad.
  - Writing utensil.

Area Setup
Team style setup with tables.

Process
1. Write categories on the sides of the Dry Erase dice (example: for a change management session, you might use leadership, resistance, process, etc.).
2. Divide participants into groups of five or fewer members each. If you have a very small group, the participants can conduct this activity in a single group.
3. Distribute one game kit to each group.
4. Explain the rules of play. 20 minutes are allotted for game play. Tell each team:
   - Elect one team member as the timekeeper and give the person the timer.
   - Elect one team member as scorekeeper and give that person the note pad and writing utensil. The scorekeeper should record all group members' names on the pad, leaving room to record and total scores from each round.
5. Continue to explain the rules.
   - Group members will take turns playing or play as pairs.
   - The player's turn begins by tossing the Thumball® five times and recording the letter under the player's right thumb for each toss. The player then rolls the category die once.
   - The object of the game is to list one term starting with each letter. All terms should fit within the category that was rolled on the die. If change categories are listed on the die, participants would list an item that fits in the change category rolled on the die for each letter. If personality profile categories are listed on the dice, participants would list characteristics of a person that fits in that category, one for each letter. For example, if a participant rolls the dice and gets the change category "leadership" and tosses the Thumball®, receiving A, I, I, C, and V, correct answers could be alignment, involvement, inspiring, communicate, and vision—among others.
   - Other group members determine whether the answers are correct. The facilitator should be called in to settle any accuracy disagreements.
   - If the participant can list one correct answer for each letter, then the scorekeeper will award all 5 points. If the participant can't list all five, he or she receives 1 point for each answer he or she can provide.

- Participants should be given 30 seconds (more or less if the topic requires) to answer. The 30 seconds should start after the letters are selected and the die rolled. The timekeeper is responsible for calling "start" and "stop."
- The person with the highest score in each group at the end of the game is the winner.

6. Set the timer for 20 minutes. Ask the participants to begin play.
7. Roam around the room to observe, answer questions, and settle any accuracy disagreements.
8. When the time is up, debrief by giving participants the opportunity to share their experiences.

Insider's Tips

- If time and topic permits, have participants give a definition or example for each term they list.
- If you do not have enough categories to fill the die, write in special instructions such as "player chooses category."
- Play a sample round and ask the entire group to give the answers before dividing the participants into smaller groups.
- Consider offering a pass for difficult letters like Q, X, and Z.

Submitted by Amy Drennen

Amy Drennen has been an instructional designer and trainer at Yazaki North America Inc. since 2000. She enjoys applying adult learning principles to make learning more effective by creating fun experiences that reach all types of learners. She feels her biggest accomplishment in the training world was helping to create a shift in her corporation's learning culture through her innovative designs and constant striving to educate class participants about learning styles. This shift can be seen by comparing participants scoffing at kinesthetic toys at the beginning of her career to a recent complaint that there weren't enough toys to go around.

Pleasure Island Review

Objectives
- To review information covered in the training session.
- To give participants an opportunity to practice locating important information in training materials.

Audience

Thirty or fewer participants.

Time

30 minutes.

Materials and Equipment

- Forty to fifty review questions based on class content, including ten more difficult bonus questions.
- Time Timer.
- Two Extra Large Game Dice.
- Pleasure Island Game Board.
- Game pieces can be made by laminating clip art and placing Velcro on the back.
- Flip chart or Dry Erase easel.

Area Setup

Any training room configuration can be used, but an arrangement with clearly defined teams works best.

Preparation

Create the review questions in advance. Create at least ten questions that are more complex/difficult than the others. These will be used as bonus questions.

Process

1. Divide the group into two to four teams. Ask each team to identify a team captain. Assign one game piece to each team and place them to start.
2. Explain the rules of the game. Each team will be asked a question. The team captain should collaborate with the team members to determine the answer. Answers will only be accepted from the team captain.
3. If the question is answered correctly, the team may roll one die and advance down the road the number of spaces indicated on the die. If the question is answered incorrectly, the team may not advance.
4. Special spaces exist on the Pleasure Island Game Board, for example, a gone fishing bonus, golf bonus, losing a map, and getting lost. Follow the specific directions.

5. The first team to reach the finish or the team farthest down the road at the end of 20 minutes wins.
6. Set the timer for 20 minutes.
7. Ask the captain of each team to roll one die. The team that has the highest roll goes first.
8. Ask questions and move pieces according to the rules of the game. End the game when the timer reaches 0.

Insider's Tips

- Participants often do not realize that they are learning because they are having so much fun with this game. Because of this, it is important to explain the objectives of the activity and ask them to identify what they learned at the end.
- Encourage participants to use their class materials to look up the answers to the questions. This will make them more comfortable with using the materials back in their work environments.
- If you wish, you may make your own game board. Game boards can be made with design software, printed, and mounted on foam core with Velcro dots on spaces. Trainer's Warehouse Flip-Chart Stickers can be used to decorate the game board.

Submitted by Amy Drennen

Amy Drennen has been an instructional designer and trainer at Yazaki North America Inc. since 2000. She enjoys applying adult learning principles to make learning more effective by creating fun experiences that reach all types of learners. She feels her biggest accomplishment in the training world was helping to create a shift in her corporation's learning culture through her innovative designs and constant striving to educate class participants about learning styles. This shift can be seen by comparing participants scoffing at kinesthetic toys at the beginning of her career to a recent complaint that there weren't enough toys to go around.

Squeeze Play Course Review

Objectives
- To review material covered in the course.
- To introduce game-show excitement to a learning event.

Audience
Any size group.

Time
30 to 45 minutes or more (depending on number of questions).

Materials and Equipment
- Eggspert Selector and Buzzers or Who's First Gameshow Buzzer and touch pads.
- Index cards with course review questions.

Area Setup
Six teams of participants organized by table or random assignment. Create a game area in front of the room, with the buzzer system on a tabletop.

Process

1. Prepare review questions for the course material covered so far, or have the participants create these review questions by distributing index cards and asking for one question per card. Questions can be open-ended, true-false, or content-specific.
2. Place a buzzer or wireless touch pad in front of each team.
3. Read the first question, instructing the representatives to buzz when they think they have the answer. If the first answer is wrong, say "Nice try, but we need another answer" and allow the others to buzz and guess. Continue until the right answer is given.
4. If no representatives guess correctly, open the question to the audience. If the correct answer does not emerge, answer it correctly.
5. Encourage participants to rotate turns at the buzzers/touch pads.
6. Have everyone give a round of applause to close off the exercise.

 nsider's Tip

-   Keeping score is optional and probably not important (however, the table teams will do it anyway).

Source

Inspired by Donna Betty, Charles Cadwell, and Joe Fehrman.

Submitted by M.K. Key, Ph.D.

A licensed clinical-community psychologist, M.K. has over thirty years of experience in organizational quality. She teaches, consults, and speaks on topics such as leadership, customer value management, tools for change corporate culture, team development and facilitation, mediation of conflict, and creativity. Prior to forming Key Associates in 1997, she was vice president of the Center for Continuous Improvement with Quorum Health Resources, Inc. Her doctoral, master's, and bachelor of arts degrees, Phi Beta Kappa, *cum laude,* and honors in psychology, have all been with Vanderbilt University. She has served for years as adjunct associate professor of Human and Organization Development at George Peabody College of Vanderbilt. She has authored several books, including *Managing Change in Healthcare: Innovative Solutions for People-Based Organizations,* and *Corporate Celebration: Play, Purpose and Profit at Work* with Terry Deal.

Dartboard Learning Review

Objective
- To review material covered in the session.

Audience
Any group.

Time
25 to 45 minutes.

Material and Equipment

- One dart board.
- One set of three darts for each participant.
- General Rules posted on a flip chart as follows:
  - Each person should have one set of three darts.
  - Each person launches three darts, then removes them before the next person launches.
  - There should never be more than three darts on a dartboard at one time.
  - To determine who goes first, have each team launch one dart; whichever is closest to the bulls-eye goes first.
  - Inner bulls-eye is worth 50 points; outer bulls-eye is worth 25 points; outer highlighted spots double the points; and the inner highlighted spots triple the points.

Process

1. Tell participants they will play Dartboard Learning Review as a review.
2. Divide the group into four teams. Assign each team a group of numbers (e.g., 1 through 5, 6 though 10, 11 through 15, 16 through 20). Whenever a team member hits one of the assigned numbers, give the team an opportunity to answer a question. If members answer correctly, award them 10 points.
3. Apply standard point doubling/tripling if they land on "highlighted" spots.
4. If they hit another team's number, give them an opportunity to answer an easy 5-point question. (Optional: if they answer the question incorrectly, you can award the 5 points to the team whose number they hit—if that team can answer correctly). You can end this game whenever a certain number of points are accumulated, or after each team has answered five or ten questions.

Variations

- Require each team to hit each of its numbers three times. Each time team members do, award 10 points if the question is answered correctly. In this version, you will not ask them a question if they hit another team's dedicated number. When a team "closes" a number (hits it the third time) offer a bonus question for 25 points. In this version, play ends when the first team has closed all of its numbers. At the end of the game, tally all points to determine the winning team. In standard dart games, players typically use numbers 20 through 15 and the bulls-eye. This might be another way to keep it simple, if you don't want to keep track of each team's dedicated numbers.

- You may use categories to determine questions. Determine which numbers will correspond with which categories (e.g., 1 through 5 for quality, 6 through 10 for methodology, 11 through 15 for numeric facts, 16 through 20 for people). When a team hits a numbered spot, ask a category-appropriate question. Award 10 points for every question answered correctly. Award double and triple points as noted on the flip chart when landing on a highlighted spot. Play to 300 (or whatever other number you choose). The first team to reach the target number wins.
- Another dart board game is 301. Assign each team 301 points. Each team's goal is to work its way down to 0 points. The first to do so is the winner. As each team hits a number, ask team members a question; if the question is answered correctly, deduct the appropriate number of points. Usually, the object is to get to exactly zero; however, in your classroom version where you want to reward learning more than skill, you might choose to play until the first team passes (or hits) zero. If you're facilitating this game, you might like to break your questions into three or four levels of difficulty so that low-point and high-point spaces can be awarded appropriately.
- Dart Game Roulette begins by asking an individual or team a question. If the individual answers correctly, have him/her launch a dart to identify the number of points received for the correct answer. Play to 300 (or whatever other number you choose). The first team to reach the target number wins.

Insider's Tip

- If you look online for dart games, you'll find over fifty variations (www.mostdartgames.com is an excellent resource).

Submitted by Susan Doctoroff Landay

Susan Doctoroff Landay is currently the president of Trainer's Warehouse. She joined her father in 1997, in what was then a fledgling business. Prior to that, Sue spent two and half years consulting and training in the field of negotiation and another two years marketing a business history consulting company. She graduated from Yale College (BA in 1986), the Kellogg Graduate School of Management at Northwestern University (MBA in 1992), and Ringling Bros. and Barnum & Bailey Clown College (MFA in 1987). Susan values using humor to enhance presentations.

Whaddaya Know™?

Objectives
- To aid retention of new learning material.
- To improve recall and reinforce learning.
- To build team spirit.

Audience
Any group.

Time
30 to 60 minutes, depending on number of rounds played and difficulty of questions.

Materials and Equipment
- Whaddaya Know™? Game Board.
- Who's First Gameshow Buzzer (optional).

Area Setup

Set group into teams of two to six players. If playing with buzzers, set a "buzz in touch pad" in front of each group.

Preparation

1. Prepare your "questions" by category and write or print them onto white sheets or cards. *Note:* questions can be written in any format. On the television version of the game show, questions are structured such that the answer is on the card and the player needs to come up with the question that goes with it. For example, the card would read: "July 4, 1776." The player's correct response would be "When was the Declaration of Independence signed?" Facilitators can also feel free to use multiple-choice, true-false, or open-ended questions.
2. Insert "questions" back-to-back with the colored number points, so that you can reveal them when someone says, "I'll take "Category I for 300.""
3. If needed, prepare an answer grid.

Process

1. Explain to participants that teams will select game board questions with varying point values in each category (i.e., Sales for 100 points or Sports for 200 points). If a team buzzes in and answers a question correctly, the team is awarded the points assigned to that question and can choose the next question. If a team answers incorrectly, the team loses the point valued assigned to the question. The other teams will be offered the opportunity to answer the question.
2. Explain that the game is over when all questions are answered, the pre-allotted time has run out, or when you select a "final question." The team with the most points is the winner.
3. Randomly select a team to go first and ask the team to select a category and point value.
4. Read the "question" revealed on the back of the point value.
5. Have players "buzz in" when they know the correct response. Option: use a buzzer system (like Who's First?) to allow players to indicate when they know the answer. Alternatively, have them hold up their hands, ring a bell, or blow a whistle to indicate that they want to answer the question.
6. Give the first responder the opportunity to answer correctly (e.g., What is the preeminent quality award?). State whether the answer is correct or not.
7. Add or deduct points to the player's point tally according to whether the response is correct or incorrect.

8. If the answer was incorrect, give the second responder an opportunity to play. Reward points accordingly.

9. The player who answers correctly can choose the category and point value for the next round of play.

Insider's Tips

- To make the most of Whaddaya Know™? as a learning game, feel free to interrupt play when a question is answered incorrectly. Take a moment to explain the correct answer. Do the same if teams disagree about whether an answer is right or wrong. In this way, the game can successfully reinforce lessons and new material.

- Insert hidden bonus question into the back of a random category/point value. When players select these questions, invite all teams to wager and win extra points.

- Create a "daily double" question somewhere on the board. The question asked at this point in the game will be worth double the points indicated on the game board.

- Include a "final question" at the end of your game to allow teams to wager points.

- Use a buzzer system so that you don't have to wonder whose hand went up first.

- Use a stopwatch or timer to limit the amount of time a player/team has to respond.

- Over a multi-day course, have teams create games for one another. Making up questions really challenges participants to "know their stuff."

Submitted by Susan Doctoroff Landay

Susan Doctoroff Landay is currently the president of Trainer's Warehouse. She joined her father in 1997, in what was then a fledgling business. Prior to that, Sue spent two and half years consulting and training in the field of negotiation and another two years marketing a business history consulting company. She graduated from Yale College (BA in 1986), the Kellogg Graduate School of Management at Northwestern University (MBA in 1992), and Ringling Bros. and Barnum & Bailey Clown College (MFA in 1987). Susan values using humor to enhance presentations.

Bull's Eye Bowl

Objectives
- To review content.
- To create an out-of-chair game experience.

Audience
Six or more participants.

Time
25 to 45 minutes.

Materials and Equipment
- One target bowl (soup bowl 4 inches or larger).
- Four Koosh® balls, Urchin Balls, or other non-bouncing balls (it is recommended that you buy two or three extra balls as backup).
- One four-question game sheet per team for each round of play (created in advance based on the content).
- Masking tape (to create the throwing line).
- One watch or stopwatch.
- One whistle or noisemaker (chimes, etc.).
- One conference table (to hold the target bowl).
- Flip chart and markers.

Area Setup
See the preparation instructions below.

Preparation
1. Place a conference table in front or center of classroom.
2. Create a throwing line by stepping off two paces (about 7 feet) from one edge of the conference table. Using the masking tape, create a two-foot-wide throw line on the floor, parallel from the edge of the table containing the target bowl.
3. Place the target bowl on the table, 10 to 12 inches from the edge nearest the throwing line.

Process
1. Divide the group into two to five teams of three to five players per team.
2. Seat each team in its own area or table.
3. Distribute a game sheet to each team. Inform the participants they have 2 minutes to respond to the four questions.
4. Call time after 2 minutes and then collect the game sheets. Go over the correct answers, reviewing the game sheets and awarding one target throw for each correct answer. Announce the number of throws earned by each team.
5. Have each team select a thrower. Invite the first team's thrower to stand at the throwing line.
6. Hand the thrower the number of balls earned by the team's correct answers. The team's thrower attempts to throw each ball into the target bowl.

7. Score as follows:
   - Each throw into the target bowl earns 5 points**.
   - Each throw within 12 inches of the target bowl earns 1 point.
   - All throws outside 12 inches of the bowl earn 0 points.
   - **Note: All throws stay on table or in target bowl until the team completes all throws at the target. Teams may ask to remove the balls from the target bowl to "make room" for the next throw. Advise the team that if you remove the ball, you also have to deduct the points earned by the throw.
8. Tally the first team's points and post on the flip chart.
9. Invite the second team's thrower to the throwing line. Continue the same for all teams.
10. You may wish to conduct a second round for all teams. The team earning the most points wins.

Submitted by Linda M. Raudenbush, Ed.D., and Steve Sugar

Linda M. Raudenbush holds a BA in mathematics and secondary education from St. Joseph College, an MS in applied behavioral science from Johns Hopkins University, and an Ed.D. in human resource development from George Washington University. Linda has more than twenty-five years of experience in training, organization development, and leadership coaching in both private and public sectors. Linda holds an ACC in leadership coaching granted by International Coaching Federation. She has been adjunct professor and is currently employed as an internal HRD/OD consultant and leadership coach at the U.S. Department of Agriculture. Linda is an active volunteer in her community, having been nominated as the Maryland Volunteer of the Year for 2003 and 2004, and was awarded Volunteer of the Year in 2005 for Faith-based Initiatives.

Steve Sugar writes "fun with a purpose" activities that have helped thousands of learners to experience classroom topics in a more meaningful way. Steve holds an A.B. in economics from Bucknell University and an M.B.A. in economics, statistics, and management from George Washington University. Steve served two tours as a Deck Watch Officer in Vietnam for the U.S. Coast Guard. Steve currently teaches business and education courses for the University of Maryland Baltimore County (UMBC). Steve is the author or co-author of *Training Games* (an ASTD Info-line), *More Great Games, Games That Teach, Games That Teach Teams, Games That Boost Performance,* and *Primary Games.* Steve has developed three game systems featured by Langevin Learning Services—the Management 2000/ Learn It board game, the QUIZO game system, and the X-O Cise dice game.

Is the Answer Correct?

Objective
- To review content material by individual and/or group.

Audience
Three to twenty participants.

Time
30 to 60 minutes, depending on group size.

Materials and Equipment
- Two to four Scratch 'n See tickets per person.
- One coin per person.

Area Setup
No special arrangement is needed.

Preparation
1. Write two to four content review questions per person, depending on group size and allotted time for review.
2. Using the Scratch 'n See software template, write the review question in the "optional text" area and the correct or incorrect answer in the "circle text" area.
3. Print off tickets and cover "circle text" areas with gold seals.

Process
1. To review at the end of the program, have each participant take two to four tickets and a coin.
2. Taking individual turns, go around the group and have each person read his or her question, scratch off the answer, read the answer, and tell the group whether or not the written answer is correct, or have the person read the review question, answer it, scratch off the answer, and verify substitute the revealed answer is correct or incorrect.

nsider's Tips

- True/false or multiple-choice answers work best.
- Keep the activity moving quickly to avoid participants over-thinking an answer.
- Allow brief explanation or discussion if incorrect answer was given. Solicit correct answers from the group.

Submitted by Marjorie Treu
As president of Team Fusion, Marjorie Treu has twenty-three years of adult education experience in the travel, banking, manufacturing, and service industries. Her main focus is on executive and management development, leadership development, sales and sales management, and all aspects of human resources training. Current emphasis is on organization development with a passion for working with team leadership through all stages of team formation, coaching teams in trouble, and experiential team building. Marjorie holds a bachelor's degree in education from the University of Wisconsin-Milwaukee and a PHR certification. She serves on the board for the Southeastern Wisconsin chapter of ASTD, most recently as president.

Chapter 12

Closings

Bringing closure to a training session is a lost art. Too often sessions end with an evaluation and the trainer begins to straighten the room. A good closing incorporates an evaluation to be sure, but it includes much more. It also allows participants to gain closure by:

- Celebrating the completion of the session.
- Confirming that the learning objectives were met.
- Discussing how the content will be applied back at the workplace.
- Pausing to acknowledge and say farewell to the rest of the participants.
- Committing to applying concepts and making changes for success.

An excellent training session may be diluted by a lack of closure. Don't let your participants walk out the door without providing them a means to wrap up all they learned and identify ways to implement the learning back at the workplace. The activities in this chapter will help you do that.

The Good Apple Award

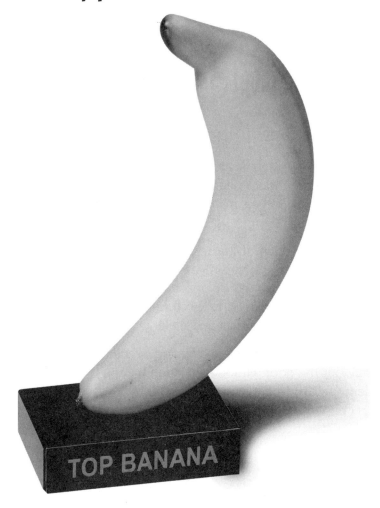

Objectives
- To acknowledge accomplishments.
- To thank attendees for their participation.

Audience
Any size group.

Time

5 to 10 minutes.

Materials and Equipment

- Small apples (can use Trainer's Warehouse Squeeze Apple, real apples, ornaments, etc.), Top Bananas, or mini Oscars, one for each participant.

Area Setup

Have an item at each place setting/chair.

Process

1. For acknowledgement, ask participants to form pairs and to tell each other why they are "good apples" ("top bananas" or "deserve an Oscar") as a result of the training session.
2. As the trainer, thank everyone for their participation, and say that they are "good apples" for taking the time to listen and to committing to implementing what they learned.

nsider's Tip

- To show appreciation or thanks makes participants walk away with a good feeling and "awards" that they can show off to others. We cannot overuse the words "thank you." Everyone who receives an award feels appreciated and will show the award to those who have not yet received one!

Submitted by Marci Goldshlack

Marci Goldshlack is director of corporate training for the Division of Organizational and Human Resource Development for Philadelphia Workforce Development Corporation in Philadelphia. She has over twenty years of experience in the field of organization and staff development. Her creativity, passion, and dynamic personality motivate others to share her mission. Her mission is this: to enhance the skills and knowledge needed to perform at one's maximum potential.

Crazy, Cool, Creative Closing

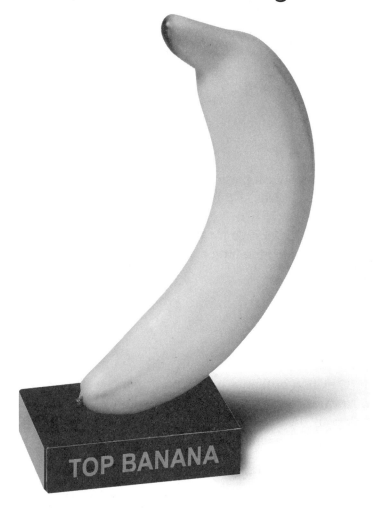

TOP BANANA

Objectives

- To end the workshop on a rewarding, playful note.
- To hold a closing ceremony for the workshop.

Audience

Up to twenty participants.

Time

15 to 30 minutes.

Materials and Equipment

- One large box for each subgroup.
- Stick-on labels.
- Pens or markers.
- Balloons.
- "Tunes for Trainers" CD.
- Rewards for participants, such as Top Banana, various lapel pins, Magic Light Bulbs, items from the Stress-Free Debrief Essentials Set, play money, or items from the Classroom Prize Pack. In addition, look around your office and home for more items: mirror, egg timer, pillow, pins, ruler, sneakers, soap. Be sure you have enough rewards so that each participant can receive one.

Area Setup

Chairs facing the front of the room.

Process

1. Before the session, fill up a box of miscellaneous items for each team.
2. Have participants form groups of four or five. These could be groups that worked together during the workshop. Give each team a box of items and some stick-on labels.
3. Ask participants to decide how each item might be used as a reward. Instruct them to write on a label the reason for awarding that particular item and to attach the label to the item. Give a few examples of ideas from this list:
   - Mirror for the person who was reflective.
   - Broad-brimmed hat for the person who had grand ideas.
   - Ruler for the person who grew the most.
   - Egg timer for the person who was most patient.
   - Rubber band for the person who stretched the most.
   - Joke book for the person who helped us laugh.
   - Pillow for the person who needs a rest.
   - Old sneakers for the person who led us in exercise.
   - Pins for the person who helped us keep the room neat.
   - Soap in a box for the person who spoke out frequently.

4. After they have determined the reasons for each award, in the total group, have each team tell the others the name for each reward and lay the awards out on a table as they are presented.

5. Assign each team another team to honor in the upcoming award ceremony. Privately, they reflect on the people in their assigned group and decide which award each person should receive. As they make these decisions, they remove each of the items from the main table and attach a second label with the person's name.

6. When the work teams have made their decisions, rearrange the room for the ceremony. Put some music on. Bring out balloons and even bottles of bubbles to blow.

7. Build some excitement for this special celebration. Start with rousing music. With fanfare, introduce the first work group to present its awards. Encourage clapping as prizes are given out. Continue until everyone has received a prize.

8. Tie what they have shared into how this information will be useful after the workshop.

nsider's Tips

- Celebrations and closing ceremonies at the end of workshops often include giving gifts and awards to people who deserve recognition and rewards. Although the engraved plaque and attractive certificate have their place, some celebrations can be more playful.
- This activity will help participants use their creativity to think of rewards that use common items but are linked to worthwhile recognition. This will be particularly appropriate as the last activity of your workshop.

Source
Inspired by *Connections*, published by HRD Press (currently out of print).

Submitted by Lois B. Hart, Ed.D.

Lois B. Hart, Ed.D., is the founder of the Women's Leadership Institute, a unique, year-long program of mentoring, coaching, and training executive women. She is president of Courageous Leadership Consortium, and for thirty-three years, a president of Leadership Dynamics. Lois is a lifetime member of the American Society of Training and Development—Rocky Mountain Chapter. Lois earned her BS from the University of Rochester, her MS from Syracuse University, and her Ed.D. from the University of Massachusetts. She has written twenty-three books and tapes, including *50 Activities for Developing Leaders, Vol. I and Vol. II* (co-authored with Dr. Charlotte Waisman), *Faultless Facilitation: A Resource Guide* and *Instructor's Manual, Learning From Conflict,* and *Training Methods That Work.*

"Peers Cheer Peers" Awards Ceremony

Objectives
- To celebrate learning at the end of a training event.
- To provide participants with a reminder of an enjoyable learning experience.

Audience
A class, preferably fewer than thirty individuals.

Time
30 to 60 minutes, depending on size of group.

Materials and Equipment
- Fiddles Deluxe set.
- Blank awards certificates and pens.

Area Setup
Space for each individual to address the group.

Process

1. Distribute a blank award certificate and a pen to each learner.
2. Ask each participant to complete a certificate, noting what skill or special learning they feel they have proudly acquired during the training. Tell them to leave the faculty or authorizing signature blank.
3. Gather up the completed certificates and redistribute them to different members of the group.
4. Ask the new certificate owner to sign the certificate, draw an object from the Fiddle Diddle set, and design a brief one- to two-minute ceremony to award the certificate, with the object, to the learner.
5. Give an example, e.g., "I proudly present you with this glitter wand for magically turning difficult feedback sessions into helpful coaching events."
6. Give 5 minutes prep time. Instruct participants that they must call the learner up, present the certificate and the object, and make an award speech.
7. Ask for volunteer presenters. Go around until everyone has been recognized.

Insider's Tips

- This activity can be very uplifting at the end of a training event.
- Make sure that individuals take their certificates and prizes home. You will see many proudly posted.

Source

Inspired by Lois B. Hart, *50 Activities for Developing Leaders,* Human Resource Development Press, 1994.

Submitted by M. K. Key. Ph.D.

A licensed clinical-community psychologist, M.K. Key has over thirty years of experience in organizational quality. She teaches, consults, and speaks on topics such as leadership, customer value management, tools for change (improvement and innovation), corporate culture, team development and facilitation, mediation of conflict, and creativity. Prior to forming Key Associates in 1997, she was vice president of the Center for Continuous Improvement with Quorum Health Resources, Inc. Her doctoral, master's, and bachelor of arts degrees, Phi Beta Kappa, *cum laude,* and honors in psychology, have all been with Vanderbilt University. She has served for years as adjunct associate professor of human and organization development at George Peabody College of Vanderbilt. She has authored several books, including *Managing Change in Healthcare: Innovative Solutions for People-Based Organizations* and *Corporate Celebration: Play, Purpose and Profit at Work* with Terry Deal.

It's Your Choice

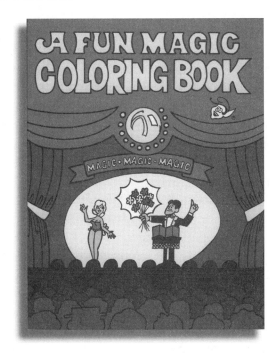

Objectives

- To provoke attendees to consider their responsibility to choose to apply their new skills and knowledge to the job.
- To end with fun and pizzazz.

Audience

Any group.

Time

5 minutes.

Materials and Equipment

- One Magic Coloring Book.
- A chair or platform to stand on so everyone can see your movements (if a large group).

Area Setup

A space where everyone can see you.

Process

1. Explain to everyone that you want to share with them some thoughts around how they may feel about the end of the learning experience.
2. Hold the Magic Coloring Book in your left hand with the open pages facing your left.
3. Fan the pages of the coloring book by placing your thumb on the bottom corner of the open pages while saying, "Here is how your work will be improved if you apply none of what you've learned back on the job." Your participants will see blank pages.
4. Fan the pages of the re-closed coloring book this time by placing your thumb on the top corner of the open pages while saying, "Here is how your work will be improved if you apply just one or two of the tips you've learned back on the job." Your participants will see black and white pages. Give them a moment to be amazed.
5. Gesture with your right hand and say, "Wait until you see what happens when you continue to apply all that you've learned in this session!"
6. Fan the pages of the re-closed coloring book—this time by placing your thumb on the middle of the open pages while saying, "See? If you apply all you've learned, and continue learning, your work will improve dramatically!" Your participants will see full-color pages. Give them a moment and then make a dramatic bow.

Insider's Tips

- This activity is a wonderful way to end on a high.
- This is an extremely easy magic trick, but be sure you practice a few times in the mirror to see what your audience will see.
- Remember the acronym BTM—Bottom, Top, Middle—to remember where to fan the pages.

Source

I believe I saw this trick the first time in a Bob Pike workshop.

Submitted by Lou Russell

Lou Russell is president and CEO of Russell Martin & Associates, a twenty-year-old consulting and training company headquartered in Indianapolis. She is the author of *The Accelerated Learning Fieldbook, Project Management for Trainers, Training Triage, IT Leadership Alchemy, Leadership Training,* and *The 10 Steps to Successful Project Management*. She is a frequent contributor to *Training, Computer World, Cutter Executive Reports*, and *Network World*, among others, and publishes the monthly Learning Flash online newsletter and a column for *Inside Indiana Business*. A popular speaker, Lou addresses national and international conferences such as ASTD, Training Directors Forum, Project Management Institute, Project World, and LotuSphere. She holds a computer science degree from Purdue University, where she taught database and programming classes, and a master's in instructional technology from Indiana University.

The Real Challenge

Objectives
- To reinforce learning.
- To identify barriers to success and counterattack strategies.

Audience
Any group setting of twelve to thirty working on a process or learning and honing skills.

Time
15 to 30 minutes.

Materials and Equipment
- One set of ten to twenty content and creative thinking questions.
- Scoreboard (computer, overhead, or flip chart and marker) with a matrix of question numbers and team numbers.
- Seven sets of dice.

Area Setup
Place scoreboard where everyone can see it.

Process
1. Organize the group into six teams of two to five people, assign each team a number from 1 to 6, and give each team a set of dice. Have each team decide on a "Team Rep" who will record team answers and correctness on behalf of the group.

2. Ask ten to twenty questions, one at a time, for all six teams to answer. (Some will be based on content and some on creatively addressing the topic.)

3. After each question, throw two die to decide which two Team Reps will report the team answer aloud. The Team Rep(s) who correctly answer(s) the question aloud throws the team dice to determine how many points the team will receive for that correct answer. The Team Rep then records that number on the scorecard in the front of the room. (If your throw of the dice produces a double, such as two 6s, then only that one team would answer and would score twice the number of points for a correct answer.)

4. When all questions have been answered, tally the team columns and announce the winner(s). Collect the dice from the other teams and give a set to each member of the winning team as a prize.

5. Debrief the activity with the following questions. (You may wish to capture responses on a flip chart.)
   - How many teams gave the same or more correct responses as the winning team?
   - Why didn't your team win?
   - What artificial or real barriers (such as dice) in your own environment could get in the way of successful application of what you've worked on in this session?
   - What counterattack strategies could minimize the effects of such barriers? (You may wish to have individuals think through their own barriers.)

Insider's Tips

- This activity is a great culminating activity.
- You could also use trivia questions on any topic and make this an opening exercise. After questioning at the end of the exercise, you would ask, "As you go through this workshop, keep track of any barriers you think may prevent you or the team from implementing your learning here. At the end of the workshop, we'll take some time to address them."
- Create a fun, but competitive game environment.

Submitted by Edie West

Edie West is an independent facilitator and writer with more than thirty years in the teaching/training/consulting field. She has written two books published and distributed internationally by McGraw-Hill: *201 Icebreakers* and *The Big Book of Icebreakers*. She has also contributed articles to publications such as *Training for Dummies* and *90 World-Class Activities by 90 World-Class Trainers*. In addition, she has designed and facilitated programs on a variety of topics. From 1996 to 2002 Edie served as executive director for a national board sponsored by Congress and the President. In this capacity, she continued to promote the defining and acquisition of skills for the workforce and those interested in entering the workforce. Today, Edie's focus is on writing, designing, and encouraging success.

Section 3

Training and Consulting Topics

This section presents training and consulting activities that evolve around a specific topic. Topics included, in alphabetical order, are:

- Change management.
- Communication and trust.
- Creativity.
- Customer service.
- Organization knowledge.
- Personal development.
- Problem solving.
- Process and projects.
- Supervision, management, and leadership.
- Teamwork and team building.

Chapter 13

Change Management

Change is all around us and not likely to go away. Trainers face change every day—whether as a part of their surroundings, such as changes in outsourcing, or as a part of the delivery they conduct. In fact, many trainers are involved in their organizations' change efforts.

Organizational change is not easy. It requires a process for implementation. It requires understanding of organizational culture. It requires an understanding and appreciation of reactions and resistance to change. It requires knowledge of organizational systems. It requires knowing how to measure success. And it requires skills to implement and evaluate the change effort.

Wise trainers are ever prepared for the changes that come their way. One of the key responsibilities trainers have is to assist employees to prepare for and deal with the changes that they face in an organization. The three activities presented here will help you do exactly that.

Change That Tune

Objectives
- To experience change first-hand.
- To identify what makes change so difficult.

Audience
Any group of ten to twenty-five experiencing change in teams of four to six people each.

Time
20 to 30 minutes.

Materials and Equipment
- Collection of Shakers—one per participant.
- Flip chart and markers.

Area Setup
Any setup you are using for your training.

Process

1. Form small groups or, if participants are already in teams, have them work in their teams.
2. Tell each team to think of a short song all members know. You may wish to suggest songs like "Mary Had a Little Lamb," "Jingle Bells," "Happy Birthday," or "Row, Row, Row Your Boat."
3. Tell them to practice singing it once while tapping their shakers to the beat. Allow 3 to 4 minutes.
4. Have each group sing and play its song using the shakers. Encourage lots of applause and reinforcement after each team performs.
5. State that doing things the way we've always done them is easy. We don't have to think very hard, don't need to find new ways to coordinate with others, and don't need to learn new skills. Doing something differently due to a change is more difficult. Tell them that they are to change the tune and rhythm of the song they just sang and be ready in 5 minutes to sing it for the group. Allow about 5 to 7 minutes for them to practice.
6. Have each team sing its "new" song. Again lead applause. After the laughter has subsided, debrief the activity by asking:
   - Which song was easier? Why?
   - How is singing an old song to a new tune and rhythm like the change you are experiencing?
   - What would have made this exercise easier? (Capture these ideas on the flip chart.)
   - Which of these ideas could be used back on the job to make change easier? How could you implement each?
   - What can you do as a result of this exercise?

Submitted by Elaine Biech

Elaine Biech is president and managing principal of ebb associates inc, a firm that helps organizations work through large-scale change. Elaine has been in the training and consulting field for twenty-five years and is the author and editor of dozens of books and articles, including *Training for Dummies* and *Thriving Through Change*. A long-time volunteer for ASTD, she has served on ASTD's National Board of Directors, was the recipient of the 1992 ASTD Torch Award, the 2004 ASTD Volunteer Staff Partnership Award, and 2006 ASTD Gordon M. Bliss Memorial Award. She currently authors ASTD's Ask a Consulting Expert Column and is the editor of the prestigious Pfeiffer Training and Consulting *Annuals*.

Shaping Our Fortune

Objectives

- To develop team members' excitement and optimism about a new, challenging project.
- To create an inspired picture (vision) of a successful outcome.

Audience

Any group that is undertaking a new, extended project. Best used with six to eighteen people.

Time

45 to 90 minutes, depending on group size.

Materials and Equipment

- For each participant, one to three empty fortune cookies from Fortune Cookie Debrief set.
- For each participant, one to three blank strips of paper that can be written on and placed inside empty fortune cookies.
- One pen or fine-point marker for each participant.
- Vinyl Fortune Cookie Takeout Box that comes with the set or other unique container.
- Flip-chart stand with markers.

Area Setup

Enough space for participants to sit, write, and move around.

Process

1. At the beginning of a new group project, provide background about the group's mission, project sponsorship, roles, timeframes, etc.
2. Once participants understand the purpose and scope of the project, provide each person with one to three empty fortune cookies, one to three blank strips of paper, and a pen or fine-point marker.
3. Tell them to imagine that, before the project began, a wise seer was sought out for his remarkable ability to foresee the future. Explain that this seer made a detailed prediction that this project would be remarkably successful. He envisioned very specific ways that this endeavor had worked out perfectly, including how the team had worked together, what upper management said about the results, how customers/clients were impacted, what other stakeholders were saying, what creative approaches were taken, and so on. (Tailor your comments to specific elements that fit the group's project.)
4. Tell participants that they will now tap into the special insight of the seer. Ask them to project themselves into the future, a few weeks after the project has been completed. Explain that, by all accounts, including their own, it is a great success. Instruct participants to write on a single strip of paper one specific

element that this success entails (based on the prompts given or on anything else they "see" in their picture of success). Tell them to insert this one strip into a single fortune cookie. If they've received two or three strips and cookies, they can create additional comments about their picture of success.

5. Collect the fortune cookies in the takeout box or a comparable container.

6. Enlist the support of several members of the group. Ask them to draw cookies from the container, one by one, and read the inserts aloud to the group. Another alternative is for each member to draw a cookie, read the message inside, and pass the container to the next member, who does the same. You may capture the ideas on a flip chart or sort them into categories and create a list of them later for the group. When needed, you or group members may ask the person who contributed the idea for clarification of his or her vision of success.

7. With the group, summarize the total picture of success that group members have created. Ask for their reactions.

8. As the project nears completion, you might revisit the fortune cookie technique, using selected debriefing questions to draw out team members' perspectives on how the project actually fared (e.g., questions related to appreciating, communicating, leading, etc.). You might also create your own debriefing questions related to their initial "vision of success" ideas.

Insider's Tips

- It will help to offer one example of a specific vision of success as a model (e.g., "Positive customer feedback about X is two times higher since project completion" or "Every member of this team requests an opportunity to work together again").

- Emphasize that only one description of success should be written per strip/per cookie.

- Encourage people to write their visions of success statements in the present tense (i.e., looking into the future and describing something that **is** true or **is** happening).

- Remember that a vision represents aspirations and a compelling picture of the future. These ideas are not specific measurable outcomes. However, they may spark ideas for setting measurable objectives.

Submitted by Sunny Bradford, Ph.D.

Sunny Bradford, Ph.D., is principal of Bradford Consulting Associates, a training and organization development firm founded in 1990. Dr. Bradford has worked extensively with non-profit, government, and Fortune 500 companies. She specializes in leadership development, team effectiveness, culture assessment, workforce diversity, and large-scale change. She has served as feedback specialist with the Center for Creative Leadership, is a certified workplace mediator, and is an Achieve Global trainer. Dr. Bradford has given presentations for the American Management Association, National OD Network, and various ASTD chapters. She is also an adjunct faculty in the master's in organization leadership program at Antioch University New England Graduate School.

Chapter 14

Communication and Trust

Communication continues to be the most delivered topic in training. It tops the list of most surveys as the most valued skill for success. It is the number one requirement in almost all job descriptions. Yet poor communication is often at the root of many personal and organizational problems and issues.

Why is good communication so important? There are hundreds of reasons. Consider these:

- Builds trust.
- Ensures that the correct information is quickly conveyed.
- Facilitates more effective and efficient problem solving.
- Builds credibility with colleagues, customers, and friends.
- Improves working relationships.
- Increases productivity by ensuring work gets done right the first time.
- Avoids arguments, prevents misunderstandings, and reduces hurt feelings.
- Ensures that individuals learn skills and knowledge to do their work better and faster.
- Reduces stress.

That's just a few of the dozens that you could name. It does point out the wide range of consequences—both good and bad—communication can have on your personal and professional life. Perhaps one of the most important reasons is the first one listed. Good communication builds trust and trust is integral to all successful relationships. It is easier to have a positive relationship with someone and to communicate well if trust exists in the relationship, yet building trust is a mystery to many people. It doesn't need to be.

The four activities in this chapter span the gamut from non-verbal communication to communication in teams to feedback.

The Power of Non-Verbals

Objective
To vividly show how powerful non-verbals are to communication.

Audience
Any group; especially useful for building a team.

Time
15 minutes.

Materials and Equipment
- Call Bell.

Area Setup
Participants stay in place.

Process
1. Have participants pair up. Choose who will be person "A" and who will be person "B."
2. Ask person "A" to tell person "B" something that happened to person "A" last week. Tell the "A's" to select a topic that they are passionate about. It can be family, job, or friend-related. Just pick a topic they enjoy speaking about.
3. Tell person "B" to act bored. Suggest that the person look at the floor, doodle, slump, avoid eye contact, write, or do whatever shows boredom. Allow 3 to 5 minutes for this step. Ring the bell.
4. Ask all the "A's," "How hard was it to tell your story? Did your energy go away? What happened to your passion?"
5. Have the "A's" tell their stories again. This time tell the "B's" to act very interested. Suggest that they maintain eye contact, lean forward, smile, and nod. Again allow about 5 minutes.

6. When the stories have ended, ask the "A's," "How did you feel that time?"
7. Make the point that, even when the participants know that they are being set up, and they know that "B" is acting, the non-verbals are still hugely powerful.

Insider's Tips

- This activity is good energizer any time you use it.
- If using this as an energizer, you may wish to shorten the storytelling to a minute or two.
- You may wish to have A and B switch places for a second round.

Submitted by Cindy Lee Hall

Cindy Lee Hall is president and CEO of CLI, a training company that couples subject-matter experts with professional trainers to offer relevant, motivational, and educational training. Cindy Lee has been in the training and consulting field for fifteen years and has written and published over twenty-five training courses. She is also a squadron commander and Lt. Colonel in the Virginia Air National Guard.

Constructive Feedback Key Pointers

Objectives

- To learn and use three key points to give effective constructive feedback.
- To give constructive feedback that does not put others on the defensive.

Audience

Maximum of twenty-four, divided into groups of three.

Time

Contingent on number of triads—approximately 45 minutes from start to finish.

Materials and Equipment

- A flip-chart page or PowerPoint slide with the three key points listed:
  1. Be specific, not general.
  2. Use objective words, not judgmental.
  3. Discuss behavior, not personality.

- Collection of Shakers, with one hand shaker per person (if possible, have the same hand shaker for each person in a triad so that the sound is distinctive).
- A list of eight to twelve unacceptable feedback comments related to the participants' jobs or the specific communication need for each team.

Area Setup
No particular way; just so people can be in groups of three.

Process
1. Explain that there are two main deterrents to giving constructive feedback. First is that people usually avoid it because they do not know how to give it without causing people to be on the defensive, and past experiences have been confrontational. Second, usually people wait too long to give the feedback. When feasible, feedback should be given promptly within 24 to 48 hours of the unacceptable behavior occurring.

2. Show the flip-chart page or PowerPoint slide and provide a mini lecture about each point, one at a time with an example, to illustrate acceptable use.
   - Specific, not general
     General: You are not responding to customer calls on time many mornings.
     Specific: Our policy is to be ready to take customer calls at the call center at 8:30 AM and in the past two weeks you have not been ready to receive calls until 8:45 or later.
   - Objective, not judgmental
     Judgmental: Your attitude is poor. You are too easy on your staff. You lack initiative.
     Objective: I need you to find time each day to help the new person learn how to use the Excel sheet so she/he is ready to be assigned to the new project that starts a week from today.
   - Behavior, not personality
     Personality: You are a controlling person.
     Behavior: I want you to find three routine tasks that you normally do and delegate them to someone else on your team in the next two weeks.

3. Ask participants to think of at least two more common "unacceptable" feedback comments. As a large group, practice reworking the comments. Ask whether each one meets the key points. If the answer is "yes," demonstrate okay with a hand shaker.

4. Divide the group into triads and distribute each team's list of unacceptable feedback comments.
   - Round One: Have the triads work together on the first comment to make it acceptable, meeting all three points. When they have finished, have them share their changes with another triad. If the triad approves, all six shake their hand shakers. Allow about 10 minutes for this round.
   - Round Two: Each person selects a statement of choice (other than the first one) to reword verbally. Each one reads it to the two others in the triad. If it meets all three points, the first time they shake the hand shakers as a form of recognition. If not, the person either redoes that one or selects another one and tries again. The objective is for each person to be recognized for his or her efforts. Allow about 10 minutes for this round.
5. Lead a discussion to bring closure to the activity.
   - What happened within your triad?
   - How easy or difficult was this activity? Why?
   - What did you learn about giving feedback?
   - What will you do differently as a result of this activity?

Insider's Tips

- This is not easy, and the participants may very well need more practice before moving into their triads.
- Help them to understand that this is a very common hindrance to anyone in supervision at any level and the reason they are unfamiliar with the process is because role modeling for acceptable feedback is rare.
- Tell them over and over that this is a learned skill that they are all capable of acquiring.
- The smaller the group, the more individual attention you can give to people.

Submitted by Harriet Rifkin

Harriet Rifkin has twenty-five years of experience in human resource management, training and development, and particularly in leadership development. Her skill as a facilitator and executive coach to many organizations has proven consistently successful. Her leadership roles have included an officer of employee relations and communication in the financial industry and corporate director of human resources for an architecture and engineering firm. She has published on writing employee handbooks and human resource policy manuals and has received several leadership awards. Harriet has been an external resource to organizations for several years, giving her clients the tools they need to be effective leaders and therefore engaging their most important asset—their people!

SNAP

Objectives
- To practice communication skills and build trust.
- To practice concentration.
- To explore risk taking.

Audience
Any group that can be divided into pairs or triads.

Time

10 to 20 minutes.

Materials and Equipment

- Each pair or triad will need the following:
- One mouse trap.
- One blindfold.
- A cube of ice and a plate or napkin (if you use this activity as an "icebreaker").
- Time Tracker or other timing device.

Area Setup

Tabletop or floor, with chairs being optional.

Process

1. Divide the group into pairs or triads.
2. Demonstrate how to set a mouse trap.
3. Explain that the challenge is to work in pairs. One team member, Snap Trapper, attempts to set a mouse trap while blindfolded. The Snap Trappers receive coaching from their partners, the Snap Coaches. The Snap Coach cannot touch the mouse trap or the hands of the Snap Trapper during this exercise. If using triads, the third person acts as an observer.
4. Distribute materials (or you may have put them out on the tables to pique your participants' curiosity).
5. Set the Time Tracker for 3 minutes at green and 30 seconds at yellow.
6. Complete one round and switch roles.
7. Debrief the activity with some of the following questions.
   - If triads were used, ask the observers what they saw.
   - What were you thinking when you were the Snap Trapper?
   - What were your thinking when you were the Snap Coach?
   - Tell us a story about the biggest risk you have ever taken and the results.
   - How do you respond to new challenges? Is this different at work or home?
   - How do you respond to risks? Are they real or perceived risks?
   - What did you learn about yourself regarding communication, trust, and risk taking?
   - How can you apply your learning?

Insider's Tips

- You may experiment with the amount of time allowed.
- If many were unsuccessful during the first round, allow a second round.
- If used as an icebreaker, put a cube of ice on the part of the trap that catches the mouse. The objective is to set the trap before the ice melts. You may want to set the trap on a paper plate or napkin to catch the melting ice.
- Reward Snap Trappers and Snap Coaches with a chunk of cheese and crackers.

Submitted by Bruce G. Waguespack, Ph.D., CPLP

Bruce G. Waguespack is an assistant professor at the Jack and Patti Phillips Workplace Learning and Performance Institute at The University of Southern Mississippi, where he teaches graduate courses and is a facilitator in the Training and Development Certificate Program. His innovative teaching style is grounded by practical, real-life experience. He was the corporate manager for training and development at Georgia Gulf Corporation for seven years. His consulting company, Potential Unlimited, designs and aligns performance improvement strategies that achieve key organizational objectives. Bruce served two terms as president of the Baton Rouge chapter of ASTD and is a CPLP pioneer.

Super Forts for Super Teams

Objectives
- To engage participants in a creative team challenge.
- To explore how communication impacts success.

Audience
Two teams of four to eight participants each. Additional teams can be added by increasing materials and space. Especially beneficial for team building, communication, and managing up to a hands-off, passive supervisor.

Time
60 minutes.

Materials and Equipment
- One Super Fort by Cranium® building set per team.
- Instructions for six different structures, cut and folded on pieces of sturdy paper inside a basket or bowl.
- Stopwatch or timer.

Area Setup
An area with enough space to build two fairly large structures.

Process
1. Separate participants into Team A and Team B, each with a distinct work area. Provide teams with Super Fort building materials. Ask for a volunteer in each group to be an observer. Tell participants that, from this point on, observers may neither actively engage in the activity nor offer suggestions. They may take notes and will have an opportunity to share observations later.
2. Set the Stage. Ask a member of each team, deemed the "Supervisor," to pick a set of instructions from the basket/bowl. Each team now has a plan for one of six Super Fort structures (Ship, Castle, Space Ship, Tree House, Playhouse, or Racer). Tell the teams they have two tasks—to build the structure and to create a commercial to promote the product to the other team.
3. Communicate and Build. State that only Supervisors may view instructions, and they cannot actively engage in the task. Delegation of building goes to the rest of the team. Supervisors may only answer closed-ended (yes or no) questions from the team. The team must determine how to build the structure through well-formed questions. Allow 30 minutes for this portion of the activity, giving signals when half the time has passed and when 5 minutes are left. When time is up, building must cease.
4. Presentation Preparation. Once the structures are complete (or when 30 minutes is up, whichever comes first), tell the teams they have 10 minutes to plan commercials to promote their structures and their purpose. The commercial should integrate all members of the team in some capacity and include a demonstration of the structure's use.

5. Presentations. Bring the teams together. Have them take turns presenting their commercials. Observers become judges, determining which team displayed the most collaboration, accurately constructed the product, and created a compelling, entertaining commercial.

6. Debrief. Ask the observers to share insights and observations with their specific teams. This can be done simultaneously, with teams seated separately. After 5 minutes, bring the teams together. Lead a discussion including a selection of the following, or related, questions:

   - How were individuals' talents assessed and employed to maximize team success?
   - "Manage up" is a term sometimes used to describe how employees attempt to get their supervisors involved in managing a project, giving instructions, or providing in put. What are the challenges in "managing up"?
   - What techniques were used to manage up a hands-off, passive supervisor?
   - What strategies did you use to communicate with the supervisor?
   - What assumptions may have limited your success?
   - What did you learn about your own communication style?
   - How is this activity similar to what happens at work?
   - How does communication impact success of a project?
   - What can you apply from this experience back to the workplace?

Insider's Tips

- Super Forts are uniquely flexible and easy to use. The large size is ideal for kinesthetic learning.
- This activity is ideal to break up stretches of lecture-based learning, infusing a group with energy.
- The dynamic nature of the activity provides a light-hearted, memorable way to emphasize how clear communication and the ability to manage up can contribute to a team's success.

Submitted by Devora Zack, MBA

Devora Zack is president of OCC, a leadership development firm with more than seventy-five clients, including Deloitte, America Online, DHS, OPM, Ann Taylor, SAIC, USDA, and the U.S. Treasury. OCC provides seminars, coaching, and consulting in leadership, change, communications, and team building. Devora is visiting faculty for Cornell University and program director for the Presidential Management Fellows Orientation. Her articles have been featured in Pfeiffer *Annuals* for three years. Devora has an MBA from Cornell, BA from the University of Pennsylvania, and certification in neurolinguistic programming and MBTI. She is a member of MENSA and Phi Beta Kappa and has U.S. secret clearance.

Chapter 15

Creativity

Einstein stated that "imagination is more important than knowledge." If that is true, we should all spend more time learning how to be more creative. Corporate training had been around for over half a century when psychologists studying imagination concluded that creativity could be learned and fostered. Soon after, Alex Osborn, father of brainstorming, formed the Creative Education Foundation, started publishing the *Journal of Creative Behavior,* and established the Creative Problem Solving Institute to teach executive creative problem solving. This set the stage to recognize the importance of creativity.

Today creativity training has its peaks and valleys of support. Creativity is recognized as a critical skill for problem solving and innovation of products and services. While brainstorming is still at the foundation of creativity, many other tools are available. Even though creativity is taught in organizations, many have difficulty fostering creativity in their workforces.

In spite of the fact that creativity isn't always viewed by organizations as the most critical skill, trainers often want ways to encourage their participants to think more creatively, to tap into their right brains, and to start their creative juices flowing. The activities in this chapter will help you tap into creativity in five different ways, from the wild and wacky to the sublime. Thinking creatively enhances employees' ability to solve problems, plan strategically, improve processes, develop new products, and hundreds of other things that make an organization more successful.

Brainstorming 101

Objective
- To practice thinking beyond the conventional and to think creatively.

Audience
Five to twenty-five people.

Time
15 to 30 minutes.

Materials and Equipment
- Four to five interesting objectives, such as:
  - Classroom Prize Pack.
  - Fiddle Diddles set.
  - Fiddler's FlexiBlox.

- Fiddler's Klixx™.
- Collection of Shakers.
- Stress-Free Debrief Essentials Set.

Area Setup
Participants can stay seated.

Process

1. Introduce this activity as a way to challenge one's thinking. Ask whether any-one knows about the school program called "Odyssey of the Mind." If no one volunteers, share the origins and purpose:

    > Sponsored by NASA, Odyssey of the Mind is a school program designed to foster creative problem-solving skills in schools from kindergarten through college. Students use a variety of tools to solve problems in many areas. Students learn lifelong skills such as working with others as a team, evaluating ideas, making decisions, and creating solutions while developing self-confidence from these experiences early in life.

2. State that Odyssey of the Mind is NASA's contribution to helping school-age children learn to think creatively. Encourage the team to think creatively dur-ing this activity.

3. Select one of the items (for example, a hand shaker) and ask, "What could this be? It could be a hand shaker (traditional thinking) or it could be a whip to beat eggs. Or it could be a back scratcher. What else could it be?"

4. Tell the team that you are going to pass "whatever this is" around the room, and ask each person to offer an idea as to what it could be. (Make it okay to pass if someone doesn't have an idea to share quickly.)

5. Hand the hand shaker to the person next to you and ask that person to think creatively. Ask, "What could this be?"

6. When the first item has been passed to all participants, introduce one or two of the other items. Debrief the activity with the following questions:
   - What inspired your creativity?
   - What made it difficult to be creative?
   - What made it easy to be creative?
   - How can you use these techniques in your personal or professional life?
   - What do you need to do to be more creative? Or do you need to be more creative?
   - What will you do next?

nsider's Tips

- The zanier the object(s) the better!
- Set the tone with your first example by giving the traditional use of the item and then a few examples that really demonstrate a creative use for each item.

Source

A similar version of this activity was published in *The 2004 Pfeiffer Annual: Consulting,* as "Odyssey: Thinking Creatively."

Submitted by Kristin J. Arnold, MBA, CMC, CPF, CSP

Kristin J. Arnold, MBA, CMC, CPF, CSP, specializes in engaging people in the work they do together. An internationally acclaimed speaker, trainer, and high-stakes meeting facilitator, she has worked with thousands of managers and executives to achieve extraordinary results. She is a columnist and author of dozens of books and articles, including the *Extraordinary Team* Series, and has been featured in numerous publications such as *Harvard Business Update, USA Today, T+D (ASTD's Training & Development), Training, Professional Speaker,* and *Team Management Briefings.* Kristin currently serves on the National Board of the National Speakers Association (NSA), where the use of Fiddle Diddles are extremely popular!

Creative Idea Generation

Objectives

- To create a list of ideas that address a problem.
- To creatively identify categories for planning.

Audience

Any group of ten to fifteen.

Time

30 minutes.

Materials and Equipment

- Classroom Prize Pack in a paper bag.
- Flip chart and markers.

Area Setup

Any, although a close U-shape works best.

Process

1. Clarify the definition of the problem you are solving. Post it on the flip chart.
2. Pass the bag of prizes to one of the participants and have the individual reach into the bag to draw out one item without looking.
3. Pose the question, "The problem is like a _____ because. . . ." For example, if the person drew out a toy car and the problem the group is solving is to identify how to move the organization to another office building efficiently and effectively, the statement would be, "The move to the new building is like a car because. . . ."
4. Have the group members complete the statement and post their ideas on a flip chart. Some sample conclusions might be "It has many moving parts" or "It requires someone to steer." Once the flow of ideas slows, have someone else draw another item out of the bag and complete the same steps capturing all ideas. Repeat with three to six items, depending on time allowed for each and total time available.
5. Go through the lists and have the participants identify which areas need further development. In the car example, the team might agree that someone needs to be identified to "steer" the move.

Insider's Tip

- If ideas are generated too quickly to post, ask for a volunteer to help you keep momentum flowing.

Submitted by Elaine Biech

Elaine Biech is president and managing principal of ebb associates inc, a firm that helps organizations work through large-scale change. Elaine has been in the training and consulting field for twenty-five years and is the author and editor of dozens of books and articles, including *Training for Dummies* and *The ASTD Trainer's Sourcebook: Creativity and Innovation*. A long-time volunteer for ASTD, she has served on ASTD's National Board of Directors, was the recipient of the 1992 ASTD Torch Award, the 2004 ASTD Volunteer Staff Partnership Award, and 2006 ASTD Gordon M. Bliss Memorial Award. She currently authors ASTD's Ask a Consulting Expert Column and is the editor of the prestigious Pfeiffer Training and Consulting *Annuals*.

Brainstorming Boost

Objectives
- To enhance team brainstorming skills used in decision making.
- To identify opportunities to augment current brainstorming outcomes.

Audience
Perfect for supervisory, management, and team lead training programs or to kick off project team development. Participants should be divided into subgroups of three to five members each.

Time
15 to 30 minutes.

Materials and Equipment
- Flip chart for the facilitator.
- One white board or poster board or flip-chart page for each group and two markers.
- One Fiddler's FlexiBlox for each group.
- Time Tracker or stop watch.
- Prizes from the Classroom Prize Pack (optional).

Area Setup
Space to break into groups of three to five.

Process
1. Break the large group into smaller groups of three to five. It is especially helpful if you can divide the groups so that the members come from different disciplines (technical, human resources, marketing, etc.) and do not currently work together.
2. Provide each group with a whiteboard, flip-chart paper, or poster board and two markers.
3. Set up the scenario by explaining that during the manufacturing of one of the company's products a mistake was made. Now the company has over one million items that need to be sold or the company will lose a great deal of money. The board of directors has chosen this group to identify ways to use this product so that it can be sold to the general public.
4. Before you hand out the Fiddles, provide each group with the rules for this brainstorming activity, which follow. *Note:* It is helpful to post these rules on a flip chart.
   - Generate as many ideas as possible in a 5-minute period.
   - Don't evaluate the idea during brainstorming.
   - Piggyback on ideas as much as possible (if someone comes up with one idea such as topping ice cream with M&M's, piggyback on that with topping ice cream with Butterfingers pieces). Choose one person to act as a scribe (this person may brainstorm as well as write others' ideas on the board).
   - Choose another person as a monitor (this person should brainstorm as well as remind people not to evaluate or discuss ideas).
   - The team with the most ideas at the end of the 5 minutes wins!

5. Hand out the Fiddles and begin the brainstorming activity. Set the Time Tracker for 5 minutes.

6. After time has expired, congratulate participants on their many ideas and ask each group to read the list on its board.

7. Debrief the activity with the following questions. (You may wish to capture responses on a flip chart.)

   • Was anyone surprised with the number of ideas they generated? If so, why?
   • What was particularly successful in the brainstorming activity?
   • What typically bogs down brainstorming when it is used to problem solve?
   • Would anything you did today help the brainstorming be more effective? Why or why not?
   • What would you do next with these ideas? (Discuss, research further, evaluate are the typical responses.)
   • What have you learned from this activity that you can you take back and use in your workplace?

8. Hand out prizes from the Classroom Prize Pack to everyone (optional).

 ## Insider's Tips

• This activity can be noisy and generate a lot of energy, so take care that you do not disturb those in adjacent rooms.
• It can be a good icebreaker early on in building team cohesiveness.
• The group may want to know other ideas that have been generated for the FlexiBlox. A few include teething ring, massage tool, interesting paperweight, and toddler play toy. Be sure to add your own as you use this activity.

Submitted by Teri Lund

Teri Lund is a partner at Strategic Assessment and Evaluation Associates. SAEA works with organizations to identify how to better maximize business results through better planning and linking performance to outcomes. Teri has been in the training and consulting field for twenty years and is the author of several books and articles. The most recent, *Ten Steps to Strategic Planning,* was published with her business partner, Susan Barksdale, in January 2007. Teri has presented at a variety of conferences including International Society of Performance Improvement, ASTD, American Training and Improvement, and ADQ. She is currently working on another book.

Opposite Brains

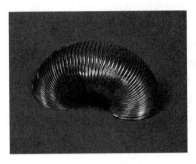

Objective

- To generate ideas related to a topic from two perspectives.

Audience

Any size group.

Time

15 to 25 minutes.

Materials and Equipment

- Slinky® Jr. for half the participants.
- Mini-Slinky® Jr. for half the participants.
- Two flip charts and markers.

Area Setup

Room for participants to work in two teams.

Preparation

Identify a problem or topic and two different perspectives of the problem. This could be as simple as the pros and cons of a potential solution.

Process

1. Provide each participant with either a Slinky® Jr. or Mini-Slinky® Jr.
2. Have the participants divide into two teams based on which Slinky they have.

3. Assign each team one of the two prepared perspectives on the problem/topic. Based on the perspective they are given on a topic, ask each team to brainstorm for 5 minutes and list their thoughts on a flip chart.
4. Call a short break to assign the next step. Tell the team with the Mini-Slinky to decrease, downsize, or minimize its ideas and continue to add to its list. Tell the team with the Slinky Jr. to expand or increase its ideas and continue to add to its list. Allow another 5 minutes for this step.
5. Have each team report back its ideas.
6. Debrief the activity by using the team reports as a stepping-off point for your discussion on the topic. Use the following questions to add a deeper perspective:
   - How did two teams affect the outcome of the first round?
   - How did adding a size dynamic impact the lists?
   - What can you glean from the results?
   - What else could you do to impact the list of ideas?
   - How could you implement what you learned in other situations on the job?

 nsider's Tip

- This activity could be used to generate thoughts about changes in an organization. Teams could discuss current versus new ways of doing business or if the business is going in too many directions versus being focused.

Source
From Mundane to Ah Ha!—Effective Training Objects by Linda Eck Mills © 2005.

Submitted by Linda S. Mills
Linda S. Mills is the author of *From Mundane to Ah Ha!—Effective Training Objects* and owns Dynamic Communication Services. She is a professional speaker who specializes in linking common objects to the information presented so it has immediate and relevant implications to the work and lives of participants. Her high-energy workshops in active training and presentations, time management, and communication skills guarantee audience involvement and create a powerful learning opportunity. She provides meeting planners with confidence that training will be memorable and guarantees to keep an audience involved and awake even after lunch or you don't pay her speaking fee!

Getting to Know You Feud

Objectives
- To foster innovation and creativity.
- To identify similarities and differences about how individuals think.

Audience
Any size group divided into subgroups of five per group; can be used for any group, but especially useful for building a team.

Time
30 to 60 minutes for the activity, plus 30 minutes for the debriefing.

Materials and Equipment
- *Cartoons for Trainers* by Lenn Millbower.
- Slim-Line Answer Boards or Whiteboards on a Stick (two per team).

Area Setup
Any setup would work: groups could be clustered around tables, they could be in designated areas of a room in chairs, *etc.* However, it is essential that there be enough room so that groups cannot hear each other.

Process

1. Identify an emcee for the activity. (A trainer may play this role, but it is also good for a team member to take on this role.)
2. Divide the participants into subgroups of five members each. (The total number of subgroups will depend on how many participants you have. It's preferable to have a larger number of subgroups rather than making the subgroups with more than five members each.)
3. Ask each group to develop a team name and write it on its Answer Board.
4. Provide each team with a cartoon from *Cartoons for Trainers*.
5. Ask each team to develop a theme from the cartoon and create a "Top 7" list for its theme. The theme can be connected to any topic the session is exploring. For example, if the session is on *change management* and the cartoon is a picture of two characters talking, a team may develop a theme of listening and create a Top 7 list of the worst situations for listening. Allow no more than 10 minutes for this step. Ask teams to record their lists on their Answer Boards.
6. Have each team hand in its Top 7 lists to the emcee.
7. The emcee explains that each team will then work with another team's theme. The second team will work with the first team's theme, the third team with the second team's theme, and so on. The first team will work with the last team's theme. When a team is presented with another team's theme, the team will have 5 minutes to develop its own Top 7 list, with the goal being to try to match the original team's Top 7 list. At the end of 5 minutes, the lists are compared. For each answer that matches, the team is awarded 1 point. (The emcee keeps score.)
8. Depending on the time available, several rounds may be played by providing each team with a new cartoon and repeating the steps above.
9. The team with the most points at the end of the rounds that are played is the winner.
10. Debrief the activity by exploring the following questions:
    - What made this activity successful?
    - What made this activity difficult?
    - What insights did you gain into the way others think that you didn't realize before?
    - How do the time frames illustrate real-world team issues?
    - How do innovation and creativity influence productivity?

- In successive rounds (if played), did you change your strategy in developing your Top 7 list?
- How did group members collaborate? How did this affect creative thinking?
- Did the competition between the groups help or hinder the group process?
- How can the experience be remembered and transferred to the workplace?
- What specific tactics observed during this activity could be used during creative problem solving in the workplace?

Insider's Tips

- This is an activity that can be used at the beginning, end, or middle of a session because the objectives of what you are accomplishing can be changed. For example, you can use it to spark discussion on a sensitive topic or use it to apply new concepts.
- It may be difficult to get participants to think in metaphors, so ensure you are using cartoons that have enough detail for themes to be developed by anyone.

Submitted by David Piltz

Dave Piltz is the director of Training Services and StrataKey Division of The Learning Key®, a company that specializes in developing innovative learning solutions. He has been creating and offering programs in leadership, organizational and educational change, communication, teamwork, customer service, and personal and professional effectiveness for over fifteen years. He has worked as a director of residence life, graphic illustrator, technical trainer and writer, and an internal OD training specialist. Dave holds a degree in aerospace engineering and has completed graduate courses in administration, leadership, counseling, industrial engineering, and workforce education. In addition, Dave holds certifications in MBTI® and game design.

Chapter 16

Customer Service

We have all come to expect excellent customer service. Whether you are grabbing a burger at McDonald's, cashing a check at your local bank, or getting your car repaired, you have high expectations of the service you receive.

Customer service is critical for any business that wants to be successful. Research (and common sense) tells us that it takes a great deal more to acquire a new customer than to keep one that we already have. So good customer service doesn't cost, it pays. As trainers, helping all the employees of your organization understand their role in customer service can be challenging and exciting.

The two activities in this chapter provide a conduit for trainers to use to help participants understand who their customers are (whether they are internal or external to the organization) and then to identify and address four different customer styles.

Customers—Up Close and Personal

Objectives
- To identify customers' needs and desires.
- To identify ways to better serve customers.

Audience
Fifteen to twenty participants who serve the same customer base.

Time
20 to 40 minutes, depending on number of participants.

Materials and Equipment
- Slim-Line Answer Boards for individual activity.
- Tabletop Whtieboard for group activity.
- Plenty of Dry Erase markers in various colors.

Area Setup
Classroom, preferably with four or five participants per group at round tables.

Process

1. Provide each participant with an Answer Board and a variety of Dry Erase markers. If this is a small group activity, provide each table with a Tabletop Whiteboard.

2. Ask participants to identify their customers and then to draw a picture that illustrates who their customers are. Provide participants with an example you have drawn. For example, you might draw a stick figure person carrying a heavy load (loaded down with problems) trying to cross a river swarming with alligators. The figure may have huge ears and eyes signaling the person is looking and listening for solutions to problems. Allow 10 minutes for this step.

3. Have participants share and explain their drawings to their tablemates. If this is a group activity, skip this step and ask for a volunteer from each table group to share with the class.

4. After all participants have displayed their work, ask clarifying questions and compliment their insights. Your questions might include:
   - How accurate were the customer depictions based on what you know about them?
   - What surprised you about the pictures?
   - What similar customer needs, desires, or other themes ran through the pictures?
   - What can we apply from this activity?
   - What are some concrete examples of how we can better serve our customers?

5. Summarize by asking each person for one thing he or she will implement when returning to the workplace.

Insider's Tips

- This exercise can be modified by asking participants (especially of service organizations) to draw pictures of their product as seen by their customers.
- Start with a couple of stick drawings of your own to illustrate class objectives. Since some people are self-conscious about their artistic ability, this can help put them at ease.

Submitted by Niki Nichols

Niki Nichols is a trainer and facilitator specializing in change management—personal and organizational change. Niki has worked in the private, non-profit, and public sectors, with stints in healthcare, hospitality, and education. She has written several articles on the topics of management development and change management for *The Journal of Rural Health*. She has a master's degree in human resources development.

"Role" of the Die

Objectives
- To identify four different customer styles.
- To develop adaptability when working with different customers.

Audience
Any sized group of employees with (internal/external) customers, divided into triads.

Time
30 to 45 minutes.

Materials and Equipment
- One Dry Erase Die per triad.
- One fine-point Dry Erase marker per triad.
- One Customer Styles Worksheet per participant.
- One flip-chart stand with paper and markers.

Area Setup
Room should be arranged to allow participants to engage in classroom discussion but also quickly break into groups of three.

Process
1. Distribute one copy of the Customer Styles Worksheet to each participant. Briefly review each of the four customer styles: Demanding, Personable,

Systematic, Perfectionist (see worksheet for descriptions). As you review each style, have participants raise their hands when you read a description that matches their own personal customer styles.

2. Emphasize that there is no good or bad customer style. Stress that an important skill for participants to have is to be able to flex to meet the needs of their diverse customers. Brainstorm different do's and don'ts for adapting to each customer style. Have participants record these ideas in the appropriate columns on their worksheets.

3. Explain that participants will now have the opportunity to see what each of these styles looks like in action while practicing their flexing skills. Divide participants into groups of three. Distribute a Dry Erase Die and marker to each triad. Ask a volunteer from each triad to write the names of the four customer styles on four sides of the die (one style per side) with the word "wild" on the other two sides. As a class, agree on a customer service scenario. This scenario will be used for all three rounds during the following skill practice.

   • Round 1: Have one person from each triad volunteer to play the role of the customer, one person the employee, and the other the observer. Instruct the person playing the customer from each triad to roll the die to determine the style that he or she will exhibit during the skill practice. If the die lands on wild, the observer will choose the style. Allow 3 minutes.

   • Round 2: Have the participants in each triad switch roles and roll the die again to determine the customer's style. Repeat the same process as was followed in Round 1. Allow 3 minutes.

   • Round 3: Repeat the same processes as were followed in Rounds 1 and 2 so that every participant in each triad has had the opportunity to be the customer, employee, and observer. Allow 3 minutes.

4. Debrief this skill practice with the following questions. You may wish to capture the responses on a flip chart and encourage participants to take notes on their worksheets.

   • Go through each of the four different customer styles and ask: What behaviors did you observe that worked particularly well with this customer style? What behaviors did you discover that did not work so well with this customer style?

   • What are some of the positive benefits of "flexing" your approach to adapt your customers' diverse styles?

   • How will you apply what you learned to your job?

Insider's Tips

- This activity may provoke some participants to share "war stories" of difficult customers. Gently redirect them to the focus on the goal of this activity. For example, encourage them to identify this customer's style and then have the class brainstorm different ways for adapting to this style.
- Although the triads may ask for more than 3 minutes to complete the role plays, avoid extending the time limit. A shorter duration will help sustain participants' energy, interest, and engagement.
- Allocate time carefully so that you can conduct a thorough debriefing conversation. This will strengthen participants' learning and give them additional insight on how to apply their new flexing skills.

Source

The four customer styles are influenced by the research of Carl Jung and William Marston.

Submitted by Travis L. Russ, Ph.D.

Travis L. Russ is an independent consultant and has designed and delivered learning solutions for a wide range of organizations in the public, private, and academic sectors. His expertise includes leadership development, communication improvement, and instructional education—training trainers. Travis holds a Ph.D. in organizational communication from Rutgers University.

Customer Styles Worksheet

Flexing Behaviors

Style	Description	Do	Don't
Demanding	Constantly in a hurry.		
	Dislikes details and instructions.		
	Demands fast, immediate results.		
	Direct and to the point.		
Personable	Enjoys socializing with everyone.		
	Outgoing and friendly—a "people person."		
	Loves new products and trends.		
	Finds it hard to say, "No."		
Systematic	Very patient.		
	Doesn't become upset easily.		
	Avoids change, prefers consistency.		
	Becomes nervous when forced to decide.		
Perfectionist	Likes to discuss details and logistics.		
	Prefers to shop around.		
	Prefers facts over opinions.		
	Knows exactly what he or she wants.		

Chapter 17

Organization Knowledge

Employees who understand their organizations are better able to address their organizations' needs, customers' requirements, and supervisors' expectations. Learning about an organization should occur right from the first day on the job—during new employee orientation. Knowledge grows naturally as an employee continues to work at a job—as the grapevine takes roots, the communication channels reveal themselves, the informal leaders emerge, and the corporate values come alive.

In the same way, when a new supervisor is hired, employees are curious about who this person is and his or her management style. The activities in this chapter give trainers a leg up on what they can do to focus clarity on the organization, the leaders who manage the organization, an organization's culture, and the introduction of new terminology.

The Good, the Bad, and the Ugly New Manager

Objectives
- To help a work group get to know a new supervisor/manager in a positive way.
- To help a new manager get to know his/her staff better.

Audience
An intact work group (including the manager) that is working with a new manager.

Time
30 to 40 minutes.

Materials and Equipment
- Two Dry Erase Dies (cubes).
- A fine tip Dry Erase marker.

Area Setup
Ideally, if the team is small enough, sit in a circle. At the least, space is required to roll the dice.

Preparation

1. Write six different managerial topics of interest to the group on one cube, e.g., leadership, work style, communication, meetings, recognition, or corporate values.
2. Write six adjectives such as good, bad, ugly, fun, frustrating, etc., on the second cube.

Process

1. Have the new manager introduce himself/herself.
2. Announce to the manager this is a "get-to-know-you" exercise, "We thought we'd 'throw' this activity in since we would like to learn more about your 'role' and you may want to know more about us." Explain that the group has two dice: one with various managerial topics and one with adjectives. Tell the manager that group members will be rolling the dice and that the manager should respond with whatever comes to mind.
3. Select a participant from the audience to roll both of the dice. Ask the manager to respond to the two words that appear.
4. Select someone else in the audience to roll the dice for the next round. Continue for several rounds or about 15 minutes.
5. Ask the manager if he/she would like a turn. Ask the manager what issues or topics he/she would like on the topic die. Ask one of the participants to change the words on the die. You may offer suggestions to the manager if desired, such as bosses, recognition, work assignments, performance, work space, equipment, or training.
6. This time the manager may roll the dice and select someone to respond. After several rolls, wrap up the activity, thank the manager, and return to the original agenda.

![puzzle piece] nsider's Tips

- Be sure to inform the new manager what is going to happen at the meeting.
- This activity could also be used for a newly formed team to learn about each others' working preferences.

Submitted by Elaine Biech

Elaine Biech is president and managing principal of ebb associates inc, a firm that helps organizations work through large-scale change. Elaine has been in the training and consulting field for twenty-five years and is the author and editor of dozens of books including *90 World-Class Activities by 90 World-Class Trainers, Thriving Through Change, and Training for Dummies.* A long-time volunteer for ASTD she has served on ASTD's National Board of Directors, was the recipient of the 1992 ASTD Torch Award, the 2004 ASTD Volunteer Staff Partnership Award, and 2006 ASTD Gordon M. Bliss Memorial Award. She currently authors ASTD's Ask a Consulting Expert Column and is the editor of the prestigious Pfeiffer Training and Consulting *Annuals.*

Developing Core Values

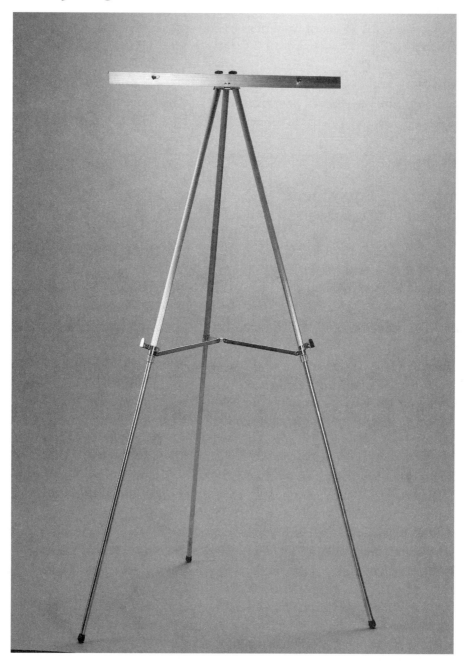

Objectives

- To determine the core values that are most valuable to the team or the organization.
- To determine the areas of weakness in current core values' expression or articulation.

Audience

Any size or group—whenever possible mixed function and hierarchy.

Time

2 hours.

Materials and Equipment

- Flip-chart stand and paper.
- Markers.
- Flip-chart stickers.
- 3" × 3" Post-its® (several for each participant).

Area Setup

If fewer than twenty people, around a conference table; if over twenty, six to eight individuals per table.

Process

1. Explain that there are certain core values that everyone would agree are supported by the organization. They may not be the published values, but they are the ones on which people are rewarded or punished. Have everyone write down three of those core values.
2. Use a round robin to create and post a list on the flip chart. Leave at least 10 inches of white space on the right side of each flip-chart page. Post the pages on the wall.
3. Ask everyone to identify three ways in which those core values are (or might be) institutionally violated regularly. They should not identify personal behaviors, but actual policies, practices, ways of doing business, etc. Have them write one on each of three Post-its.
4. Have participants post the violations next to the value statements. Ask for volunteers to debrief on these. Use the flip-chart stickers to identify those values that appear to require better support.

5. Have the group break into three- or four-person teams and design one new practice or one revised policy to support each core value. If there are many values, you may wish to use a prioritization process to select the top few values. Alternatively, you may also want to assign one value to each small group.
6. Have each team share its new practice. Document the new practices and code them to match the core values they are meant to express.
7. Have the same group consider which core values would be most vital to the success of the business (that is, to its customer value proposition or its business model).
8. Summarize the activity with these questions:
   - What has become more clear to you as a result of this activity?
   - How did this experience help you better understand the organization?
   - What responsibility do you have as a result of this activity?
   - What can we do next?

 ## nsider's Tips

- Ensure that everyone understands that core values guide behavior, not just ethically, but also with respect to the business.
- Prepare leaders to bring full participation and responsibility to the process.

Submitted by Amie Devero

Amie Devero is the founder of The Devero Group, a boutique management consulting firm specializing in producing unprecedented results with its clients utilizing strategy mapping and balanced scorecards, as well as long-range visioning, planning, core values, and organizational alignment. As a central part of her strategy consulting, Amie helps organizations create strategic core values and drive them into every aspect of the organization. This approach is outlined in her forthcoming book, *Powered by Principle*, in which she demonstrates that such organizations outperform the market over the long-term. Amie was educated at Bennington College, Harvard University, and the London School of Economics and holds two master's degrees.

Spinning the Organizational Culture

Objectives

- To create a dialogue about organizational topics or issues.
- To explore assumptions made about the existing and future organizational culture.

Audience

Six or more players, supervisory to executive level.

Time

60 to 90 minutes.

Materials and Equipment

- Three Dry Erase markers (black).
- One Turn 'n Learn Game Wheel, mounted on an easel or a flip chart.
- Six to twelve topical statements about the organization, prepared in advance by the instructor. These statements should identify recent events or key occurrences that have affected the organization. Sample statements:
  - Company Market Share Increases 20 Percent.
  - Manufacturing Division Wins Local Environmental Award.
  - Computer Technology Unit Solves Customer Need.
  - Computer Mentoring Program Is Industry Benchmark.
  - Company Loses Key Customer.
  - New Strategic Plan Issued.
  - Supply Price Increases.
  - New Chair Announced.
  - Company Profits Drop.
  - HR Announces Job Openings.
  - Company Introduces New Executive Training Program.
  - Sales Territories Reorganized.
- One watch or stopwatch (optional).
- Flip-chart easel and markers.

Area Setup

An area large enough to have a table for each team.

Preparation

1. Write in key words or the number of each statement on each pie section of the game wheel.
2. Set up the game wheel on a wallboard or flip-chart easel, making sure that the wheel turns freely.
3. Post complete numbered statements on the wall.
4. Post the following questions on the flip chart:
   - What do you know about this topic?
   - What concerns does it raise?
   - What positive outcomes has the topic delivered or could it deliver in the future?
   - How is the topic/issue related to the organization's culture?
   - Could it affect the culture in the future? If yes, how?

Process

1. Divide the group into two or more teams of three to five players each. Seat each team in its own area or at a table.
2. Spin the wheel for each team and assign the selected statement. (If the spin duplicates topics, spin again.)
3. Inform teams they have 15 minutes to respond to the questions posted on the flip chart regarding their topics.
4. Have each team give a 5-minute presentation on its scenario.
5. Focus the participants on what they have learned from this exercise. Use the following questions to help guide the discussion:
   - What did you experience as you discussed your assigned topic?
   - What did you learn?
   - How do official announcements and communications affect employees?
   - What is your version of what works and doesn't work for making these types of announcements?
   - How do these events strengthen or weaken the current organizational culture? The future?
   - What will you do differently as a result of this experience?
6. If time permits, conduct additional rounds.

Insider's Tips

- Write your questions in advance and post the questions for participants to see.
- Conduct the discussion in a large group, after the activity is finished.
- After participants discuss and respond to the debriefing questions, you may wish to offer your observations, highlighting situations you observed during the activity.

Submitted by Linda M. Raudenbush, Ed.D., and Steve Sugar

Linda M. Raudenbush holds a BA in mathematics and secondary education from St. Joseph College, an MS in applied behavioral science from Johns Hopkins University, and an Ed.D. in human resource development from George Washington University. Linda has more than twenty-five years o experience in training, organization development, and leadership coaching in both private and public sectors. Linda holds an ACC in leadership coaching granted by the International Coaching Federation. She has been adjunct professor at National-Louis University and Strayer University and is in her eighteenth year of part-time teaching at the University of Maryland, Baltimore. She is currently employed as an internal HRD/OD consultant and leadership coach at the U.S. Department of Agriculture. Linda is an active volunteer in her community, having been nominated as the Maryland Volunteer of the Year for 2003 and 2004, and was awarded Volunteer of the Year in 2005 for Faith-based Initiatives.

Steve Sugar writes "fun with a purpose" activities that have helped thousands of learners to experience classroom topics in a more meaningful way. Steve holds an A.B. in economics from Bucknell University and an M.B.A. in economics, statistics, and management from George Washington University. Steve served two tours as a Deck Watch Officer in Vietnam for the U.S. Coast Guard. Steve currently teaches business and education courses for the University of Maryland Baltimore County (UMBC). Steve is the author or co-author of the following books: *Training Games* and the Info-line, *More Great Games, Games That Teach, Games That Teach Teams, Games That Boost Performance*, and *Primary Games*. Steve has developed three game systems featured by Langevin Learning Services—the Management 2000/Learn It board game, the QUIZO game system, and the X-O Cise dice game.

Organizational Lingo Crossword Puzzle

Objectives
- To understand an organization's terminology and operational definitions.
- To accurately use organizational terms and acronyms in domestic and global communications.

Audience
- All employees new to the organization (can be incorporated into new employee orientation).
- All employees who need to know new terminology or acronyms related to a new product launch, merger/acquisition, reorganization, etc.

Time
25 minutes.

Materials and Equipment
- Puzzle Power CD.
- A completed crossword puzzle for the facilitator.

- A blank crossword puzzle for each participant.
- A pen or pencil for each participant.
- Prizes for winners (e.g., "throwable" foam light bulbs, brains, stars).
- Stopwatch or timer.
- Computer with LCD screen (optional).

Area Setup
U-shaped arrangement.

Preparation
1. Prepare the puzzle to be completed.
2. List all terms and accurate definitions to be included.
3. Enter the data using crossword puzzle software (Puzzle Power) according to user tips (easy!).
4. Make printouts that contain both "Down" and "Across" clues, one containing a completed puzzle for facilitator, the other containing a blank puzzle for copying.
5. Make enough copies of the blank puzzle so that each participant can have his or her own copy.

Process
1. During the session, introduce participants to some new or unfamiliar words and terms that are commonly used in day-to-day organizational communication and that all participants are expected to understand and use as a result of this training.
2. After you have delivered the content, provide each person with a blank puzzle and a pen or pencil and ask them all to write their names at the top.
3. Explain the activity and its importance. Be sure to emphasize that this is a game so that they don't perceive it as a test or quiz.
4. Tell participants they will have 10 minutes to read the clues and fill in as many of the terms as they can. (Offer an example: read the clue for 1-Across and show the 1-Across blocks to be filled in.)
5. After 10 minutes, call time. Ask participants to pass their puzzles two persons to their right (double-check that names are on puzzles).
6. Review results by asking for a volunteer to read the 1-Across clue and give its correct term, as all check the puzzle passed to them. Continue asking for correct responses in a clockwise rotation around the table until all "Across" and "Down" clues/terms are accurately identified.

7. Have participants total the number of correct terms on the puzzle they were given and note that number in a circle at the top next to the person's name. Have them pass puzzles back to their owners.
8. Ask for a show of hands of who identified all terms correctly. Acknowledge them with a "nice job" and toss each a "throwable" foam toy.

Insider's Tips

- Emphasize that the activity helps boost retention and is not a quiz or test.
- Have an ample supply of prizes in case everyone earns one.
- As a visual reinforcement for the group during the answer session, project a blank puzzle using a laptop and LCD projector, and display each correct term as it is given.
- Offer support when an incorrect term is given, e.g., "This one is a bit obscure. Who else has a guess for 4-Down?" This helps reduce embarrassment and keeps it moving.
- You may also wish to use this as a concluding review exercise.

Submitted by Johanna Zitto, CPT

Johanna Zitto, CPT, is president of JZ Consulting and Training Inc. A former global training manager with Pitney Bowes and Arete Publishing, she's been consulting and training more than twenty years, improving sales performance, developing strong leaders, building cohesive teams, and raising customer service satisfaction. She enjoys tailoring games and fun learning activities that link performance improvement goals and business goals. A past president of the American Society for Training and Development (ASTD) Philadelphia/Delaware Valley Chapter, Johanna earned Human Performance Improvement (HPI) Certification from ASTD and was awarded the Certified Performance Technologist (CPT) designation by the International Society for Performance Improvement (ISPI).

Chapter 18

Personal Development

As trainers, many of us are also life-long learners developing our skills and talents to be better employees as well as human beings. So whether it is learning more about one's communication style, discovering how positive thinking can move one closer to success, identifying the kind of work that comes naturally, or understanding how one's personal traits contribute to or prevent teamwork, we develop ourselves to be better contributors to our families, our organizations, and the world.

For those teaching specific personal development classes, such as conflict management, communication styles, stress management, and others, the six activities in this chapter are fun, energizing, and practical.

Trainers may also find themselves coaching others in a one-to-one situation about personal attributes or identifying resources for small groups to work together more productively. Although the activities in this chapter are written for groups, most activities can be adapted for individuals and address a range of self improvement topics.

See the Light to the Power of Positive Thinking

Objectives
- To engage and guide participants to focus on positive aspects of their environment.
- To discover individual attitudes about positive thinking.

Audience
Ten to forty participants. Training is targeted for participants from the same organization. Facilitators can adjust the debriefing and instrumentation for participants from multiple organizations. May be used as a session opener or for use in training involving change, problem solving, customer service, or organization culture.

Time
45 to 60 minutes.

Materials and Equipment
- One (or more) low-cost flashlights that use at least two "AAA" or larger batteries.
- One Trainer's Warehouse Magic, Light Bulb.
- One copy of the See the Light Mini-Assessment for each participant.
- One copy of the See the Light Scoring Sheet for each participant.
- One copy of the See the Light Debriefing Sheet for each participant.
- A pen or pencil for each participant.

- Flip chart and markers for facilitator.
- Trainer's Warehouse Squeezable light bulbs for some or all participants (optional).
- TimerTools™ software if using presentation software (optional).

Area Setup

Any room large enough for the entire group and subgroups to work without disturbing each other. Participants need suitable writing surfaces on which to fill out worksheets.

Process

1. Begin by introducing the activity as an exercise to engage participants in positive thinking.
2. Show the participants the Magic Light Bulb and explain that your goal as the facilitator is to get enough positive energy in the room to light this ordinary bulb in your hand.
3. Explain that first the participants must do a problem-solving exercise and that you need one (or several) volunteer(s). Hand out one (or more) flashlights with the batteries installed incorrectly (such that they will not work). Ask participants to examine the flashlights and try to get them to operate, paying close attention to how they as individuals solve the problem. Ask that they remain quiet about how they solved the problem but to signal you when they are finished.
4. Patiently allow several minutes for the problem to be resolved. While they are problem solving, continue to explain that a positive reflection on the organization is preferred to a negative reflection and that sometimes we should pause to discover what is going well instead of focusing on what is not going well.
5. Once the participants with the flashlights have them operating, provide a short debriefing. Ask participants what they did to make the flashlights operate. Someone will say that he or she "moved [or changed] the batteries." Acknowledge that the batteries were the problem and that both batteries needed the positive ends positioned correctly to make the flashlight operate. This is also true for getting groups and teams to be positive. Now the group can "see the light" to the power of positive thinking.
6. Hand out the See the Light Mini-Assessment and a pen or pencil to each participant and clearly explain the directions. Allow 5 to 10 minutes and ask participants to remain quiet when finished. Stress that first reactions and honest answers yield the best results on this instrument.

7. When all participants are finished or time is called, hand out the See the Light Scoring Sheet and give instructions for completing it, prompting participants for any questions before beginning. Instruct participants to carefully transfer their scores, paying close attention to reversing only asterisked items. Allow 5 minutes for scoring.

8. Break participants into subgroups of four or five people. Each subgroup should begin by selecting a recorder and a speaker. Distribute a copy of the See the Light Debriefing Sheet to each participant and have the subgroups discuss their answers to the questions. At least one person in each subgroup should record reactions to the questions. Allow 15 to 20 minutes for subgroup interaction.

9. Reassemble the entire group and facilitate a debriefing by soliciting and recording themes from the subgroups on a flip chart. Focus on items that can improve the positive outlook and energies of the organization or department. Allow 10 to 15 minutes for the debriefing.

10. To begin the wrap-up, ask for a show of hands for those who scored in the "very good" category on the See the Light Scoring Sheet. If no one responds, then continue backwards category-by-category until someone raises a hand. Option: Hand out a squeezable light bulb to the high performers. Indicate that they can "see the light to the power of positive thinking."

11. As the facilitator, reflect on what can be done to improve the positive energy and express that the group is already on its way to improvement. As you wrap up, show the Magic Light Bulb again. This time demonstrate that through the power of positive thinking the bulb can light. Consider saying, "I can feel the power of positive thinking in this group. See the light to the power of positive thinking" as you make the bulb light.

Insider's Tips

- It is important that you, as the facilitator, be able to make your presentation convincing enough to begin to draw out positive attitudes from the audience.
- To use this activity as an energizer, consider having participants say in chorus "See the light to the power of positive thinking" whenever someone offers a positive statement or comment. The chorus can be commissioned by the facilitator saying "light" or "flashlight" after a positive statement is offered.

- Consider variations for the conclusion such as having the group assemble in a circle with outstretched arms touching fingertip to fingertip. You are in the center of the circle. As the group touches fingertip to fingertip, the Magic Light Bulb lights.

Submitted by Dennis E. Gilbert

Dennis E. Gilbert is the president of Appreciative Strategies, LLC, a human performance improvement training and consulting business. He combines his expertise in private for-profit business management with his experience in the non-profit educational sector to deliver outstanding results through consultation and training interventions. Dennis's extensive background in management and education are the culmination of over twenty years of experience with both for-profit businesses and non-profit institutions of higher learning. An accomplished executive, manager, consultant, and trainer, he delivers exceptional human performance improvement solutions to businesses and organizations. His focus is on leadership development, communications, and group dynamics.

See the Light Mini-Assessment

Directions: Please read each statement and provide your initial reaction without in-depth thought. Your facilitator will give you additional instructions shortly. Please remain quiet when finished.

Circle the number that best matches your initial reaction—with a "1" representing total disagreement and a "5" representing complete agreement.

1 = Total Disagreement   3 = Neutral   5 = Complete Agreement

Statement	Your Assessment				
1. I start my day with an open mind and enthusiasm toward work assignments.	1	2	3	4	5
2. My workload is much more demanding as compared to other employees in the same work area.	1	2	3	4	5
3. When working on an assignment, I only do what I am told without asking questions for clarification.	1	2	3	4	5
4. When starting my work day, I scan my immediate environment to see whether others have started their work.	1	2	3	4	5
5. When I notice others not pulling their fair share of the workload, I discuss it with other co-workers.	1	2	3	4	5
6. I attack problems as if they are opportunities to improve.	1	2	3	4	5
7. I find myself shutting out others while forming a rebuttal when others are speaking.	1	2	3	4	5
8. I need my co-workers' help to get my work done.	1	2	3	4	5
9. When discussing problem resolutions, I listen patiently while trying to put myself in the other person's place.	1	2	3	4	5
10. If I answer my telephone, it is going to be another problem resulting in more workload.	1	2	3	4	5
11. I support this organization, and it supports me.	1	2	3	4	5
12. In staff meetings, I remain quiet and never offer any input.	1	2	3	4	5

See the Light Scoring Sheet

Directions: Please transfer your scores from the mini-assessment, reversing scores marked with an asterisk according to the following scale:

5 = 1 point 4 = 2 points 3 = 3 points 2 = 4 points 1 = 5 points

Statement	Score	Statement	Score
1. *		7.	
2.		8. *	
3.		9. *	
4.		10.	
5.		11. *	
6. *		12.	
Total - A		Total - B	
Total A + B =		_____ your score	

Assess your results by marking the appropriate block with an "X."

"X"	Score	Assessment
	52–60	Big problem with negativity
	41–51	Trouble with staying positive—refocus to be more positive
	30–40	Doing okay—strive to be more positive
	22–29	Doing well—some room for a more positive attitude
	12–21	Very good—you are a positive influence to others!

See the Light Debriefing Sheet

Directions: In your subgroup, discuss the following three questions. At least one person in the subgroup should record combined group answers or thoughts.

1. Which statement did you relate to the most? Why?

2. How would you rate the organization (department, group) on this exercise?

3. What can be done to improve the positive outlook and energies at your organization?

If Life Gives You Lemons . . .

Objectives

- To identify techniques to change adverse events at work (lemons) into positive outcomes (lemonade).
- To help participants recognize and understand workplace conflict and resulting misunderstandings.

Audience

Eight to ten people.

Time

35 to 55 minutes.

Materials and Equipment

- One sheet of blank paper for each participant.
- A pencil or pen for each participant.
- One copy of If Life Gives You Lemons, Make the Best Lemonade You Can for each participant.

- A flip chart and markers.
- Flip-chart highlighter tape or a highlighter pen.
- When Life Gives You Lemons Trophy (Note: you may want to have two or three in case of a tie).

Area Setup
One table to seat eight to ten people and a chair for each person.

Process
1. Give each person one sheet of blank paper and a pencil.
2. Ask each person to list and/or describe at least three personality characteristics, skills, or special abilities he or she uses to help reduce tension/conflict or resolve disagreements or misunderstandings at work. Encourage them to write down their first impressions quickly. Otherwise, too much time will be spent in deliberation.
3. Ask all participants to spend 2 or 3 minutes discussing their lists with one or two participants closest to them.
4. Ask each person to read his or her list and write the statements on the flip chart, omitting duplications. By a show of hands, ask participants to vote for the most useful items listed on the flip chart. Tell participants they are each allowed three votes. Write the number of votes for each item and select the top ten items. Use the flip-chart highlighter tape or a pen to mark the top ten.
5. Have participants form triads and spend 5 minutes discussing the top ten items with members of their subgroups.
6. Distribute copies of If Life Gives You Lemons, Make the Best Lemonade You Can and have participants read it silently.
7. Ask participants to compare the examples on the handout with the ten-item group list.
8. Bring closure to the exercise with these questions:
   - What did you discover when you compared the items on the group's list to the handout?
   - What can you surmise from the differences and similarities?
   - How will this information help you and your team in the future?
   - Pause for a moment and think about a situation when you turned a negative situation around—you made lemonade out of lemons. Who will share a situation?

9. After all participants have shared their situations, ask for a nomination from the group for the best lemonade turnaround. Once you reach agreement, give the Lemon Trophy to the nominee.

10. Have participants spend 5 minutes listing on the back of their handout at least three steps they will take to improve their ability to resolve conflict or reduce misunderstandings at work.

11. Ask for a couple of volunteers to share their plans (but do not force this if no one wants to do so.)

Insider's Tips

- Established work teams can use this exercise for team building.
- Useful as an icebreaker for newly formed groups or teams.
- If there are multiple groups in one large room, items on each group's flip chart could be shared with all group members present. This process will take longer, but would provide numerous insights helpful for all groups, not just one group.

Submitted by Elizabeth A. Smith, Ph.D.

Elizabeth A. Smith, Ph.D., is founder, Community Medical Foundation for Patient Safety, a Houston, Texas-based non-profit. She taught numerous management courses at the University of Houston Clear Lake, Houston Baptist University, and Rice University. She has published over forty peer-reviewed articles and six books in psychology, management, and health care. Major books are *Creating Productive Organizations* and *The Productivity Manual*. She also co-authored *Your Owner's Manual for Health Care Survival*. Elizabeth belongs to Sigma Xi, the American Society for Quality, the American College of Healthcare Executives, and the Gulf Coast Association for Healthcare Quality.

If Life Gives You Lemons, Make the Best Lemonade You Can

People who take the first step and apply some of the concepts developed by your group and presented below can reduce the level of interpersonal and group conflict experienced at work. Using positive words and reflecting the other person's words and opinions shows you are really listening to what is being said. This simple listening and reflecting process often helps change negative events into positive attitudes and outcomes.

By "putting yourself in the other person's shoes," you can develop creative ideas about ways to handle various tense situations. The ideas presented below and the list from the group discussion provide ways to help reduce conflict, reach an understanding, or result in a compromise.

Examples

1. Always listen to what the other person is saying and be sure you totally understand what is being said.
2. Think positive, even though it may be hard to do so at first.
3. Take the first step to identify the *real* problem.
4. Ask what you can do to move from negatives to positives. Every small step in the positive direction is a major achievement. Small steps add up and become big steps.
5. By accepting some of the blame for the situation, such as acknowledging that you may have misunderstood what happened or not remembered certain details, you set a more conciliatory tone. The other person is then more likely to start thinking in positive terms.
6. Be patient and don't jump to conclusions.
7. Demonstrate empathy for the other person and the conflict situation or problem.
8. Balance humor with humility.
9. Since not all problems or conflict situations can be totally resolved, "meeting in the middle" or comprising on certain issues means that each person gives a little.
10. If things are not going well, take a break. If possible, postpone the meeting for at least a day. If the next meeting does not go well, ask a person who knows about the problem and the conflict situation to attend all future meetings.

The Object of My Discussion

Objectives
- To reveal personal aspects and traits.
- To give and receive feedback.

Audience
Two or more. For larger groups, you may wish to set up multiple teams.

Time
20 minutes.

Materials and Equipment
- Classroom Prize Pack, Fiddle Deluxe, Debrief Essentials, etc.—the more the better.

Area Setup

Prepare a place to spread out objects where participants can view and handle them easily.

Process

1. Introduce the objects. You may wish to dump them out of a box, bag, or bucket for effect.
2. Inform participants that they are to examine the objects and select two: one to represent a talent, interest, or aspect of their personality that they are particularly proud of and a second to represent an aspect they would like to develop further. Allow about 5 minutes.
3. Have participants take turns displaying their objects and explaining their selections. For example, "I chose a hand, because I believe I'm very even-handed."
4. As an alternative, or a follow-up activity, participants can select an object to represent an aspect of another participant that they find to be particularly admirable or they wish to emulate.

nsider's Tips

- When introducing the activity, encourage participants to keep their revelations positive. Reinforce that this is intended to be a pleasant way to learn about each other.
- Try to collect as wide a selection of objects as possible to encourage creative thought.
- You may make the activity more challenging by not allowing duplication of objects. Just don't let participants fight over them!

Submitted by Randy Woodward

Randy Woodward is the director of training and development for Ho-Chunk Casino in Wisconsin Dells, Wisconsin. In addition to his background in training, he worked for many years as a manager in the hospitality industry. Ho-Chunk has been named one of *Training* magazine's Top 100 Companies each of the past six years.

Truth or Chicken

Objectives

- To provide an opportunity to disclose a difficult situation.
- To create an environment conducive to offering advice.

Audience

Groups of four or five people.

Time

30 minutes to one hour.

Materials and Equipment

- One rubber chicken or squawking rubber chicken for each group.

Area Setup

Groups should be sitting at a round table or other setting so all are facing each other.

Process

1. Inform participants that this is an exercise in disclosure. When it is their turn, they will be asked to discuss a task they have been reluctant to tackle, a problem they've been avoiding, or a situation they've been uncomfortable dealing with. Honesty is key, and confidences will be respected.
2. Hand a rubber chicken to each group. Ask one member of each group to spin the chicken to indicate the first participant. (As an alternative, the member may hand off the chicken to another player.)
3. The selected participant reveals the subject he or she has been "chicken" about.
4. Ask the other participants to offer advice or assistance to help address the concern. Reinforce that these suggestions must be positive and constructive.
5. Have the participant spin the chicken to select the next player.
6. Repeat until everyone has had an opportunity to share.
7. Bring all the groups together and bring closure with these questions:
   - How did you feel about sharing your situation?
   - How did you feel about hearing others' situations?
   - What will you do differently as a result of this activity?
   - How can you transfer your learning to others in the workplace?

 nsider's Tips

- Participants in this activity should be reasonably comfortable with self-revelation.
- Participants in this activity should be comfortable with the other members of the group.
- Not recommended for low-trust environments.

Submitted by Randy Woodward

Randy Woodward is the director of Training and Development for Ho-Chunk Casino in Wisconsin Dells, Wisconsin. In addition to his background in training, he worked for many years as a manager in the hospitality industry. Ho-Chunk has been named one of *Training* magazine's Top 100 Companies each of the past six years.

I Appreciate My Job

Objectives
- To have participants think positively about their jobs or careers.
- To emphasize what is going right, not what is wrong.
- To create an opportunity to practice appreciative inquiry.

Audience
Any size group, but the larger group is divided into groups of three to five people. Members of the group should be part of the same occupational group.

Time
Minimum of 35 minutes, but could be longer with more time for discussion and reflection.

Materials and Equipment
- A copy of the I Appreciate My Job handout for each participant.
- A pen or pencil for each participant.

- Whiteboard or flip chart and markers.
- One light bulb-shaped Post-it® pad for each subgroup.

Process

1. Distribute a handout and a pen or pencil to each person. Ask participants to form small groups of three to five and to answer the questions on the handout. Give each group a pad of the light bulb Post-it® Notes. Have them write one idea per Post-it. Allow 15 to 20 minutes.
2. While the groups are discussing the questions, post five flip-chart sheets on the wall with one question listed at the top of each sheet.
3. With the full group, review some of the questions on the handout, gaining input from as many small groups as possible. As they discuss their responses, have members of each group post their Post-its on the appropriate flip-chart sheets.
4. Have the group cluster similar responses.
5. Use the responses as a basis for debriefing.
    - What did you observe about this discussion?
    - Appreciative Inquiry is a process that focuses on the positive aspects of a topic. How did a positive focus affect your discussion?
    - What did you notice about the clusters of similar responses?
    - How else might you use Appreciative Inquiry?

nsider's Tips

- Encourage positive thinking and looking for what is working.
- Think about your job in relation to your past, present, and future goals.

Submitted by Marty Yopp, Ph.D., and Michael Kroth, Ph.D.

Marty Yopp and Michael Kroth are both professors of adult and organizational learning at the University of Idaho Boise Center. Both have academic and experiential background in human resource development, organization development, and leadership. They have used an Appreciative Inquiry model to elicit positive responses about what people like about their jobs or careers at three professional conferences.

I Appreciate My Job

Respond to the following questions by identifying several things you like about your job, career, or profession.

1. What characteristics or attributes contribute to making your workplace a positive place to be?

2. What about your career makes you feel good about yourself?

3. What are some of the things that you enjoy doing that are associated with your job or career?

4. What external benefits are associated with this career?

5. What would make your job or career even better?

Express Expressions

Objectives
- To provide an opportunity to explore personal attributes.
- To experience negotiating for mutual gain.
- To use personal attributes as a basis for team building.

Audience
A group of three to fifteen participants.

Time
30 minutes.

Materials and Equipment
- One deck of Expression Cards.

Area Setup
A space large enough for participants to move about freely.

Process

1. Give one participant the deck of Expression Cards. Tell the participant to shuffle the deck and distribute an equal number (up to five cards each) to all participants. (Larger groups will have fewer cards per person.) Place extra cards face down in a central location.

2. Tell participants to look at their cards. Explain that the objective is to find and obtain cards that best illustrate various aspects of their own personalities. Give the group members 5 minutes to negotiate card trades with each other.

3. Participants can replace any or all of their cards with an equal number of the unclaimed extra cards. Because the extras pile is face down, these cards are unknown commodities. When a card is selected from the extras pile, it cannot be traded back. The newly acquired card can, however, be transferred to another participant if part of a successful negotiation.

4. When trading is over, ask participants to organize their cards in order of importance to them. Provide 5 minutes for participants to prepare a brief presentation to the group regarding why they selected the cards currently in their possession and what each represents. Keep presentations fast-paced, particularly in larger groups.

5. If you use this exercise primarily to explore personal attributes, lead a group discussion with questions such as:
   - What attribute is most important to you? Why?
   - What was most important to you during this exercise?
   - What did you learn about yourself?
   - What imbalance did you identify? Is it important to you? Why or why not?
   - What will you do as a result of this exercise?

6. If you use this exercise for team building or a negotiations class, lead a group discussion with questions such as:
   - What techniques did you use or observe while negotiating for cards you wanted? What worked or did not and why?
   - What cards did you want yet could not acquire? What occurred?
   - Did anyone agree to a trade that was not one-for-one? Why?
   - Did you learn something about a colleague that broke down a previous impression?
   - What mattered to you the most during the negotiation and how did this impact your behavior?

- Who risked trading a known card with an unknown from the extras pile? What was the result? How can this be compared to taking risks at work?
- Did you learn something unexpected about yourself?

Insider's Tips

- With existing work groups, the discussion about preconceptions will be quite different than for newly formed groups. You can change the debriefing from previous impressions to what you guess about others before knowing them.
- This activity can be adapted in many ways. For example, cards can be distributed at the beginning of a multi-day training and traded informally throughout the program. Participants share final cards at the program conclusion.
- As an energizer, have groups randomly select three to five cards, then present a skit encompassing how themes on their selected cards are symbolic of their work or team.

Submitted by Devora Zack

Devora Zack is president of OCC, a leadership development firm with more than seventy-five clients, such as Deloitte, America Online, DHS, OPM, Ann Taylor, SAIC, USDA, and the U.S. Treasury. OCC provides seminars, coaching, and consulting in leadership, change, communications, and team building. Devora is visiting faculty for Cornell University and program director for the presidential management fellows orientation. Her articles have been featured in Pfeiffer *Annuals* for three years. She has an MBA from Cornell, BA from University of Pennsylvania, and certification in neurolinguistic programming and MBTI. She is a member of MENSA and Phi Beta Kappa and has U.S. secret clearance.

Chapter 19

Problem Solving

Solving problems is what life is all about. Whether the problem is a small one, such as what to prepare for dinner, or a large one, such as whether to change jobs, solving the problem using the smallest number of resources and resulting in the best outcome is the measure of success.

Learning the principles of problem solving, decision making, and successful implementation is a trio required of all successful people. A good problem solver uses a process to define the problem, generate solutions, evaluate the solutions, and implement the resolution. The contributors to this chapter address the process and each of the aspects of problem solving. They consider problem solving from a personal perspective and from a team perspective.

Problem Solving Line Up

Objectives
- To learn what valuable resources other people can be when making decisions.
- To learn to listen without judging.

Audience
Any group; especially useful for building a team.

Time
50 to 65 minutes.

Materials and Equipment

- TimeTracker or other timing device set for 5 minutes.

Area Setup

Space to move around.

Process

1. Divide the group into two teams. Line each team up so that every person on one team is facing and directly across from another person on the other team. If there are an odd number of participants, ask one to observe the action with you.

2. Ask each person on Team One to think of a problem he or she needs help solving. (If there are eight people on Team One, there should be eight problems.) Allow a couple of minutes for each person to identify a problem.

3. Have each person on Team One state his or her problem to the person across from him or her on Team Two. (All Team One members will be talking at the same time to their counterparts on Team Two.)

4. Tell participants on Team Two to give advice to their counterparts on Team One. Explain that they are not to try to talk them into taking the advice; they are not to repeat the advice over and over. Just state their advice, add how to implement it, and stop talking.

5. Tell participants on Team One to listen to the advice. They should not explain that they have tried it already or why they can't take the advice. They should not say anything except "Thank you!"

6. Tell participants that you will set the TimeTracker for 5 minutes. Once it sounds the end of time, all the conversations should cease. Ask if there are any questions. Set the TimeTracker, say "go," and ensure that all Team One members are stating their problems.

7. When all of the "advisors" have finished giving advice (or when time is up), the Team One person who is at the end of the line will walk to the other end of the line. The Team One members will slide to the right so that they are facing new people on Team Two. Team Two does not move. This way every person on Team One with a problem will have a new "advisor."

8. Repeat these steps four times or until every person on Team One has talked to at least four people on Team Two.

9. Now reverse the process and have each person on Team Two think of a problem. Set the TimeTracker for 5 minutes and have Team Two

participants state their problems and participants on Team One give advice to their counterparts. Repeat four times. Have participants return to their seats.

10. Debrief using these questions:
    - What did you learn about problem solving from this exercise?
    - What worked? What rules enabled this? How do you relate this to problem solving?
    - How will you use this information for solving problems in the future?

Be sure to include comments from the observer (if you had one) during the debriefing.

 # Insider's Tips

- If you have time, you may conduct more than four rounds for each group.
- This activity is a great energizer during slump times, such as right after lunch.
- This activity vividly illustrates the power of involving others in decision making. It also makes a great point about listening to what is being said without judging or criticizing the advice.

Submitted by Cindy Lee Hall

Cindy Lee Hall is president and CEO of CLI, a training company that couples subject-matter experts with professional trainers to offer relevant, motivational, and educational training. Cindy Lee has been in the training and consulting field for fifteen years and has written and published over twenty-five training courses. She is also a squadron commander and Lt. Colonel in the Virginia Air National Guard.

Cat-A-Pult™ Challenge*

Objectives
- To identify problem-solving skills.
- To practice team skills.

Audience
Any group in sub-teams of five or six people.

Time
60 to 90 minutes.

Materials and Equipment
- One Cat-A-Pult launcher per person.
- A pencil and paper for note-taking for each group.
- One target for each team, e.g., a cup or paper marked with an X.
- One copy of the Assembling, Adjusting, and Launching Your Cat-A-Pult for each participant.
- One copy of the Notes for Successful Facilitation for the trainer.
- One flip chart and markers (optional).

---

*Cat-A-Pult™ is a registered trademark of Trainer's Warehouse.

Area Setup

Enough open floor/table space for each team to work independently without getting in each other's way.

Preparation

Read the Notes for Successful Facilitation and practice with the Cat-A-Pult™ so you can answer questions and assist the participants.

Process

1. Tell the teams they will be involved in an activity that requires them to work through a series of challenges as a team. Divide the group into teams of five or six people and provide a copy of the Assembling, Adjusting, and Launching Your Cat-A-Pult™ handout to each person. Give each team one Cat-a-Pult™ set. Note that there are five launchers per set, so if you have any teams with six people, you may want to ask the sixth person to be a team coordinator or an observer.

2. Have participants assemble the launchers and figure out how they work. Tell participants that each Cat-A-Pult™ is designed to launch a small foam cat. The Cat-A-Pults™ can be adjusted in four ways. (*Note:* you may wish to post this guidance on a flip chart.) Allow 10 minutes for this step.
   - Placement: Where it is set relative to the other launchers.
   - Force: The green knob has five settings (1 is weakest; 5 is strongest).
   - Trajectory: The orange knob has five settings (1 for the shortest, steepest arc; 5 for the flattest, longest arc).
   - Rotation: The body rotates 360 degrees on its base.

3. Tell participants they are to prepare for their first challenge. Ask participants to create a simple chain reaction where each cat will take one "flight." The challenge is to arrange, aim, and adjust the launchers such that each flying cat will trigger the next cat, one after the other. The fifth Cat-A-Pult™ must be aimed at a landing pad, such as a piece of paper marked with an X. They will launch the first cat by dropping one of the extra cats provided straight down onto the flat, round trigger plate. Launchers can be set up linearly or in any other formation. Tell them that their goal is to set up a five-cat chain reaction that can be successfully repeated 80 percent of the time. Allow 10 to 15 minutes for this challenge.

4. Tell the teams that they are to prepare for their next challenge. State that the teams will create a complex chain reaction. Tell them that the chain reaction is required to include at least three crisscrossing trajectories. Allow about 15 minutes for this challenge.

5. Tell the teams to prepare for their final challenge. State that they will be required to create a "closed circuit," that is, arrange the launchers such that the last cat to take "flight" will re-launch the first cat, setting off the circuit again and again by continuously reloading cats. Allow about 15 minutes for this challenge.

6. Debrief the activity with these questions:
   - What happened as each challenge was presented?
   - What helped the process?
   - What hindered the process?
   - What did you learn about your team? Yourself?
   - What problem-solving skills did you observe on the team?
   - What problem-solving skills were absent on the team?
   - What suggestions do you have to improve how your team solves problems?
   - What will you do differently on your team as a result of the Cat-A-Pult™ Challenge?

Variations

- After the participants have set up one simple chain reaction, have them destroy it and then race the clock to see how long it will take them to set one up again.
- Have them create a multi-level chain reaction, that is, place the launchers at different heights.
- Once groups have mastered the simple chain reaction, you can vary the challenges in many ways. You could:
  - Ask them to set up a new chain reaction in a limited time period, say 5 minutes.
  - Prohibit talking and ask them to complete the task without saying a word!
  - Bring multiple teams together by asking three teams to come together to create a fifteen-cat chain reaction. Again, limit time to 10 minutes.
- If you have time, you could create an extended chain reaction with multiple groups.

Insider's Tip

- Cat-A-Pult™ can also be used to model probability, risk assessment, and a variety of physical laws, including force, direction, and trajectory.

Submitted by Susan Doctoroff Landay

Susan Doctoroff Landay is currently the president of Trainer's Warehouse. She joined her father in 1997, in what was then a fledgling business. Prior to that, Sue spent two and half years consulting and training in the field of negotiation and another two years marketing a business history consulting company. She graduated from Yale College (BA in 1986), the Kellogg Graduate School of Management at Northwestern University (MBA in 1992), and Ringling Bros. and Barnum & Bailey Clown College (MFA in 1987). Susan values using humor to enhance presentations.

Notes for Successful Facilitation

Cat-A-Pults™ are packed in five-launcher sets. So a team of five players is quite natural. If you want to form larger groups, the sixth person may be designated as an observer, charged with the task of watching the group interaction and making notes for later discussion. If assigning smaller groups, five or fewer, ask players to pay attention and make some mental notes of how they are working together.

The Cat-A-Pults™ require some assembly and practice to make them work consistently. For the maximum challenge, distribute the launcher parts, but not the assembly instructions. Most groups will figure out how the parts go together without them. The trickiest of the three-step assembly process is the last step, which is often missed—that is, locking the flat plate (not the base) onto the launcher mechanism and lifting it up until it snaps into place. If it isn't snapped, then the Cat-A-Pult™ will not perform consistently and creating a chain reaction will be difficult.

If you want to minimize the duration of this exercise, you might want to distribute the launchers pre-assembled. Another time-saving technique would be to show the assembly instructions.

Here's the simplest way to set up a chain reaction:

1. Adjust knobs on all Cat-A-Pults™ to the same settings—i.e., both green and orange knobs at the two setting.
2. Set, load, and fire first Cat-A-Pult™. Watch where the cat lands (before bouncing!).
3. Place your second Cat-A-Pult™ so that the trigger plate is right where the first cat landed.
4. Reload Cat-A-Pult™ "1" and see if it now lands on the second trigger plate. Adjust as needed.
5. Reload Cat-A-Pults™ "1" and "2." Fire the first Cat-A-Pult™ again. Watch where cat "2" lands.
6. Continue in this manner until all Cat-A-Pult™ launchers are in place.

Assembling, Adjusting, and Launching Your Cat-A-Pult™

Assembling Cat-A-Pults™ in Three Easy Steps

Cat-A-Pults™ have three parts that need to be connected: a body, a trigger plate, and a base.

Step 1—Body: Make sure the launch arm is in its release (up) position.

Step 2—Trigger Plate: Snap the trigger plate onto the body, sliding the small notch in the trigger plate over the latch near the top of the launch arm. When the latch is partially inserted, press down with your finger so the latch goes under the lip on the trigger plate. Continue to slide the trigger plate in until it locks, but don't force it. When the pieces are lined up right, they will snap together easily.

Step 3—Base: Secure the body to the base by pressing firmly on the pivot at the bottom of the body and snapping it into the hole at the center.

Adjusting Information

Green knob: Force Adjuster controls how fast and how far your cat will fly.
   1 = weakest setting   5 = strongest setting
   Orange knob: Trajectory Adjuster controls the arc of the cat's flight.
   1 = Steep: shortest distance, highest arc   5 = Flat: longest distance, flattest arc
   Body rotates 360 degrees, so you can launch it in any direction. Each "click" represents one degree.

Launching Your Cat-A-Pult™
Ready

- Load a foam cat onto the end of the launch arm so that it fits snugly.
- Press the end down until the launch arm locks in the "ready" position.
- *Note:* consistency of each launch can be improved by setting and releasing each Cat-A-Pult™ ten times on the maximum spring tension settings of 5. This ensures that all the components are aligned appropriately.

Aim

- Aim the Cat-A-Pult™ away from you.

Fire

- Drop an extra cat onto the trigger plate from 6 to 12 inches above.
- The cat should fly over the trigger plate.
- Warning: Hitting the trigger plate hard will affect the accuracy of the Cat-A-Pult™. It can also break the Cat-A-Pult™.

STAR Principle

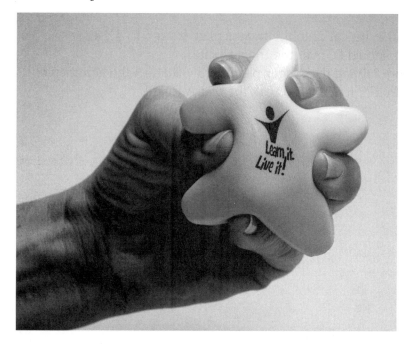

Objective
- To learn a principle for problem solving and successful implementation.

Audience
Any group or size.

Time
20 to 30 minutes.

Materials and Equipment
- Squeeze Star, Smiley Star, or Learn/Live Star—one for each participant.
- Star Post-it®—one for each table.
- A pen or pencil for each participant.
- Blue poster board(s) to represent sky on easel(s) or the wall.

Area Setup
Participants working at round tables.

Process

1. Set up your training session so that you discuss the STAR principle— Situation, Task, Action, Result—for problem solving. For example: Describe the *situation* in detail by giving the overall context. Describe the *task* that you were responsible for or you want to accomplish. What *action* needs to be taken to resolve the situation? What was the end *result* of the action that you took or what *result* do you need?

2. Ask participants to think of a recent task in which they used the STAR principle. Ask whether any of the four aspects were missing.

3. Divide the group into four subgroups and assign each one of the STAR aspects. Have them identify:
   - What is important to remember about this aspect?
   - How can you be more successful in implementing this aspect?
   - What specific lessons have you learned from past problem-solving experiences?
   - What key idea are you taking from this discussion?

4. Ask each of the groups to report out, rewarding each with some of the star items.

5. Have participants write one thing they will remember to do in the future on a star Post-it® and place it on the blue poster board. Allow time to share this information with the entire group.

nsider's Tips

- Tell the group you want to make them "stars" at doing something.
- Decorate the room with stars to make the "STAR" principle more memorable.

Submitted by Linda S. Mills

Linda S. Mills is the author of *From Mundane to Ah Ha!—Effective Training Objects* and owns Dynamic Communication Services. She is a professional speaker who specializes in linking common objects to the information presented so it has immediate and relevant implications to the work and lives of participants. Her high-energy workshops in active training and presentations, time management, and communication skills guarantee audience involvement and create a powerful learning opportunity. Linda provides meeting planners with confidence that training will be memorable and guarantees to keep an audience involved and awake, even after lunch or if you don't pay her speaking fee!

True Colors

Objectives
- To practice non-verbal group problem solving.
- To form groups for subsequent activities.

Audience
A group of twelve to twenty-four people; useful for team formation and team building.

Time
15 to 20 minutes.

Materials
- Colored Name Pins (enough to divide the whole group into three to four small groups, each with a different color).

Area Setup
Space to move around.

Process
1. Have the group form a circle, facing outward, as you stand in the middle of the circle.
2. Explain that you are going to pin a colored name pin to each person's back (or, as an alternative, the pins can be attached to a looped piece of

yarn so that the cord can be placed over each person's head with the pin hanging down the person's back). Share the following guidelines for the activity:

- Individuals must not attempt to find out what color pin they are wearing.
- If asked, individuals must not identify the colors of their neighbors' pins.

3. Randomly place a colored pin on the back of each participant.
4. After asking all the participants to turn around and face inward, identify two tasks for each individual to complete. These two tasks are to, **without talking, writing, or looking** at her or his own pin:

- Find out what color pin he or she has.
- Find all of the other individuals with the same color pin and form a subgroup.

5. After asking whether any of the group members need clarification of the instructions, ask the group to proceed.
6. When all group members have successfully found the other members in their color pin group, stop the activity. Then, one group at a time, asks the members of each color group to identify their color and then to individually turn around so that everyone can verify that each group member does, indeed, have the same color pin.
7. After congratulating all of the group members, lead a debriefing session guided by the following questions:

- When the task was first described, and before group members began attempting to solve the problem, what were your initial thoughts and feelings about this task?
- Once the group members began attempting to solve the problem, what strategies did group members employ to successfully solve the task?
- Are there any other strategies not employed that might have successfully solved the problem? If so, what strategies?
- How is this challenge most easily solved? What are the implications of defining this challenge as an individual and not a group task?
- What group skills have to be effectively employed to successfully complete this challenge?
- What implications can be gleaned from this activity as they relate to teamwork? To problem solving?

8. If desired, the groups' members can remain in their newly formed color pin groups for the next activity.

Insider's Tips

- Careful structuring and clear directions, as well as reinforcement of guidelines, are important for this activity to be successful.
- If you want the group to also experience the impact of participant inclusion and exclusion, one or two of the group members can be given a colored pin that does not match the others. How the other group members react to these "outsiders" adds a lot of provocative food for thought and discussion. *Note:* If this dimension is added, the "outsiders" may be privately taken aside before the activity and alerted to their roles.

Submitted by Terry Murray

Terry Murray is an assistant professor in the Humanistic/Multicultural Education Program at SUNY New Paltz. This graduate program is based in approaches that are experiential, reflective, democratic, and inclusive. Terry has developed a number of experiential activities for use in his courses. In addition, he has worked for many years as a trainer and consultant with educational institutions and not-for-profit organizations.

Spaghetti and Gum Drops

Objectives
- To encourage group problem solving.
- To practice effective team functioning behaviors.

Audience
Large group divided into subgroups of six to ten.

Time
55 to 60 minutes.

Materials and Equipment
- Each small group needs the following:
  - One pack of raw spaghetti.

- One pack of gumdrops.
- One raw egg.
- One Painter's Hat.
- One platform (large paper plates work fine).
- One Timer Tool Clock set for 30 minutes.
- Fiddles as prizes.

Area Setup
Table tops or open floor space.

Process
1. Divide the group into teams of six to ten members each.
2. Explain the challenge. Your team has been contracted to complete a special project funded by the National Society of Spaghetti Architectural & Structural Designers (NSSASD) and the USDA Eggstra Special Project Division. Your mission is to design a structure that can support (hold) a raw egg at the height of one full-length spaghetti stick. The structure must stand on its own while holding the egg for at least a countdown of ten. The height will be measured and recorded in the NSSASD book of records.
3. You can repeat the challenge in plain English. Build a structure to support the raw egg, at least as tall as a spaghetti stick and the structure must stand on its own, with the egg, for a count down from ten by the whole team . . . all together.
4. Distribute materials to the participants. Tell them they have 30 minutes.
5. Set the Timer Tool Clock for 30 minutes. Observe the teams' work.
6. When time is up, reconvene the whole group and process the lessons learned using the following questions:
   - How was leadership determined?
   - Was there clear leadership?
   - How were decisions made?
   - Was the atmosphere competitive or cooperative?
   - Was everyone involved? How?
   - Was there a plan? Did it work?
   - What effect do these aspects (leadership, decision making, atmosphere, involvement, planning) have on successful problem solving?
   - What are some key concepts about solving problems brought out here?

- Does your team function like this at work?
- What improvements can you make to the way your team solves problems?

nsider's Tips

- Play energizing music while the teams work.
- Give awards (e.g., least material, most material, group or person who ate the most gum drops, tallest).

Submitted by Bruce G. Waguespack, Ph.D., CPLP

Bruce G. Waguespack is an assistant professor at the Jack and Patti Phillips Workplace Learning and Performance Institute at The University of Southern Mississippi, where he teaches graduate courses and is a facilitator in the Training and Development Certificate Program. His innovative teaching style is grounded by practical, real-life experience. He was the corporate manager for training and development at Georgia Gulf Corporation for seven years. His consulting company, Potential Unlimited, designs and aligns performance improvement strategies that achieve key organizational objectives. Bruce served two terms as president of the Baton Rouge chapter of ASTD and is a CPLP pioneer.

Go for the Goal: Influencing Performance to Reduce Shortage

Objectives

- To identify policy discrepancies presented in photos of actual workplace incidents.
- To briefly explain appropriate corrective action(s) and/or preventive measure(s).
- To estimate cost savings the corrective action(s) and/or preventive measure(s) contribute to shortage reduction goals.

Audience

Four teams of three to four participants from the same organization.

Time

45 minutes.

Materials and Equipment

- One What Kind of Shortage Is It? handout for each participant.
- One Go for the Goal Rules of the Game handout for each participant.
- One Go for the Goal: Your Role in Shortage Control handout for each participant.
- Thirty to forty-five digital photos of typical incidents that result in store and department shortage, saved in a slideshow format (e.g., PowerPoint or Keynote). *Note:* Be sure to screen these pictures carefully to avoid or be prepared for internal shortage discussions that may display the participants themselves or others participants know.
- Leader notes of correct responses for each photo: procedure discrepancy, corrective action(s) and/or preventive measure(s), and cost savings estimate.
- Laptop computer, LCD projector, screen, wireless remote to project slides.
- Buzzer system with color-coded touch pads (e.g., Trainer's Warehouse Who's First? Buzzers).
- Stopwatch or other timing device.
- Flip chart or whiteboard and felt-tipped marker for scorekeeping. (See the Scoreboard Format Sample at the end of the activity.)
- Prize for each winning team member (e.g., $3 break coupon).

Area Setup

Spacious enough for teams to form comfortably around a U-shaped conference table and whisper ideas among themselves; access their team buzzers; and see the projected photos and scoreboard clearly.

Process

1. Distribute a copy of the What Kind of Shortage Is It? handout to each participant and review the content.

2. Introduce the game by expressing confidence in participants' knowledge about and experience with shortage issues in their store and their potential to exceed their department and store shortage reduction goal. Tell them that, to show what they know (and dust off any cobwebs), they are going to play a game called Go for the Goal!

3. Group participants into teams of three or four.

4. Ask each team to claim the nearest buzzer touchpad. Tell them the color of the touchpad determines the color of their team, e.g., red, blue, green, etc. Demonstrate how the buzzers work (the color of the first team to buzz blinks; the back-up team's color lights up solid). Allow teams to take turns buzzing in to assure that all touchpads work.

5. Explain that a shortage example will appear on the screen and that the examples are actual photos of shortage culprits in their stores.

6. Distribute a copy of the Go for the Goal Rules of the Game handout to each participant. Review the rules and explain that the work of the team is threefold:
   - Identify the cause of shortage depicted in the photo.
   - State an appropriate corrective action and/or prevention.
   - Estimate the cost savings toward the department or store goal. (10 minutes.)

7. Show the first slide and announce the color of the first team to buzz in. For example, "All right! Let's hear from the blue team!" Listen for a correct (or close enough to be acceptable) response. If correct/acceptable, congratulate the team with a, "Way to go! Nice job!" as you place a point on the scoreboard.

8. If a team responds incorrectly to the shortage cause or fix/prevention, proceed to the backup team whose light is blinking by saying something like, "Good try, team. Let's hear from the blinking team." If the blinking team responds correctly, congratulate them as you place a point on the scoreboard.

9. Reset the light unit, advance to the next photo, and announce the first team to buzz in.

10. If a team calls out a response but has not buzzed in, remind the group that points are only awarded to the team that buzzes in, and that calling out helps other teams to buzz in and use their great ideas to earn the point.

11. If a team argues with the facilitator/judge's ruling, tell them that argument with the judge results in an automatic point loss and deduct 1 point from their score.

12. If a team buzzes in and doesn't respond right away, start the stopwatch to enforce the 5-second rule. If they don't respond within 5 seconds, deduct 1 point from their score. Then invite the backup (blinking) team to respond.

13. Continue playing until a team reaches 10 points (or until 20 minutes has elapsed, whichever comes first). End the game by saying something like, "We have a winner! Let's have a round of applause for the winning team and all of you for your winning ideas!"

14. Award the winning team members prizes.

15. Distribute copies of the Go for the Goal: Your Role in Shortage Control handout to each participant.
    - Allow participants 5 minutes to complete this individual exercise.
    - Invite a volunteer to share one item from his or her list with the group. Record the item on a flip chart and thank the first volunteer.
    - Proceed in a round-robin process to invite and chart responses from remaining participants.
    - Thank participants for their past shortage-control efforts and their commitment to make an even greater difference.
    - Share information about when, where, and how to access the latest shortage goal numbers so they can track their department's progress regularly after the session.

Insider's Tips

- Create a variety of slideshows based on the composition of the audience. For example, if most participants work the night crew, select photos most relevant for them; if they are cashiers and customer service, select the photos most relevant to their jobs.
- Various forms of recognition can be used for winning team members besides coupons. For example, a team photo could be taken and posted on the employee bulletin board and/or published in the next company newsletter.

Submitted by Johanna Zitto, CPT

Johanna Zitto, CPT, president of JZ Consulting and Training Inc., specializes in improving sales performance, developing strong leaders, building cohesive teams, and raising customer service satisfaction. A twenty-year practitioner, Johanna has earned the American Society for Training & Development (ASTD) Human Performance Improvement (HPI) Certificate and the International Society for Performance Improvement (ISPI) Certified Performance Technologist (CPT) designation. A former ASTD chapter president, Johanna was published in *WHO'S WHO in Sales and Marketing* for sales training achievements.

What Kind of Shortage Is It?

As you know, there are many causes of shortage in your store. The most common are:

- Theft—eating food not paid for; switching labels to pay a lower price; stealing money or products; etc.
- Inaccurate Scanning—improper discounting; false voids; unauthorized refunds; not checking under the cart; etc.
- Back Door Receiving—paying for items not received; paying higher price than book price; approving receipt of damaged or incorrect items; leaving door open; etc.
- Incorrect Pricing—incorrect shelf signs; item entered into system incorrectly; price changes not updated; etc.
- Employee Mistakes—damage caused by mishandled product loading or unloading; mishandling cutter during pack out; excessive trimming; improper bagging; inaccurate inventory-taking; misuse of supplies; mistakes in container selection; etc.
- Customer mistakes—customer-caused breakage or omissions.
- Spoilage—improper rotation resulting in out-of-code items and spoiled perishables; unsuitable case temperatures; etc.
- Accounting Errors—mistakes, omissions, or sloppy writing in recording markdowns, damages, transfers, etc.

Go for the Goal Rules of the Game

1. Form four teams: Red, Blue, Green, Yellow.
2. A shortage example will be shown on screen. Try to identify (a) apparent cause of shortage, (b) what employees can do to correct and/or prevent it, and (c) estimated cost savings toward shortage control goal.
3. First team to buzz in and answer correctly wins 1 point. An unacceptable response, as deemed by the judge, results in a second team getting a chance to respond. If the other team answers correctly, they earn 1 point.
4. If a team buzzes but does not give an answer within 5 seconds of buzzing, it loses 1 point.
5. If a team or team member argues with the judge, the team loses 1 point.
6. The first team to score 10 points wins the game!

Go for the Goal: Your Role in Shortage Control

It is impossible to totally eliminate shortage in our business. However, when *everyone* works together, we can control shortage and build a stronger organization for the future.

In the spaces below, write three things you can do in your department and/or store to control shortage. You will choose one of them to share with the group before the end of the session.

My Role in Shortage Control

1.

2.

3.

Scoreboard Format Sample

Team Color	Point Tally	Total Points
Red		
Blue		
Green		
Yellow		

Chapter 20

Process and Projects

Process improvement has been on the lips of almost every employee since the mid-1980s. Today you are more likely to hear about Six Sigma teams. The concepts are the same. Organizations are clear that doing business in the 21st century, in a global economy, against excellent competitors requires ongoing process improvement. This means that everyone in an organization must have knowledge about how to reduce waste, save time, reduce expenses, increase sales, boost productivity, and improve quality.

Trainers are expected to incorporate the principles of process improvement and project management in most classes that they design and conduct. They also are expected to convey the importance of empowering employees to get involved with process improvement.

This chapter presents trainers with an opportunity to involve participants in identifying processes that require improvement, root causes, and the effect of time pressures. Participants are also introduced to the concept of internal customers and suppliers.

Bright Idea

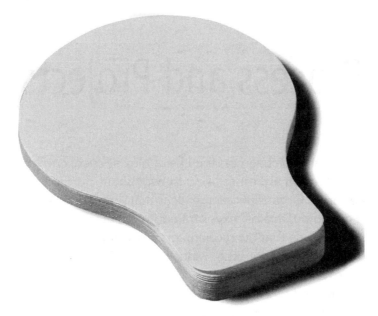

Objectives
- To visually identify places to improve a process.
- To make suggestions for improving a process.

Audience
Members of a group who work in a similar process.

Time
60 minutes.

Materials and Equipment
- Four or five flip-chart sheets taped to a wall.
- 3-inch × 3-inch Post-its®.
- A pen.
- Lightbulb Post-its®.
- Lightbulb throwable, one for each participant.

Area Setup

Need one long wall without windows for hanging flip-chart pages.

Process

1. As you begin, give all participants Lightbulb throwables to keep their hands busy (and their brains engaged).
2. Review the symbols for a simple flow chart: circle = start and end; rectangle = step in the process; diamond = decision step.
3. Identify a process that needs to be improved. Have the participants list the steps in the process. Use a dark pen to write each step on a Post-it. Use the appropriate symbol as noted in Step 2. Try to phrase decision steps so that each has a yes or no answer.
4. Hang the steps (Post-its) on the flip-chart sheets in order from left to right.
5. If someone identifies a step that is out of order or is missing, simply rearrange the Post-its to indicate the correct order.
6. Once all the steps have been posted, have one of the participants walk the group through the process.
7. Ask the group to stand and, working in pairs, identify where the process bogs down, causes delays, creates confusion, or generates rework.
8. Once they have identified the problem step, pairs should identify what they believe to be a root cause and a potential solution. Tell them to write this information on a lightbulb Post-it and to place it at the appropriate step. If more than one pair selects the same step, all responses should be included.
9. Review the lightbulbs and state that these ideas will be forwarded to a process improvement or Six Sigma team for evaluation.

Submitted by Daniel Greene

Daniel Greene is vice president of operations for ebb associates inc, a firm that helps organizations work through large-scale change. He brings a Deming foundation to his work in process improvement and has worked with clients such as Lands' End, Newport News Shipbuilding, and the Navy's FISC, Honolulu. In a former life he was a fighter pilot for the U.S. Navy.

Puzzling About Systems Thinking

Objectives

- To experience the importance of systems thinking.
- To create a dialogue about how various aspects of the whole affect systems thinking.

Audience

At least fifteen participants; can be facilitated with forty or more participants.

Time

30 to 50 minutes, depending on group size.

Materials and Equipment

- One 500-piece puzzle with fairly intricate (interesting or complex) picture. (For example, I have used one with a picture of Times Square and one with the characters from the *Wizard of Oz*.)
- Answer Boards—one per participant.

- Mr. Sketch® markers.
- One Dry Erase marker for each participant.
- Flip chart.

Area Setup

Individuals should be seated so they can be easily placed in smaller subgroups.

Preparation

Prior to the participants arriving, hand select one puzzle piece for each participant in the program. Choose a puzzle piece that will not make it easy to identify the puzzle picture. Select a wide range of pieces—colors, shapes, pictures, etc. Set aside. Then choose a second (additional) puzzle piece for each participant—this time select pieces that provide more "information," i.e., provide more details that start to identify the picture. Set them aside.

Process

1. Introduce the exercise by saying,

   "When facing complex problems, many of us were taught to break the issue down and study the individual parts in the belief that the whole is merely the sum of its parts. Systems thinking takes a different approach, believing that in order to understand a whole, you must understand the connections between individual parts and how they work together. It has applications to both our personal and professional lives. In the organization, we have many systems; understanding the connections between teams and departments is an important part of understanding our business."

2. Go on to define the term "system" for the group as "a collection all partici-pants of parts that interact with each other to function as a whole."

3. Ask people to give examples of systems. Have all participants think of one or two systems that they are a part of now, what their roles are in those systems, and how their efforts affect those systems. They can be work or non-work related, as seen in the examples.
   - The sales department is a system. My role in that system is to _____. If I don't do that, then _____.
   - My family is a system. My role is to _____. If I change, then _____.

4. Transition into the exercise by saying, "The best way to understand something is to experience it first-hand. Let's look at systems thinking through a quick exercise."

5. Distribute the first puzzle pieces you reserved (face down) to all participants. Instruct them not to look at their puzzle pieces until everyone has one.

Once distributed, ask participants to turn their puzzle pieces over, "identify" their picture, and write it on their answer boards. (This is an individual exercise at this point in time.)

6. Ask participants to display the responses on their Answer Boards. Allow enough time for everyone to read all responses. (At this time, it will likely be difficult for people to identify the picture.)

7. Distribute the second puzzle pieces you reserved (face down) to all participants. Ask four or five participants who are sitting near each other to share their puzzle pieces with each other. If you have a group of five, they collectively have ten puzzle pieces at this point in time. Have them give their best guess based on the collective information they have gathered and record it on one Answer Board. Because you hand-selected some puzzle pieces for this step, the guesses should be getting "warmer." Go around the room and have each group identify its best guess recorded on one Answer Board. If you have five teams, you will record five total guesses.

8. If all of the guesses in Round Two are correct, skip to Step 11. Otherwise, proceed to Step 9.

9. Ask the entire group to gather and share all of their puzzle pieces with each other. Do not add any new pieces to the mix (unless you have to because the guesses are still off the mark). After the entire group looks at all of the puzzle pieces, have the individuals go back to their smaller teams and come up with one final best answer based on all of the information gathered.

10. Go around the room and ask each team for its answer. Record on the flip chart. At this point in time, you usually have several teams who are very close to identifying the puzzle. Again, if you have five groups, you will have five total guesses.

11. Share the picture/cover of the puzzle box. Pass it around the room. Facilitate a large group discussion and debrief by asking the following questions:
    - So what does this tell us about systems thinking? What are the key learnings?
    - What are your takeaways from this activity?

12. Discuss key learning points. List on a flip chart (as appropriate). There are many insights and you may need to structure the discussion. Insights may include:
    - Viewing an organization as a whole versus individual parts. (They could make better decisions when they started to view the whole system in this

exercise—on a smaller level, their group versus themselves; on a larger level, the entire class versus their teams.)

- Information that one group/team has is not valuable data for the organization if it is not shared. For example, one group may have a piece of the puzzle that helps them identify the "answer" early on. They may not be willing to share that information with others. (You may set this up to create some competition between the groups if you choose to facilitate it this way.)

- Competition between teams can be healthy. It can also be destructive if it is not managed well (again, you can facilitate this in a way that gets at issues of competition between teams if you choose to).

- We don't need all of the information to make good, informed decisions. Analysis by paralysis isn't necessary (e.g., they made a good decision without having all of the facts—500 pieces of the puzzle).

- An organization is only as fast as its slowest part (as evidenced when you go around the room and ask everyone to share answers to the puzzle. Some may get bogged down with this).

- Individual personalities, style differences, etc., affect the system. Sometimes an individual will share a vital piece of information and it is not heard. She/ he may even repeat it two or three times. As the facilitator, try to observe these personality/style differences at play so you can comment on them during the debriefing.

- What is rewarded is what gets attention, even if it's wrong. (You can build in a discussion about rewards if you want to. During the exercise, you can acknowledge/recognize teams or individuals to add another layer of complexity to this activity.)

- Changes made by one group affect other groups, often negatively. Examples? (Even though this is a very simple exercise, I've had people try to cheat; I've had some try to look at the cover of the box to see the picture of the puzzle; and I've had two teams work together and leave other teams out.)

13. Close by asking questions about why systems thinking in the organization is important. Why does working together as a system matter? Have people relate these concepts to the organization and their own team/department. They may talk about whether these issues exist, what's been done to alleviate them, or tell stories. Discuss the leader's role in a system and in promoting systems thinking.

Submitted by Diane Hamilton

Diane Hamilton is a partner with the Center for Organization Effectiveness and surveysbydesign.com, a management consulting firm that focuses on strategy execution and leadership effectiveness. Diane has been in the HR/OD field for over twenty-three years and has worked with clients in a variety of organizations and industries on their individual and organizational improvement and change strategies. She assesses culture and organizational effectiveness, designs performance improvement systems, designs and implements talent review processes, and coaches executives on business and interpersonal effectiveness issues. Diane is a long-time volunteer for SHRM at a local and state level and holds a SPHR certification.

Project Change Challenge

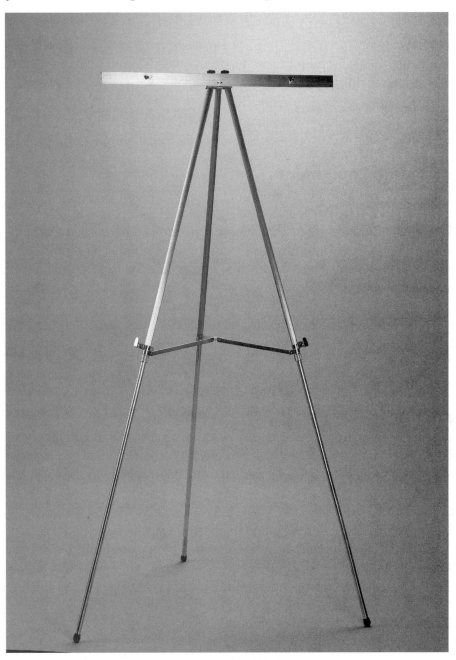

Objectives
- To identify skills needed to complete a project under pressure.
- To evaluate ethical behaviors that surface under pressure.

Audience
Any group; especially useful for cross-functional teams, time management issues, and project management teams.

Time
20 to 25 minutes.

Materials and Equipment
- Easy Snap Easel (one per team).
- Flip-chart pads (one per team).
- Mr. Sketch® markers (one each blue, green, and black for each team).
- Red Mr. Sketch® markers (one less than the total number of teams).
- One set of three envelopes for each team prepared with three different messages inside:
  1. Every sixth word must be written backwards.
  2. At least four of the words must be furniture.
  3. Every word on your list that contains more than four letters must be circled in red.
- Time Tracker or stopwatch.

Area Setup
One easel per team should be placed in a corner or distributed equally throughout the room. The easels should face the center of the room. Put all red markers in a location not accessible or visible to participants, but available to the facilitator.

Process
1. Determine in advance how many teams you want to have and ask participants to count off by that number. For example, if you want four teams, have participants count off by 4s.
2. Tell participants to form teams based on their numbers, i.e., all the 1s together, all the 2s together, and so forth.
3. Direct each team to stand at an easel.

4. Tell the teams that when you say, "Go!" they must write the alphabet on the flip chart, from A to Z.
5. The teams must then identify objects in the room *that they can all see* that start with the appropriate alphabet letter (example: M = marker). Once they have written a word for each alphabet letter, they have completed the project. The project deadline is 8 minutes away.
6. Answer questions. Set Time Tracker or stopwatch. Say, "Go!"
7. About 2 minutes into the activity, deliver the first sealed envelope to each team. Explain that the customer has revised the project scope and these are the new specifications.
8. Each team opens its envelope and reads the new specifications: "Every sixth word must be written backwards."
9. Allow the teams to begin making changes and continue with the project.
10. In about 90 seconds more, give each team its second sealed envelope and explain that a new project manager has just been named. New instructions are in the sealed envelope: "At least four of the words must be pieces of furniture."
11. Allow the teams to continue making changes and working toward completing the project. Remind all groups of the remaining time before the project deadline.
12. After another 90 seconds, announce a budget change for the project. Give each team its third sealed envelope. The new instructions read, "Every word on your list that contains more than four letters must be circled in red."
13. As noted in the setup, no red markers should be visible to participants. If a participant asks you for a red marker, give it to him or her. If participants do not ask, they do not receive a red marker. Have one less red marker than the number of teams. (Example: if there are four easels, then only three red markers are available for teams that ask.)
14. At the end of 8 minutes, announce that the project deadline has arrived and all teams must stop their work.
15. Have the participants stay with their teams. Debrief using some of the following questions:
    • Did a natural leader emerge in the process? Who took charge?
    • Describe your planning process.
    • Did anyone give up during the activity? Why?
    • How did you feel with each of the specification changes?

- How similar to reality was this activity?
- What happened when you couldn't find a red marker?
- Why didn't you ask the facilitator for a red marker?
- Why didn't you ask another team to use its red marker?
- How often do these things—new specifications, new direction, seemingly unattainable resources and short deadlines—happen to you during a project?
- What skills are required to complete a project under pressure?
- What ethical issues can surface during these types of pressures?
- What lessons will you take back to the workplace as a result of this activity?

Insider's Tips

- Be sure to emphasize that the words for the flip charts must be something they actually can see in the classroom. Participants have been known to come up with words like "ulcer" for the letter "U".
- Participants can become really frustrated during this activity and resort to looking at other teams' lists for appropriate words, moving their easels so other teams won't use their words, whispering, and substituting other colors of markers for the red one.
- Help teams realize that by working together they could finish faster and meet the new specification changes.
- Acknowledge that the level of stress during the game may be comparable to what they can feel during an actual project and say that they should deal with that stress appropriately.

Submitted by Sarah E. Hurst

Sarah E. Hurst is the training manager of Stewart & Stevenson LLC, Houston, Texas, and has been in training for over sixteen years. She is responsible for researching, developing, creating, and presenting classes on customer service, communication, leadership, project management, time management, stress management, and more. Sarah has been a member of ASTD since 1996 and is currently the vice president of membership for the Houston chapter.

Chicken, Salad, and Koosh® Ball Shuffle

Objectives
- To experience process improvement.
- To practice high performance team functioning.

Audience
Any group of twelve to thirty. Works best with about twenty.

Time
50 to 75 minutes.

Materials and Equipment

- Pack everything in a large duffle bag. This is your bag of surprises.
  - About a dozen "Koosh® balls" or tennis balls.
  - One rubber chicken.
  - Six to ten assorted raw, firm fruit and vegetables (use a variety for different shapes, colors, and sizes such as an apple, orange, grapefruit, carrot, or potato).
  - A one-gallon bucket of water balloons (eight to twelve).
  - One dozen raw eggs.
  - Blindfolds (enough for half the group).
- A stopwatch or watch with a second hand.

Area Setup

Open floor space or open outside area big enough for the group to make a large circle.

Process

Note: This activity works best when the facilitator processes it between rounds.

1. Assemble the group in a large circle.
2. Introduce the activity by explaining that the group will throw the Koosh ball around to each other in random order. The ball starts with the facilitator and ends with the facilitator and everyone gets it one time without dropping it. Play one round. This will establish the sequence to use for each subsequent round.
3. Debrief this round by asking, "How did that go? How could we improve it?" Explain that this is like any work process, a sequence of steps that a team of people complete. Ask them to describe a process at their workplace. State that many things must occur for the process to be successful, including things such as effective customer/supplier communication, improved focus and productivity, solving problems, inclusion of diversity, and others.
4. State that next they're going to practice internal customer/supplier communication. Have them decide who will be the customers and who will be the suppliers. Ask the group to practice another round or two (using the same sequence as earlier), only this time, they are to call their internal customer's name and throw the ball in such a way that the customer can catch it. Participants should strive to serve their customers, so they may want to ask their customers how they want the ball tossed.

5. Debrief by asking again, "How did that go? Where should our main focus be?" Continue by saying, "Focus should be on our internal customer/supplier relationship with our attention to the overall objective, passing the Koosh ball without dropping it in the process." Ask, "How can we strengthen our relationships with internal customers/suppliers?" Accept a few responses and state that it is time to move to another important aspect.

6. State that, on the job, they may be constantly multi-tasking, working on individual relationships, and improving productivity, while still focusing on the main goal. Play another round. This time, surprise participants by rapidly feeding eight to twelve more Koosh balls into the process. This should cause some confusion and chaos. You can warn them by explaining that they must pass each item one at a time per person, without dropping any items they are producing (balls). This represents the kind of multi-tasking they complete every day.

7. Debrief the round by asking, "How did that go? What was different about that round? Is your workplace more like that?" Expect participants to raise issues such as multiple tasks, lots to do, more on my plate than I can handle, things slipping through the cracks, balls dropping all over the place. Continue by facilitating a discussion about their work environment. Ask, "What processes are you currently involved in that could be improved?"

8. Introduce the next round by asking whether anyone is ever required to solve problems. Ask the group to play another round, and to make sure their customers are ready for the ball (task) before they throw it. Start by feeding three balls in and without delay feed a rubber chicken into the process. Continue feeding another six balls into the process. This should cause a diversion from the focus required to execute the process.

9. Debrief this round by asking, "How did that go? How was that round like your work day? Do you have unexpected problems (rubber chickens) appear in your work processes? Like what? Name some. What do you typically do about them? What did we do about this 'rubber chicken'? What are some strategies for dealing with problems in our work processes? What are the best strategies for solving problems in our processes?"

10. State that we must also respect diversity and build synergy. Play another round, but this time, feed in the fruits and vegetables, one at a time (use the real stuff but be careful).

11. Debrief by asking, "How did that go? What was different about that round?" Explain, "As long as we are working with other people, we will experience

differences, different sizes, shapes, weights, colors, races, gender, values, perspectives, and so forth. What are the advantages of differences on your team? Challenges? Do you 'synergize' or 'polarize' around differences?"

12. Introduce the next round by asking whether they are required to take risks or shift paradigms. Take out your gallon bucket of water balloons. You will get a reaction from the group. Give them a chance to choose to improve their process. Usually they choose to rearrange themselves in closer proximity to one another. Recognize the paradigm shift here. Play another round and expect they will improve performance tremendously!

13. Debrief by asking, "How did that go? What was different about that round? What made you make a significant change?" Explain, "Performance improvement can be incremental or, after a paradigm shift, it can be huge! What opportunities do you have to shift the way you think about your work processes? Are your processes aligned for high performance? How does risk influence our behavior? How does risk influence our choices to work together, to survive, to improve, and to seek excellence?"

14. State that, even with everything occurring, organizations must measure what they are doing. Introduce the next round by pulling out a dozen raw eggs (not boiled—raw). You will get a reaction from the group, but they sort of expect it at this point. Give the group the opportunity to go back to the old way of doing things. If they do, you may make the point that performance improvement sticks if the individuals truly buy in to the new way of doing things and if they are committed to make it work. Tell the group that the same rules apply: no cracked (dropped) eggs, one item (egg) passed at a time, same sequence. The effectiveness or quality measurement will be "no cracked eggs" and the efficiency measurement will be "cycle time per twelve items," e.g., how long it takes the dozen eggs to all be passed through the sequence. Ask someone to time the round. Usually someone in the middle of the sequence is the most appropriate for this task.

15. Debrief the round by asking, "Are there any cracked eggs? What was your time? How did that go? Are there some egg-handling techniques that worked better than others? Would it be a good idea to standardize one best practice for our next round? How did measurement influence our performance?"

16. Finally, introduce the last round by stating that trust is critical to high performance. Explain that every other person will be blindfolded. You may wish to make up a story about why they are "temporarily visually impaired." The challenge now is to improve their cycle time without cracking any eggs, using the

same sequence, with the blindfolded team members participating. Brainstorm ideas and prompt them by suggesting that we need to reduce the distance the eggs have to travel, to minimize the risks associated with blindfolded people handling the eggs, and to standardize best practices to improve effectiveness and efficiency. *Note:* Help them come up with the idea of forming a circle in a circle (inside circle should consist of blindfolded participants facing outward) or two lines (blindfolded facing non-blindfolded). Play the round and remember to time it!

17. Debrief the round by asking, "Are there any cracked eggs? What was our time? How did that go? Did we improve? How do we know? How did it feel to be blindfolded? How did it feel to be responsible for taking care of the eggs and blindfolded people?" Explain that trust is absolutely necessary to build a high performance team. Add that they are a high performance team! And finally ask, "What does it take to be one?"

18. Review the principles discussed.

19. Celebrate!

Insider's Tips

- Do cheers to encourage team spirit.
- Have fun and be creative.
- I have done this activity hundreds of times and it is a bit different every time. But it works every time!
- It can be used to "teach" experientially lots of different principles.

Submitted by Bruce G. Waguespack, Ph.D., CPLP

Bruce G. Waguespack is an assistant professor at the Jack and Patti Phillips Workplace Learning and Performance Institute at The University of Southern Mississippi, where he teaches graduate courses and is a facilitator in the Training and Development Certificate Program. His innovative teaching style is grounded by practical, real-life experience. He was the corporate manager for training and development at Georgia Gulf Corporation for seven years. His consulting company, Potential Unlimited, designs and aligns performance improvement strategies that achieve key organizational objectives. Bruce served two terms as president of the Baton Rouge chapter of ASTD and is a CPLP pioneer.

Chapter 21

Supervision, Management, and Leadership

The first job as a supervisor, a manager, or in any leadership role is often a surprise. When individuals become responsible for the performance of a group, their work lives change. As individual contributors, they had complete control over what to do in order to achieve better results. Once they become responsible for a group of people and their performance, that control disappears and is replaced with influence.

Supervisors, managers, and leaders are all responsible for other people's performance. Supervisors typically deal with individuals and with tasks. There is supervisory work to do at almost all levels in an organization—typically, supervisors work with their direct reports to discuss what they are going to do and how they are going to do it. Managers, on the other hand, deal more with groups and priorities and handle things like scheduling problems and how to allocate scarce resources. It is a tactical position, and the need for influence increases. Both, however, must act as "leaders." The leadership role is about purpose and direction. A leadership role deals with strategic issues and is almost entirely accomplished through influence.

Trainers frequently design and deliver courses that cater to all three roles: supervisory, management, and leadership. Each course includes skill building for various aspects of the job such as goal setting, building teams, dealing with different styles, getting work done through others, etc. The activities in this chapter can stand alone or be integrated into a leadership development course.

Appraising Performance:
A Home Building Challenge

Objectives
- To identify all the steps of the appraisal process.
- To introduce a complete performance appraisal process.
- To identify the benefits of utilizing the entire performance appraisal process.

Audience
Supervisors or leaders who must evaluate employee performance. Also good for any person in a leadership role who wants to improve team performance.

Time
60 minutes.

Materials and Equipment
- Copies of Handouts 1 and 2 for supervisor.
- One copy of Handout 1 for each participant.

- Colored popsicle sticks.
- Small flag.
- Glue.
- Clay.
- Tape.
- Colored note cards.
- Flip chart.
- Marker.
- One Right Time Timer, Meeting Minder, or other timing device.

Area Setup
Two or three tables to set up the "building area" and room to move around.

Process
1. Tell participants that they work for a home-building company. Everyone has a role or job title. One person is the supervisor. Explain the following goals:
   - Team member or "employee" goals: Build as many houses as possible following the criteria in the job description.
   - Team leader or supervisor goals: Determine the elements you will use as a basis for each employee's performance appraisal. For example, the roofer must be able to follow directions, communicate with others, have enough physical strength to carry shingles, have the ability to use glue and to fold paper. The supervisor must determine what elements are critical to job success. Later the supervisor will use these elements to evaluate the employee for the performance appraisal.
2. Tell participants that there will be three building periods of 5 minutes each. Time will be called at each 5-minute increment. At that time all completed homes will be counted. Five homes completed per period meets the requirements.
3. Gather the employees together, providing each with a copy of Handout 1, and assign each a role. (*Note:* You may allow two or three roofers, assemblers, cutters, cheerleaders, etc., but have just one quality assurance person.) If you have too many participants, let them grade the performance in the role of observer. Later, when the supervisor has finished giving the evaluation, you may ask the observers whether they agree with what the supervisor determined. Have the employees study their roles while you talk to the supervisor, telling him or her to avoid discussing or interacting with the other employees.

4. Give the supervisor the job descriptions for all employees (Handout 1) and the performance appraisal worksheet (Handout 2). Put the supervisor at a desk somewhere in the room yet out of the immediate work area, where he or she can determine the critical elements that will be evaluated.

5. Set the timer and begin the exercise. Stay out of participants' way.

6. When the timer sounds, ask everyone to stop work. They will probably not complete any homes the first time. Ask the supervisor to inspect the work and record on a flip chart how many homes are "in progress" and "complete" for the 5-minute period, using a chart like the following:

Houses in Progress	Houses Complete
Period 1	
Period 2	
Period 3	

7. Reset the timer and complete the second and third periods. When all three periods are over, tally the total houses completed and ask the supervisor to complete the performance appraisals. The supervisor will either give an acceptable or unacceptable grade. *Note:* If the supervisor drags this on, it is okay to cut it short after a few appraisals once you feel that the point has been made. The review questions will reveal how inadequate an appraisal is when you leave out the rest of the appraisal process.

8. If you used observers, ask for their observations.

9. Review the exercise as a large group, using these questions:
   - Did the supervisor know who actually performed well?
   - What did the supervisor base the appraisal on?
   - Did any employees work "outside" of their job descriptions to help the process? Did the supervisor note this?
   - What would have made the appraisal process more effective?
   - If not mentioned in answer to the previous question, ask about these elements:
     - The supervisor discussing expectations (not just a job description) with each employee prior to the work beginning.
     - The supervisor explaining how he or she would measure whether or not expectations were met.
     - The supervisor discussing obstacles with employees.

- The supervisor checking in occasionally and actually talking with employees to see how they were doing.
- The supervisor coming to the job site and actually monitored performance.
- The supervisor coaching, explaining, arranging for training, and other actions that have the potential of improving performance.
- Often, supervisors base their appraisals on work completed, in this case, completed homes. Often these appraisals are based on opinion, not fact. How effective is it to accomplish an appraisal at the end of the year and base it on work accomplished?

10. State that this exercise mimics real life Supervisors are so busy doing "office work" going to meetings, etc., that they skip the actual leading and supervising part. Make the following learning points:
   - The goal of the appraisal should be to improve performance.
   - The actual performance appraisal itself is just *one* part of an overall strategy to improve performance.
   - The most important part of an appraisal is the before-and-after work:
     - Establishing expectations prior to the work being performed.
     - Monitoring performance to ensure understanding and ability, to reward, etc.
     - Communicating with the employee during the appraisal period.
   - The appraisal is just a point in time. The "before appraisal" and "after appraisal" work is substantially more relevant than "the appraisal" itself.
   - If the supervisor wants to improve performance, he or she has to get out of the office and actually "talk" to employees.

Submitted by Cindy Lee Hall

Cindy Lee Hall is president and CEO of CLI, a training company that couples subject-matter experts with professional trainers to offer relevant, motivational, and educational training. Cindy Lee has been in the training and consulting field for fifteen years and has written and published over twenty-five training courses. She is also a squadron commander and Lt. Colonel in the Virginia Air National Guard.

Appraising Performance Handout 1

Number	Job Title
1	**Supervisor** Performance appraisals are coming up for several of your employees. Attached you will find a list of the employees and their job description. Establish the performance standards that you will use to rate their performance. Do a performance appraisal on each employee according to his or her performance on the newest American Homes project.
2 or 3	**Roofer** Must be able to: use scissors and glue. Performance Criteria: Must deliver at least three assembled roofs to builder every 5 minutes. Job Description: Fold roof (5 × 7 note card) in half so that both sides are equal. Glue six shingles on each side of roof. Hand carry completed roof to builder.
2 or 3	**Frame Assembler** Must be able to: Use glue. Performance Criteria: Must assemble and deliver at least fifteen frame assemblies to builder every 5 minutes. Job Description: Using glue, attach four studs (popsicle sticks) to each other to form a square frame assembly. Hand deliver each frame assembly to the builder. **Four popsicle sticks glued together**

1	**Quality Assurance**
	Must be able to: Count, see color, get along with people.
	Performance Criteria: Must inspect at least three houses every 5 minutes.
	Job Description: Inspect every completed house to ensure that each side is made with fifteen stacked frame assemblies. Make sure a roof is attached to each house with a flag at the peak and that walls use rainbow colors.
1 to 3	**Cheerleader**
	Must be able to: Act enthusiastic. Count.
	Performance Criteria: Must count up to 15. Must give encouragement to workers.
	Job Description: Visit job sites and cheer workers on. Count finished product and tell workers how good they are.
1 to 3	**Shingle Cutter**
	Must be able to: Use scissors to cut a sheet of shingle material into six equal-sized shingles. Deliver cut shingles to builder.
	Performance Criteria: Must deliver at least forty-eight shingles to builder every 5 minutes.
	Job Description: Use scissors to cut sheet of shingles into eight equal-sized shingles. Must deliver shingles to builder at 5-minute intervals.

Builder

Must be able to: Use glue to construct assembled frame units into walls. Use tape to attach roof. Use clay to build a flag holder.

Performance Criteria: Must build at least three houses every 5 minutes.

Job Description: Must glue and stack fifteen assembled frame units on top of each other to form a house. Attach roof using tape. Raise flag onto peak of roof using clay as a flag holder.

House walls are fifteen sticks high on all four sides

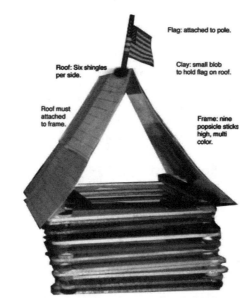

Flag: attached to pole.

Roof: Six shingles per side.

Clay: small blob to hold flag on roof.

Roof must attached to frame.

Frame: nine popsicle sticks high, multi color.

Finished house

Appraising Performance Handout 2

Performance Appraisal Review System

Name	Job Title	Critical Element	Acceptable	Unacceptable

Signature of Supervisor

Getting Things in Focus:
Koosh® Ball Mania

Objectives
- To experience the importance of focus in accomplishing goals.
- To demonstrate the debilitating effect multiple distractions have on solving problems and productivity.
- To discuss a supervisor's responsibility regarding distractions.

Audience

This works best with groups of eight or more supervisors. Large groups are divided into teams of up to fifteen.

Time

15 to 30 minutes, depending on debriefing time.

Materials and Equipment

- Six to eight Koosh® balls of various sizes and colors for each group.
- Flip-chart paper (optional; to be used during debriefing if you want to capture insights of the group).
- Markers.

Area Setup

Requires enough room for the group (or groups) to stand in a circle, with a little space between members.

Process

1. Form the group into a circle. Hold up a Koosh ball and announce that you want to create a sequence pattern by tossing the ball around until everyone has received it. Remember who you receive it from, and who you pass it to.
2. Have everyone hold his or her right hand in the air to signify they have not yet received the Koosh ball. Once they receive the Koosh, they can drop their hands and pass the ball to someone whose hand is still in the air. Complete the round, and then repeat it without hands raised to be sure everyone remembers the sequence.
3. Announce that it is time to put their memory to the test by creating a goal: see how long they can keep the sequence going without dropping the ball.
4. Once the activity has begun, subtly introduce a second Koosh ball into the group. Then continue introducing Koosh balls until you have added five or six to the mix.
5. When things get too crazy and balls are being dropped, stop the activity and conduct a mini-debriefing. Discuss the feelings and experiences when several Koosh balls were introduced into the circuit without warning. Emphasize the value of giving complete attention and focus only to the individual you are receiving a Koosh from, and who you are throwing to.

6. Begin again, starting with one Koosh ball, then slowly introducing additional balls. Recognize the impact of improvement based on the ability of the group to maintain focus.
7. Debrief, using these questions:
   - How was this activity like your work day?
   - How do distractions impact your performance?
   - How does being forewarned as opposed to being surprised impact performance?
   - As a supervisor, what responsibility do you have toward your employees with regard to distractions?
   - How will doing this activity help you be more effective in the future?

Insider's Tips

- This activity begins like another, very familiar activity. When I have seasoned participants in my group, I may say during the instructions, "This may feel like it's going to be a familiar activity, but I would just give you a heads-up to pay attention. It may surprise you!"
- The group is usually very verbal during the debriefing of this activity. It makes a tremendous impact on them in terms of the power of focus—so be sure to allow time for lots of discussion!

Submitted by Cher Holton, Ph.D., CSP, CMC

Cher Holton, Ph.D., president of The Holton Consulting Group, Inc., is an impact consultant, trainer, and speaker focusing on bringing harmony to life with customers, among team members, and in life. In addition to being one of a handful of professionals world-wide who have earned both the Certified Speaking Professional and Certified Management Consultant designations, she has authored several books, including *The Manager's Short Course to a Long Career, Living at the Speed of Life: Staying in Control in a World Gone Bonkers!, From Ballroom to Bottom Line;* and *Crackerjack Choices: 200 of the Best Choices You Will Ever Make.*

Leadership Essentials

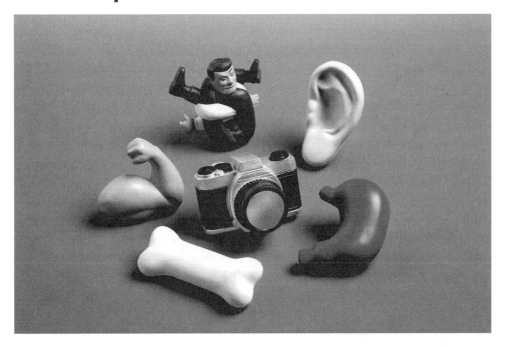

Objectives
- To introduce session participants to key leadership skills.
- To exchange perspectives on important leader behavior.

Audience
A group of no more than twelve participants who are beginning a leadership training program.

Time
2 minutes each for up to twelve participants.

Materials and Equipment
- Easel with flip-chart pad.
- Markers.
- Two Debrief Essentials Sets.

Area Setup
Open space for moving around.

Process
1. Place fourteen foam Debrief Essentials toys on a table.
2. Tell participants to stand and walk over to the table; each of them should select an item that represents a particular leadership skill or behavior.
3. Ask participants to return to their seats.
4. Ask each participant, in turn, to stand and tell the entire group what leadership skill or behavior the item he or she chose represents.
5. Record on a flip chart each skill or behavior.
6. Ask the group to brainstorm other leadership essential skills or behaviors. Record the ideas on flip-chart paper.
7. Add to the list based on any aspect of the course content that participants may have missed.
8. Lead a discussion about any leaders participants have encountered who have all the skills and behaviors that have been identified.
9. Segue into the next learning activity.

 nsider's Tips

- This should be a fast-paced exercise.
- Ask an occasional question about a particular toy and the identified behavior or skill.

Submitted by Kitty Preziosi and Robert C. Preziosi, D.P.A.
Kitty Preziosi has over twenty years of experience as a company team leader and senior consultant for achieving strategic initiatives in the areas of organization development, training, executive coaching, team building, performance management, values and competency systems, and process re-design. She is a co-owner of Preziosi Partners, Inc., and director of training/organization development or senior learning consultant for/to such organizations as Miller Brewing Company, Moss & Associates, JM Family Enterprises, The Coca-Cola Company, ABB Combustion Engineering, Bank Atlantic, Chubb, Crawford & Company, Kraft General Foods, Lexis Nexis, New South, Inc., United Technologies, and Nova Southeastern University.

Robert C. Preziosi, D.P.A., is a professor of management at the Huizenga School of Business and Entrepreneurship at Nova Southeastern University in Fort Lauderdale, Florida. He has received numerous awards, including Excellence in Teaching, Professor of the Decade, and Faculty Member of the Year. He is also president of Preziosi Partners, Inc., a consulting firm. ASTD has bestowed the Outstanding Contribution to HRD award and two Torch Awards on him. He is the editor of the 2005, 2006, and 2007 *Pfeiffer Annual: Human Resource Management* and the *2008 Annual: Management Development*. He focuses his presentations, research, and teaching on leadership, HRD, training trainers, and executive education.

Your Supervisor Hat

Objective

- To create a visual aid of leadership concepts important to each participant's development as a supervisor.

Audience

Eight to twenty participants in a supervisor or leader development program.

Time

15 minutes to create the cap; 1 to 2 minutes per participant to debrief.

Materials and Equipment

- One Painter's Cap per person.
- Several sets of fine-tipped permanent colored markers.
- Several sets of Mr. Sketch® colored markers.

Area Setup

No special arrangement is needed.

Process

1. Distribute one Painter's Hat to each participant with an assortment of colored markers.
2. Say, "During this session, you have been exposed to various leadership ideas and techniques as you build your skill level. You now have the opportunity to create a visual reminder using a Painter's Hat to take back to your office. Please take a few minutes to think about what is important for you to remember as a leader, and then draw something on your cap that will remind you."
3. Allow 15 minutes for participants to draw on their hats.
4. Stop several times throughout the remainder of the session and have participants take turns sharing what is on their caps and one thing they learned about themselves in their new supervisor role.

 nsider's Tips

- Remind participants that it's not important to be a good artist. Ideas and concepts can be shown through words, symbols, stick figures, etc.
- Address any judging comments from participants during the sharing phase. All participants will have their own unique leadership goals. There are many types of leaders.

Submitted by Marjorie Treu

As president of Team Fusion, Marjorie Treu has twenty-three years of adult education experience in the travel, banking, manufacturing, and service industries. Her main focus is on executive and management development, leadership development, sales and sales management, and all aspects of human resources training. Her current emphasis is on organization development, with a passion for working with team leadership through all stages of team formation, coaching teams in trouble, and experiential team building. Marjorie holds a bachelor's degree in education from the University of Wisconsin-Milwaukee and a PHR certification. She serves on the board for the Southeastern Wisconsin chapter of ASTD, most recently as president.

Chapter 22

Teamwork and Team Building

Most of you have been members of many teams throughout your life: athletic teams, such as baseball or tennis; volunteer teams, such as fund-raising groups or fire fighting; school teams, such as debate or the chorus; social teams, such as card clubs; or civic teams, such as the civic league or a city-wide support group. You are a member of a family, and that is a team. And you are on a variety of teams at work. Indeed, teamwork is all around us at all times.

As you think of teamwork, you are most likely confronted with an assortment of thoughts. These may include positive thoughts, such as working together, achieving common goals, and having fun. On the other hand, negative thoughts may also come to mind, such as time-consuming, personality conflicts, and difficult communication.

What is a "team" anyway? It is any group of people who are mutually dependent on each other to achieve a common goal. Trainers frequently are involved in teaching teamwork skills and facilitating team-building events. The dozen contributions in this chapter are a testimonial to the importance and the necessity of team-building activities. The fact is that you could probably use many of the activities in this book to reinforce teamwork, so don't limit your search to this chapter.

Skills on a Stick

Objectives
- To identify individual skills and talents team members bring to the team.
- To identify skills that may be missing from the team.

Audience
Any group; especially useful for building an intact team.

Time
10 to 15 minutes.

Materials and Equipment
- One Whiteboard on a Stick for each participant.
- A marker for each participant.
- "Everybody Dance" CD.

Area Setup
Space to move around.

Process
1. Provide each participant with a Whiteboard on a Stick and a marker and ask them to write their names at the top of the whiteboards.
2. Have everyone stand and walk around the room while you play music. Tell them that, once the music stops, they will all stop and find partners. They will exchange whiteboards and write one skill or talent the other person brings to the team on his/her whiteboard. Allow only 1 minute before you start the music again. Participants return the whiteboards to their owners and begin to walk around again.
3. Start and stop the music eight to twelve times, depending on the group.
4. Ask participants to return to their places and have a few volunteers read the lists of skills and talents on their boards.
5. Debrief the activity with the following questions. (You may wish to capture responses on a flip chart.)
   - Are you familiar with everyone's skills or not?
   - Were you surprised by what others thought your skills were?
   - Look around at everyone's boards. What skills does this team have in abundance?
   - What skills does the team need to build or add?
   - How could your team gain the needed skills?
   - What do you think your team needs to do next?

# nsider's Tips

- This activity is good energizer during slump times, such as right after lunch.
- It can be lots of fun and get a bit raucous, so be sure to use it during the last half of your team building when everyone is comfortable with one another.

Source
No one in particular, but I have been influenced by Bob Pike.

Submitted by Elaine Biech

Elaine Biech is president and managing principal of ebb associates inc, a firm that helps organizations work through large-scale change. She has been in the training and consulting field for twenty-five years and is the author and editor of dozens of books and articles, including *The Pfeiffer Book of Successful Team-Building Tools* (2nd ed.), *Training for Dummies, The Business of Consulting* (2nd ed.)., and *90 World-Class Activities by 90 World-Class Trainers*. A long-time volunteer for ASTD, Elaine has served on ASTD's National Board of Directors and was the recipient of the 1992 ASTD Torch Award, the 2004 ASTD Volunteer Staff Partnership Award, and the 2006 ASTD Gordon M. Bliss Memorial Award. She currently authors ASTD's Ask a Consulting Expert Column and is the editor of the prestigious Pfeiffer Training and Consulting *Annuals*.

Spinning Discovery

Objectives

- To discover something personal about team members to build a deeper team relationship.
- To reveal something about yourself.

Audience

An intact team with growth potential.

Time

30 to 75 minutes.

Materials and Equipment

- Turn 'n Learn Game Wheel.
- Dry Erase marker.
- Colored paper corresponding to the wheel.

Area Setup

Any comfortable seating, preferably in a circle.

Preparation

- Identify about fifty interesting questions and write each on a piece of colored paper, corresponding to the colors on the wheel. You may classify topics according to color. For example, all "red" questions could pertain to career and job, all blue to family and friends, green to childhood memories, and so forth. Questions might include the following:
- What was the last dumb thing you did?
- What was the smartest thing you've ever done?
- What did you excel at when you were in high school?
- What do you want to be when you grow up?
- What is your fantasy career?
- What is funny story your family might tell about you?
- What's your favorite family car?
- If you could spend an entire day doing one thing, what would it be?
- What is the best or worst family vacation you were on as a child or as an adult?
- If you could trade places with someone anywhere in the world for one year, who would it be and why?

- If you had to spend $5,000 on yourself today, how would you spend it?
- What advice would you give to your sixteen-year-old self?
- What advice would your sixteen-year-old self give to you?
- Who was the best teacher/professor you ever had and why?
- What was the worst job you had before you turned twenty?
- If you could stop one of your daily habits, what would it be?
- If cell phones and BlackBerries could no longer be used because they caused cancer, how would it change your daily life?
- What sport or hobby do you really want to try, but will most likely never have the chance?
- Are your dreams while you are asleep in color or black and white? How do you know?
- What is the longest time you have ever held your breath and why?
- If you could be mayor of a town or city, which one would it be and why?
- What do you see people do in public that really annoys you?
- Where in the United States have you not visited, but would really like to?
- What world-famous person alive today would you choose to go to dinner with and why?
- If in the middle of the night you had to rush out of your house due to a fire, what one thing would you take with you and why?
- What is your idea of a perfect day off and why?
- Which of your senses do you value most?
- What kind of emergency scares you the most?
- What do you like to do that seems out of the ordinary?
- What have you done this past year that makes you feel proud?
- What is one thing you would like to do this year?
- Which fairy tale, movie, or other fictional character do you relate to the most? Why?
- What would you like to achieve with your life?
- When do you feel most confident?
- Who is the most significant person in your life and why?
- What was your most memorable day?
- What is the name of your favorite book?
- If you could travel anywhere in the world, where would it be and why?
- Are you the youngest, middle, or oldest child in your family, and what were the advantages?
- What hobbies do you have?

Process

1. Have the team sit in a circle.
2. Select someone from the group to spin the wheel. Select a question written on the paper color that matches where the spinner stopped. Direct the question to one of the team members.
3. The person who answered the question gets to spin and ask the next question of the next person in the circle.
4. Continue until you've made at least one complete round.

nsider's Tip

- A variation is to write in prizes, or "lose your turn," or "take another turn" in the color spinner portion.

Submitted by Elaine Biech

Elaine Biech is president and managing principal of ebb associates inc, a firm that helps organizations work through large-scale change. She has been in the training and consulting field for twenty-five years and is the author and editor of dozens of books and articles, including *The Pfeiffer Book of Successful Team-Building Tools* (2nd ed.), *Training for Dummies, Business of Consulting* (2nd ed.), and *90 World-Class Activities by 90 World-Class Trainers*. A long-time volunteer for ASTD, Elaine has served on ASTD's National Board of Directors and was the recipient of the 1992 ASTD Torch Award, the 2004 ASTD Volunteer Staff Partnership Award, and the 2006 ASTD Gordon M. Bliss Memorial Award. She currently authors ASTD's Ask a Consulting Expert Column and is the editor of the prestigious Pfeiffer Training and Consulting *Annuals*.

Getting to Know You

Objectives

- To introduce members of a new team to each other.
- To break down barriers between two groups, as in a merger or an acquisition.
- To help each member of a new team share an important aspect of his or her life.

Audience

Any group; especially useful for building a team.

Time

25 to 45 minutes, depending on the size of the group.

Materials and Equipment

- Personal photos or other mementos brought from home.
- "Tunes for Trainers."
- CD player.
- Meeting Chime (optional).

Area Setup

Space to move around.

Process

1. Each person is told in the pre-meeting instructions to bring three photos or mementos that will help other people get to know who they are and what's really important to them. Family photos, pictures of children or grandchildren, awards, newspaper clippings, or recipes are just some example of what you might bring.
2. Have everyone stand and walk around the room while you play music. Tell them that, once the music stops, they will all stop and form partnerships with the closest person. They will then show what they have brought and explain why what they have brought is important to them. Start and stop the music as many times as necessary for each individual to have an opportunity to interact with every other person.
3. Ask participants to return to their places and ask for a few reactions to the process.
4. Debrief the activity with the following questions:
    *   What did you learn about the other people, especially those whom you did not know before?
    *   What preconceptions were not met?
    *   How will you build on this experience?
    *   What else do we need to do to further build the team?

Insider's Tips

*   This activity has been especially useful in bringing together groups that will have to merge.
*   The trainer needs to make certain that everyone has a chance to interact with everyone else.
*   It is a fun experience and people want it to go on and on.
*   It is possible to do this activity outdoors, but you have to make sure that people are dressed to feel comfortable sitting on the grass. If you decide to go outside, use the meeting chime to signal switching partners.

Submitted by Leonard D. Goodstein, Ph.D.

Leonard D. Goodstein, Ph.D., is a consulting psychologist based in Washington, D.C., as well as a principal with Psichometrics International, LLC, an Atlanta-based test development and distribution company. He formerly was CEO and executive vice president of the American Psychological Association and CEO of University Associates (now Pfeiffer). He also has held a variety of academic positions, including professorships at the Universities of Iowa, Cincinnati, and Arizona State, where he also served as department chair. He is a frequent contributor to the professional literature and is one of the co-authors of *Applied Strategic Planning: How to Develop Plans That Really Work*. His most recent book, co-authored with Erich P. Prien, *Individual Assessment in the Workplace: A Practical Guide for HR Professionals, Trainers, and Managers* has just been published by Pfeiffer.

Marble Run

Objectives

- To enhance problem solving.
- To improve communication on a team.
- To establish or reestablish trust in a group.
- To create awareness of required team skills.

Audience

Four to six participants per team. There is no limit on how many teams may participate.

Material and Equipment

- One Marble Run Construction Set for each team.
- Paper, clipboard, and pencil for the observer.
- Tape measure for the observer.
- Flip chart and marker.

Time

30 to 60 minutes.

Area Setup

Plenty of table space for teams to work. Floor space is okay if teams don't mind working on the floor.

Process

1. Have teams create the best Marble Run they can in 30 minutes. Tell them that their structure will be judged on four criteria: functionality, aesthetics, height, and complexity. Post these on a flip chart. Suggest that each team assign a "warden" for each of these metrics.
2. Ask for an observer to help with the judging. Give the clipboard and tape measure to the observer and tell him or her to judge the structures based on the four criteria.
3. You may wish to debrief after 5 to 10 minutes or wait until the end of the entire exercise. If you do an interim debriefing, ask such questions as:
    - How is it going so far?
    - What is hindering your process?
    - What might you do differently when you resume construction?
    If you do wait until the end, you might want to ask the observer to also take notes on some of the debriefing questions, so that he or she can be prepared for the conversation following the activity.
4. At the end of the 30 minutes, stop the teams and begin the debriefing using these questions:
    - What happened?
    - What were the results?

- What surprised you?
- What did you learn about yourself? The team?
- Do you see a consistent pattern of behavior?
- Because of this experience what might you do differently back at work? What might you continue doing? What might you stop doing? Start doing?
- What/whose help or support do you need to implement these changes?

Variations
- Assemble a Marble Run with at least three changes of direction.
- Assemble a Marble Run that reaches at least 2 feet high. Invite teams to assign members the following roles: architect, master builder, assistant, observer.
- Re-create one of the Marble Runs shown on the instruction sheet that is in the game box. Make no explicit mention of individuals' roles—simply let them emerge on their own.

Submitted by Susan Doctoroff Landay
Susan Doctoroff Landay is currently the president of Trainer's Warehouse. She joined her father in 1997, in what was then a fledgling business. Prior to that, Sue spent two and half years consulting and training in the field of negotiation and another two years marketing a business history consulting company. She graduated from Yale College (BA in 1986), the Kellogg Graduate School of Management at Northwestern University (MBA in 1992), and Ringling Bros. and Barnum & Bailey Clown College (MFA in 1987). Susan values using humor to enhance presentations.

Certifying Your Self-Image

Objectives

- To obtain feedback from teammates in order to develop a more realistic self-image.
- To enhance team communication, team building, and overall team effectiveness.

Audience

Any existing team that has continuity over time and for which long-term team effectiveness is critical.

Time

Open-ended, depending on the size of the team.

Materials and Equipment

- A supply of Certificate Paper.
- A supply of pencils, pens, or markers.

Area Setup

A private room with a conference table and chairs to accommodate all team members and a facilitator or trainer.

Process

1. Ask for a volunteer to complete a certificate with bullet points that capture his or her self-perceived strengths and developmental needs that relate to the team's effectiveness.
2. At the same time, have all the other members of the team fill in their perceptions of that individual's strengths and developmental needs on certificates.
3. Ask the person who is being focused on to read his or her certificate to the rest of the team. Have each team member read his or her certificate pertaining to that individual. Ask for all of the certificates to be passed to that individual to keep. Have the individual verbally summarize what he or she has learned from the team's feedback.
4. Moving around the table, continue the process for each member of the team as indicated above.

 nsider's Tips

- Encourage each team member to provide written feedback pertaining to both strengths and developmental needs.
- Discuss the importance of providing and receiving feedback in order to enhance learning and the development of a realistic self-image.
- Discuss the concept of a realistic self-image as one that is consistent with the way we are viewed by others who know us and work with us.
- Discuss reasons why our self-images may be inconsistent with others' views or unrealistic and what we can do to build more realistic self-images.

Submitted by Ira J. Morrow, Ph.D.

Ira J. Morrow has a Ph.D. degree in industrial-organizational psychology from New York University. He is currently associate professor of management at Pace University's Lubin School of Business in New York City, where he teaches M.B.A. students from around the world. He also consults in the field of human resources with an emphasis on management assessment.

Acknowledging Our Team Resources

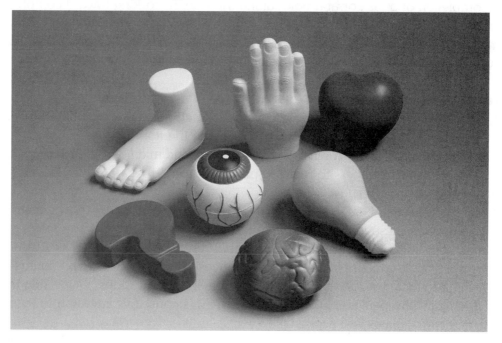

Objectives
- To facilitate team self-assessment.
- To support the identification and affirmation of resources that individual team members bring to the collective efforts.

Audience
Any work team that has spent time together working on tasks.

Time
15 to 30 minutes.

Materials
- Stress-Free Debrief Essentials.

Area Setup
Comfortable, quiet space for team discussion.

Note

This activity structures opportunities for teams to reflect on their efforts, either at the completion of a task or at a point along the way in working toward completion of their task. The Stress-Free Debrief Essentials provide concrete symbols to use in thinking and talking about their efforts. These symbols can be used in at least two ways: as a team self-assessment or for individual affirmation.

Process for Team Self-Assessment

1. Ask the team to find a spot in the workshop setting where members can sit in a circle, either around a table, in chairs, or on the floor.
2. Place a set of Stress-Free Debrief Essentials in the middle of the team circle.
3. Ask the team members to recall a specific task that they have successfully completed together.
4. Invite team members, one at a time, to pick up a symbol that most effectively represents a resource that the team has drawn on in its work. The team member holding the symbol describes that resource and how it was effectively employed. For example, picking up the question mark, the person might speak to the team members' ability to pose critical questions. Or picking up the heart, the person could describe the team's conscious attention to team member needs as well as the task.
5. State that if other team members want to add a comment related to the symbol currently being focused on, they can ask for the symbol and add their comments.
6. Allow the team self-assessment to evolve as members select varying symbols that represent critical skills, knowledge, and attitudes that the team collectively possesses and has applied in solving the task.

Process for Individual Team Member Affirmation

1. Ask the team to find a spot in the workshop setting where members can sit in a circle, either around a table, in chairs, or on the floor.
2. Place a set of Stress-Free Debrief Essentials in the middle of the team circle.
3. Ask for a volunteer, who becomes the focus person for some affirmative feedback. Team members select a Debrief Essential that represents a skill, area of knowledge, or attitude that this particular team member contributed to the team's collective effort and describe how this skill/knowledge/attribute helped the team.

4. If other team members want to add an affirmative comment related to the symbol currently being focused on, they may ask for the symbol and add their comments.

5. The activity continues until all team members have had an opportunity to receive affirmative feedback.

Insider's Tips

- If the group has had no experience in conducting team self-assessment or providing individual team member affirmations, you will want to model this process.
- Using additional debriefing and Q&A sets will provide additional symbols to draw on for this activity.

Submitted by Terry Murray

Terry Murray is an assistant professor in the Humanistic/Multicultural Education Program at SUNY New Paltz. This graduate program is based in approaches that are experiential, reflective, democratic, and inclusive. Terry has developed a number of experiential activities for use in his courses. In addition, he has worked for many years as a trainer and consultant with educational institutions and not-for-profit organizations.

The Red and Black Game

Objectives

- To enable a group to see how quickly people move to compete with one another versus cooperate with one another.
- To demonstrate the effects on performance and morale when people choose to compete versus cooperate.
- To identify the benefits of cooperating over competing.

Audience

Any group; especially useful for intact teams within a single organization, arranged in four equal teams.

Time

75 to 90 minutes.

Materials and Equipment
- One Whiteboard on a Stick for each table group.
- One marker for each table group.
- A copy of the Red and Black Game Rules handout for each participant.
- A copy of the Red and Black Game Scoring handout for each participant.
- A flip-chart easel with a flip-chart page prepared with a scoring grid (see sample Red and Black Game Flip-Chart Scoring Grid).
- PowerPoint slides and LCD projector used for highlighting the rules and scoring process (optional).

Area Setup
This game works best for four teams, with each team working at an individual table and the tables separated from one another such that the groups can discuss their strategies without being overheard by the other groups.

Process
1. Distribute the Red and Black Game Rules and walk the large group through the rules.
2. Explain to the group that there will be ten rounds and that each team will vote Red or Black for every round. Note that Rounds 5, 8, and 10 are weighted rounds and that these rounds are also negotiated rounds. Explain that, for these negotiation rounds, each group will be asked to designate a negotiator who will represent that team in negotiations with the other teams on a Red and Black strategy. Inform the group that these negotiation rounds will be more fully explained when they reach Round 5.
3. Distribute the Red and Black Game Scoring handout (this could be the back page of the Rules handout) and explain how the scoring works. Note that you will be keeping a running tally of each team's score on the prepared flip chart.
4. Distribute one Whiteboard on a Stick and whiteboard marker to each team. Indicate that, once the team decides to vote Red or Black, they should write their vote (Red or Black) on the Whiteboard on a Stick. Indicate to the teams that once they write down their Red or Black votes, they should turn their Whiteboards on a Stick face down until you ask them to display their votes.
5. Begin the game. Ask the groups to quietly discuss their votes and to then decide to vote Red or Black. Tell the groups that they will have about 2 to 4 minutes to cast their votes. Remind the group not to display their votes until directed to do so.

6. Once all groups indicate that they are ready to display their votes, ask all teams to hold up their Whiteboard on a Sticks to display their votes. Based on the votes and following the scoring guidelines, record the individual scores for each team on the flip-chart scoring grid. After the scoring is recorded, move the group into the second round—again reminding the teams to discuss their votes quietly, to write their votes on their whiteboards, and to keep their votes private until you ask them to display their votes.

7. Lead the teams through the first four rounds, recording a running tally for each team after each round.

8. At Round 5, indicate to the group that this is a weighted round and that it is also a negotiated round. Ask each group to designate someone from their team to negotiate with a representative of the other teams. Once each group has selected a negotiator, ask the groups to give directions to their representatives. Once all teams have charged their negotiators, direct the representatives to meet in another room to decide on a voting strategy. Give the negotiators about 7 to 8 minutes to come to some understanding.

9. Call time on the negotiators and bring them back to their teams. Direct each team to confer with the negotiator and to vote Red or Black as usual. When all groups indicate that they are ready to display their votes, ask the teams to hold up their whiteboard votes. Add the now weighted results from this round to the running tally for each team.

10. Continue through the remaining rounds, guiding the teams into the negotiation rounds with the same instructions as for Round 5. Keep recording the running tally for each team on the flip-chart scoring grid.

11. At the negotiation Rounds 8 and 10, each team can choose to use the same negotiator or to designate a new negotiator.

12. The Red and Black Game ends at the conclusion of Round 10—when the scores for this negotiated round are amplified by a factor of ten and a final tally is made for each team and recorded on the flip-chart scoring grid.

13. Announce and celebrate the winner with the highest score. By this time, however, there are likely to be considerable comments, said in jest, about "back-stabbing" and humorous comments about the *real* level of teamwork in the organization.

14. Debrief the activity with the following comments and questions:
    - How many of you were proud of your strategy? Was it a winning strategy? Why did you use this strategy?
    - Note that the rules never state "get as many points for your team as possible"; the rules simply say "get as many points as possible." Might this rule suggest getting as many points as possible for all teams combined?

- The only way to "win" this game is for all teams to consistently vote Black.
- Point out that if all teams voted Black every round, the individual score for each team would be 27 points, with a grand total for all teams of 108. Ask the groups to compare this with their own team's actual results and the actual grand total for all teams.
- Some of you as individuals or your entire team figured out early how the game should be played—but you nonetheless plunged into the "dark side" by engaging in competition over cooperation. Why?
- Why do we tend to assume a competitive rather than cooperative strategy when presented with this simple game?
- What are the key lessons of the Red and Black Game?
- If the playing of this game follows content on team building and the characteristics of effective teams, ask the group: Given our very recent discussion (and despite our recent discussion) of the importance of cooperation and collaboration to effective teams, what are the implications of the Red and Black Game to teamwork in this company?

Insider's Tips

- This activity is a great post-lunch energizer and is best done *following* any training content related to the characteristics of effective teams.
- Initially people may express some confusion as to what the voting process is all about (Why vote for Red or Black? What's the point of this game?). Acknowledge some of this ambiguity and give some clarification to the rules if required—but ask the group to trust you, to just start playing the game to see whether the point of the game becomes clearer.
- During the negotiation rounds, the representatives may ask you for direction on what they are supposed to do. Be vague and simply ask them to see whether they can agree on a voting strategy going forward.
- As the game progresses, you will see an increasing amount of both humor and animosity as the teams experience the results of the game, and especially when teams betray other teams following the negotiation rounds. There is almost always betrayal when the negotiators agree to all vote Black, but one or more of the teams decides instead to vote Red.
- Sometimes, toward the end of the game and usually following the negotiation Rounds 8 and 10, there may be some real expressions of anger and bitterness

by some players. The facilitator should be watchful of this and be prepared to address this directly—by using light humor and by guiding a debriefing that surfaces these feelings toward a productive discussion. If these emotions surface, it is important to use this as a teachable moment: If these emotions surface on a simple game such as the Red and Black Game, think of the emotions that we are likely to experience when the "game" is real life!

- The Red and Black Game Scoring handout can be modified for five, six, seven, or more teams. Contact the authors if you would like assistance and direction for doing so.
- The Red and Black Game is one version of the Prisoner's Dilemma. In game theory, the Prisoner's Dilemma is an approach to competition where the only way to win is to trust your opponent.

Submitted by Linda Russell and Jeffrey Russell

Linda and Jeffrey Russell are co-directors of Russell Consulting, Inc., a firm that helps its clients achieve their goals through leadership, strategy, and change. Linda and Jeff have been helping leaders build great and enduring organizations since 1987. They work internationally and are authors of numerous books and articles, most recently *Change Basics* (ASTD Press) and *Ten Steps to Effective Problem Solving and Decision Making* (ASTD Press). They publish *Workplace Enhancement Notes* and an e-newsletter, *Great Organization's Journal*. Their work in the area of change resilience has led to the development of the Resilience Quotient, which is used internationally.

Red and Black Game Rules

1. The object of the game is to get as many points as possible.
2. Each team casts _one_ vote per round. There are ten rounds. Each vote cast will be either for **RED** or for **BLACK**.
3. Each team quietly discusses each round's vote and must achieve consensus on voting either **RED** or **BLACK**—writing the choice on a Whiteboard on a Stick.
4. Each team presents the team's vote by holding up the Whiteboard on a Stick when directed to do so by the facilitator.
5. Each team's score resulting from each voting round is recorded by the facilitator as a running total for that team on the flip-chart tally sheet.
6. Rounds 5, 8, and 10 are **weighted** rounds. Each team's score for these rounds will be multiplied by the round's weighted factor:
   Round 5 = **2 times** Round 8 = **5 times** Round 10 = **10 times**
7. Rounds 5, 8, and 10 are also **negotiation** rounds. Each team (a) selects a negotiator, (b) gives negotiator negotiation advice, and (c) agrees or disagrees with the negotiated vote.

Red and Black Game Scoring

Team Vote Results	Team Point Assignments
4 black votes (all teams vote black)	Each team gains 1 point
3 black votes 1 red vote	These teams each lose 1 point This team gains 3 points
2 black votes 2 red votes	These teams each lose 2 points These teams each gain 2 points
1 black vote 3 red votes	This team loses 3 points These teams each gain 1 point
4 red votes (all teams vote red)	Each team loses 1 point

Red and Black Game
Flip-Chart Scoring Grid

This scoring grid should be created on a flip-chart sheet and posted where all teams can see the scoring results. The facilitator records a running tally for each team on this grid.

Round	Team 1	Team 2	Team 3	Team 4
Round 1				
Round 2				
Round 3				
Round 4				
Round 5 ($\times$ 2)				
Round 6				
Round 7				
Round 8 ($\times$ 5)				
Round 9				
Round 10 ($\times$ 10)				

Koosh®-Koosh®

Objectives
- To explore intra-team collaboration, coordination, and communication.
- To begin a dialogue about self-directed teams and team building.

Audience
Two or more teams of four or more players each.

Time
40 minutes.

Materials and Equipment

- Two Koosh® balls per team.
- One crumpled sheet of regular-sized (8.5 × 11) paper for each team.
- One roll of masking or painters tape.
- One timer or stopwatch.
- One noisemaker (whistle or chimes).
- Flip chart and marker.

Area Setup

- Create a three-foot equilateral triangle on the floor for each team.
  - First, establish the base with one 3-foot strip of tape. (Use tape that is easily removed, like painter's tape.)
  - At each corner of the base, place a 3-foot strip of tape.
  - Move the two strips so that they touch, creating a 3-foot triangle.

Process

1. Divide the group into teams of three or four players. For teams of four, ask one person to be an observer/recorder.
2. Have each of the three players stand at one corner of the triangle. Have the observer stand outside the triangle.
3. Hand out the three throwing objects. In each team, two players each receive a Koosh ball; the third player receives the crumpled paper ball.
4. State, "The object of this game is for your team to make as many transfers as it can within the 30-second time limit.
   - A transfer is the simultaneous tossing and catching of the three objects. All three objects must be in the air at the same time.
   - When all three objects are caught, it is scored as 1 point.
   - If any object is not caught (hits the ground), restart the tally from 0.
   - The team with the most points at the end of three rounds wins."
5. Begin the first round with the sound of the chimes. Time the round and call time at the end of 30 seconds. Have each team or observer report how many points the team scored.
6. Post the scores on the flip chart. Have the teams return to their seats.
7. Ask, "What happened?" Accept a couple of responses and then ask, "What do you need to do now?" Have each team meet for 3 minutes to discuss assignments and strategy.

8. Have teams meet at their triangles. Inform teams that this round will consist of 45 seconds and the play is the same as in Round 1.

9. When time is up, ask team or observers for the scores and post the scores from Round 2. Allow for a 3-minute team debriefing.

10. Tell teams that the next round will consist of 1 minute and that the play is the same as for earlier rounds. When time is up, post the scores from Round 3. Tally all of the scores; the team with the most points wins.

11. Summarize with these questions in a large group:
    - What did you experience? How does it relate to the content we have been discussing?
    - What did you learn about teamwork?
    - What does this tell you about self-directed teams?
    - How does this activity apply to situations you encounter at work?
    - What will you do differently because of this experience?

12. After participants discuss and respond to the debriefing questions, offer your observations, highlighting situations you observed during the game.

Insider's Tips

- You may find it easier to prepare the floor triangle by first preparing one "triangle guide" on two or more flip-chart sheets, and then using the guide to transfer each of the floor triangles onto the floor. The guide can then be stored and used for future groups.

- Requiring the three balls to be airborne simultaneously creates a need for planning (and practice) and strategy. Players quickly discover that what looks like a simple transfer requires total individual focus and team coordination to execute just one transfer (for 1 point).

- Using a differing weight mix of two Koosh balls and a crumpled piece of paper requires more technique than the transfer of three equally weighted objects, subsequently requiring more attention to planning and skill building.

- The time of each successive round is expanded to allow teams to become familiar with the requirement (toss-and-catch) and then build on their skills. In the past, teams who have been scoreless in Round 1 usually make a few successful transfers in Round 2 and then even more successful transfers in Round 3.

- Use full sheets (8.5 × 11) of regular 20-pound paper. A full sheet of paper has enough weight to be tossed and caught. Also, try to use a different color paper for each team. (This can also serve as the team identifier—"blue team," etc.)
- Use easy-to-remove tape, such as painter's tape. Hard-to-remove tape seems to annoy clean-up crews.

Submitted by Linda M. Raudenbush, Ed.D., and Steve Sugar

Linda M. Raudenbush holds a BA in mathematics and secondary education from St. Joseph College, an MS in applied behavioral science from Johns Hopkins University, and an Ed.D. in human resource development from George Washington University. Linda has more than twenty-five years of experience in training, organization development, and leadership coaching in both private and public sectors. Linda holds an ACC in leadership coaching granted by International Coaching Federation. She has been adjunct professor at National-Louis University and Strayer University and is in her eighteenth year of part-time teaching at the University of Maryland, Baltimore. She is currently employed as an internal HRD/OD consultant and leadership coach at the U.S. Department of Agriculture in the National Agricultural Statistics Service. Linda is an active volunteer in her community, having been nominated for as the Maryland Volunteer of the Year for 2003 and 2004, and was awarded Volunteer of the Year in 2005 for Faith-Based Initiatives.

Steve Sugar writes "fun with a purpose" activities that have helped thousands of learners to experience classroom topics in a more meaningful way. Steve holds a B.A. in economics from Bucknell University and an M.B.A. in economics, statistics, and management from George Washington University. Steve served two tours as a Deck Watch Officer in Vietnam for the U.S. Coast Guard. Steve currently teaches business and education courses for the University of Maryland Baltimore County (UMBC). Steve is the author or co-author of *Training Games* and the Info-line, *More Great Games, Games That Teach, Games That Teach Teams, Games That Boost Performance,* and *Primary Games.* Steve has developed three game systems featured by Langevin Learning Services—the Management 2000/Learn It board game, the QUIZO game system, and the X-O Cise dice game.

By the Numbers

Objectives
- To introduce participants to the values of working together as a team.
- To demonstrate the power of team collaboration.
- To illustrate how team efforts increase efficiency and effectiveness.

Audience
Any group or organization, especially those interested in establishing a team concept.

Time
The activity can be completed within 15 minutes, but ample time should be left to process the results.

Materials and Equipment
- Two copies of the By the Numbers handout for each participant.
- Three copies of the By the Numbers handout for each triad.
- A pen or pencil for each participant.
- Stopwatch.
- Call Bell or one of the other noisemakers.
- A flip chart and markers.
- Wastebasket.

Area Setup
Set the room up in a U-shaped format with a large wastebasket in the center of the U.

Process
1. Introduce the exercise to the participants, noting the advantages of working in teams. Give everyone a copy of the By the Numbers handout, face down, and a pen or pencil, explaining that this is a 30-second timed exercise. Indicate that there are sixty numbers on the handout. The task is to circle the numbers

sequentially, that is, 1, 2, 3, 4, and so on, until they have circled all sixty numbers. The person or group circling the most numbers will be declared the winner. Tell them the goal is to circle fifty-seven numbers in 30 seconds.

2. Have each participant try it individually. Tell the participants they will have 30 seconds to circle (in sequence) as many numbers as they can. When completed, record the scores (total numbers circled by each individual in 30 seconds) on the flip chart. Have participants throw the wadded-up sheets into the wastebasket located in the center of the U.

3. Distribute a second copy of the By the Numbers handout to each participant and give participants a chance to improve their scores. Once again record the scores (numbers circled in 30 seconds) on the flip chart and have participants toss the number sheet in the wastebasket.

4. Break the groups into triads. Point out that now participants are no longer working individually but as teams; however, explain that they need to try to achieve the goal without any verbal exchange. Distribute a copy of the By the Numbers handout to each triad. The team members are not allowed to talk to each other. Record the scores as triads (numbers circled in 30 seconds) on the flip chart. Have them discard the number sheet by tossing it into the wastebasket.

5. Distribute a handout to each triad. Tell participants they will have an opportunity to strategize for 2 minutes prior to starting the activity. Encourage them to become more of a team; allow them to verbally communicate, collaborate, and brainstorm ideas. They can physically form into a circle, if they prefer. Complete the exercise again and record the scores. Do not ask participants to discard the sheets until they have had the opportunity to look at the handout closely. After 2 minutes, have them discard the sheets in the wastebasket.

6. Complete the exercise a fifth and final time and record the scores.

7. Ask what the teams believe is the most important learning they have gained. Ask how they will implement this knowledge.

Insider's Tips

- The odd numbers are on the left-hand side of the handout; the even numbers are on the right.
- The first six numbers (1 through 6) are on the top half of the page, the next six (7 through 12) are on the lower half, the next six (13 through 18) are back on the top and it alternates for the rest of the numbers.

- The first three times, or more, some teams will still have everyone circling numbers individually. Ask them why? Explain that culturally we are individualistic and not team oriented.
- In addition, it is human nature to just attack the problem and try to beat everyone else. Explain that they need take the time to look at the problem, analyze it, share the information, and then collectively address the problem.
- Without taking the time to analyze the numbers (the odd and even sequence and the six-up and six-down sequence), the sequences will never be discovered.
- Throwing the used handouts in the wastebasket is a diversion to make the exercise more fun; however, it does point out our competitiveness as everyone tries to make the target. Once in a great while a team will let its best shooter go for the wastebasket. That is a sign of teaming.
- For fun, use a variety of Trainer's Warehouse noisemakers to indicate the end of a time period.

Submitted by Rodney C. Vandeveer and Alexander W. Crispo

Rodney C. Vandeveer received his master's of science degree in management from Indiana Wesleyan University and holds a bachelor of science degree in organizational leadership from Purdue University. He currently is an associate professor in the college of technology at Purdue University, West Lafayette, Indiana. Rodney brings thirty years of industrial experience to his teaching and training. He joined Purdue in 1994 in the department of organizational leadership and supervision. He teaches human behavior in organizations, leadership strategies for quality and productivity, entrepreneurship, and emerging world-class leadership strategies at the graduate level. He has over fifty publications and is the author of two texts published by Pearson Prentice Hall Publishing.

Alexander W. Crispo is an associate professor in the organizational leadership department in the College of Technology at Purdue University. He teaches graduate and undergraduate courses in leadership and change management. He is past president of the International Society for the Exploration of Teaching and Learning and a member of the Organizational Behavior Teaching Society. He has published and presented over fifty papers and workshops and has been recognized by his students and faculty for his teaching. He has extensive experience in the manufacturing sector, where he enjoyed a successful and rewarding career before joining academia. He earned his bachelor of science degree in industrial distribution and his master's of science in industrial management from Clarkson University.

By the Numbers

Egg Drop Group

Objectives
- To build a team.
- To encourage creative thinking and idea sharing.
- To practice project management skills (planning, division of task, execution).

Audience
Any group divided into subgroups of five to seven.

Time
60 to 70 minutes.

Materials and Equipment
- "Gotta Dance" CD.
- CD player.
- Prizes from the Classroom Prize Pack.

- Each subgroup will need the following:
  - One raw egg.
  - One GeoTwister™.
  - Approximately two dozen straws.
  - One Learn/Live Star.
  - Yarn.
  - Two feet of masking tape.
  - A landing platform (trash bag).
- Props for the presentations such as Painter's Hats, color-coded noise makers, flip-chart paper, and markers.

Area Setup
Tabletop or floor. Room for each group to design and prepare.

Process
1. Divide the group into teams of five to seven.
2. Set the stage by explaining the challenge. Say that their team has been selected to conduct research to develop an egg-carrying contraption that will cushion the fall for a raw egg to be dropped from the height of 8 feet. They will be provided with the only resources available to build such a device. Their team must also name its contraption and develop a presentation to introduce this scientific innovation to the large group (sales presentation, rap song, press conference, cheer, song, skit, etc.).
3. The only rules are as follows:
   - Only the straws can touch the egg.
   - You can only use the materials provided.
   - Everyone must participate in the presentation.
4. Distribute the materials to each team and tell them to begin. State that they have 30 minutes to complete the task.
5. When time is up, have each team present and test its contraption.
6. Debrief the activity with the following questions.
   - Was everyone involved? How?
   - Were ideas shared freely?
   - Was there a plan? Did it work?
   - What are some key concepts about teamwork brought out here?
   - Does your team function like this at work?
   - What will you do differently as a result of this activity?

Insider's Tips

- Play energizing music while the teams work.
- Make sure the sub-teams start working on the presentations early.
- Give awards such as most functional, best design, most creative presentation, funniest, etc.
- Provide an assortment of props for teams to really "ham up" their presentations.

Submitted by Bruce G. Waguespack, Ph.D., CPLP

Bruce G. Waguespack is an assistant professor at the Jack and Patti Phillips Workplace Learning and Performance Institute at The University of Southern Mississippi, where he teaches graduate courses and is a facilitator in the training and development certificate program. His innovative teaching style is grounded by practical, real-life experience. He was the corporate manager for training and development at Georgia Gulf Corporation for seven years. His consulting company, "Potential Unlimited," designs and aligns performance improvement strategies that achieve key organizational objectives. Bruce served two terms as president of the Baton Rouge chapter of ASTD and is a CPLP pioneer.

Domino Effect

Objectives
- To build camaraderie on a team.
- To discover unique attributes and build connections among participants.

Audience
A group of up to twenty-eight participants.

Time
45 to 90 minutes.

Materials and Equipment
- One set of twenty-eight Jumbo Foam Dominos.
- A large sign at front of class with Domino Rules (see Step 2).
- A container holding all participants' names on sheets of paper folded up inside.

Area Setup
Open floor space somewhere in the room (front, back or side) to play a giant game of Dominos. Pre-set all Dominos face down in this space.

Process
1. Invite each participant to take one Domino, still face down, from the pile. In groups of fourteen or fewer, each participant takes two; in groups of nine or

fewer, each takes three. Extra Dominos stay where they are. Back at their seats, participants may look at the "dot" side of the Domino(s) selected.

2. Review basic Domino rules, as summarized on the flip chart in the front of the room:
   - Do not show your dominos to others.
   - When it is your turn, match either end of a domino you have to one in play on the floor.
   - A match can only be made against the two open ends of the domino line.

3. Take one of the remaining face down Dominos and turn it up to start the game (if no extras remain, a volunteer can begin the game). Invite a participant to come forward who can match dots with one side of the first Domino (as in basic Domino rules). If an even number was matched (2, 4, or 6), the volunteer picks a name from the container at the front of the room. The volunteer identifies the same number of traits, skills, or attributes as the number of dots that he or she shares in common with the participant whose name was drawn. For example, if Sally matched a Domino with two dots, she states two items she believes she shares in common with the participant she selected. It is fine to check in with the other person selected as a match to ensure the items stated are correct.

4. When participants match odd numbers in dominos (1, 3, 5), explain they have a different job. These players must list a corresponding number of facts about themselves that they believe no one else in the room has in common with them. In other words, people matching odd-numbered dots are sharing unique, unusual traits. If someone else in the room has one of those traits, the player must come up with something else. For example, if Jacob matches three dots, he shares three facts about himself that he is reasonably certain no one else in the room shares, e.g., born in Brazil, certified scuba diver instructor, and favorite food is Brussels sprouts. If someone else says, "I was born in Brazil, too!" Jacob must replace it with a different unique trait, e.g., never received a parking ticket.

5. The Domino game continues with volunteers matching Dominos and sharing either matching traits (for even players) or unique traits (for odd players) until either everyone has a turn or no one can play a Domino. If the game is "stuck," and face down pieces are still available, the facilitator may select another extra face down piece to kick-start the game again.

6. Upon conclusion of the game, explain that the game enabled participants to learn both what they have in common with others and also surprising, unusual facts or traits about others. Ask the following questions:

- What was the most surprising unusual fact you learned about someone else?
- What did you learn you had in common with someone else that you did not expect?
- How can this knowledge help to build your team?

nsider's Tips

- This team-building activity uniquely integrates the three primary learning styles: visual, kinesthetic, and auditory. It also creatively demonstrates that we can be surprised both by the novel experiences and talents of those around us and by the things we share in common with people we may have otherwise assumed were very different from ourselves. The juxtaposition of these two alternating tasks also keeps the discussion from becoming overly repetitive.
- Emphasize that it is fine when participants make "mistakes" by thinking a trait is shared in common when it is not (Our favorite day is Saturday) or that a trait is unique (I speak three languages). These "errors" are helpful in revealing additional information and underlying assumptions (e.g., "Everyone prefers the weekend to weekdays" or "No one else speaks more than two languages in the class").
- Recognize that not all participant names will be picked out of the container, as only approximately half the players will match even-numbered dots. If you like, those remaining names can be drawn later during the training for another purpose (e.g., special roles, team leaders).
- Of course, the Jumbo Dominos set can also be used for a traditional, yet giant, game of Dominos.

Submitted by Devora Zack

Devora Zack is president of OCC, a leadership development firm with more than seventy-five clients, such as Deloitte, America Online, DHS, OPM, Ann Taylor, SAIC, USDA, and the U.S. Treasury. OCC provides seminars, coaching, and consulting in leadership, change, communications, and team building. Devora is visiting faculty for Cornell University and program director for the presidential management fellows orientation. Her articles have been featured in Pfeiffer *Annuals* for three years. She has an MBA from Cornell, a BA from University of Pennsylvania, and certification in neurolinguistic programming and MBTI. She is a member of MENSA and Phi Beta Kappa and has U.S. secret clearance.

More Than Meets the Eye

Objectives
- To identify team members' talents and interests.
- To emphasize that there is more than meets the eye when working with colleagues.

Audience
Any group of eight to one hundred participants. Useful for team building or as an icebreaker.

Time
30 to 40 minutes.

Materials and Equipment
- One Thumball® per table group.
- One easel with paper and Mr. Sketch® markers per table (if not available, substitute regular pens and pads).
- Nametags or tent cards with large first names for all participants.
- Small prizes (i.e., the Classroom Prize Pack, candy, trainer toys, gift certificates, or books).

Area Setup

Arrange the room to accommodate groups of four to ten participants each, around tables or with chairs set in circles. A minimum of two teams is necessary, and aim for teams to have equal numbers of participants.

Process

1. Provide each team with a Thumball®. Toss a ball to each table. Tell whoever catches it to pass the ball two people to the left—that person becomes team captain. Do not reveal activity flow in advance.

2. Have the groups toss the Thumball® in any order within their team. Each participant has one turn catching and throwing. When catching the ball, each participant answers the question that is under his or her thumb. If both thumbs touch the ball, select one of the options. The process takes longer with larger table groups; however, teams should be encouraged to keep it moving and say the first answer that comes to mind.

3. When groups finish sharing responses, announce that the first person at each table who can correctly recall what everyone on the team shared wins a prize. Provide time for tables to determine a winner. Ask the team captain to give a prize to the person who volunteers first at each table and provides all correct answers.

4. Have each team list participants' responses on its easel (or notepad) in no particular order and without names. Each team then trades lists with a nearby table. If there are an odd number of tables, lists can be passed clockwise. Without further interaction, groups guess which response goes with each participant on the other team. If this is a newly formed team, the guessing team can reference nametags or tent cards to identify participants on the other team. Guesses can be based on intuition, individual appearances, or past experience—if any—with those colleagues. Guesses are returned to the original table groups and scored for accuracy. For example, if there are six members on a team and three names were correctly assigned, the guessing team receives a score of 3 out of 6. The team captain determines the percent, and everyone on the team with the highest percentage of accurate guesses earns a prize.

5. Process the activity with questions such as those listed here. Adapt debriefing questions to fit overall training goals, group dynamics, size, and past history of teams (i.e., newly formed or well established).
   - What were some of the most memorable or unusual responses?
   - What responses surprised you and why?

- What assumptions were made in guessing other teams' responses?
- If you engaged again in this activity, what would you do differently?
- How can learning these new facts about colleagues improve overall morale, productivity, and communication?
- What did you learn about yourself with respect to the team from participating in this activity?

Insider's Tips

- This could be used as an opening activity, doubling as an icebreaker and team builder.
- For new teams, this can dispel stereotypes based on appearances (i.e., a man who cooks, a woman who loves handiwork). For established teams, the point can be made that colleagues we know well can still surprise us.
- Warn participants to watch personal belongings, especially drinks, as the ball tends to bounce around. I generally caution that this is not a good time to space out! The up side is that everyone stays focused and engaged in the activity.

Submitted by Devora Zack

Devora Zack is president of OCC, a leadership development firm with more than seventy-five clients, such as Deloitte, America Online, DHS, OPM, Ann Taylor, SAIC, USDA, and the U.S. Treasury. OCC provides seminars, coaching, and consulting in leadership, change, communications, and team building. Devora is visiting faculty for Cornell University and program director for the Presidential Management Fellows Orientation. Her articles have been featured in Pfeiffer *Annuals* for three years. She has an MBA from Cornell, BA from University of Pennsylvania, and certification in neurolinguistic programming and MBTI. She is a member of MENSA and Phi Beta Kappa and has U.S. secret clearance.

Primary and Alternative Uses for Activities

Activities P = Primary Use A = Alternative Use	Page	Openings	Icebreakers	Energizers	Participation Encouragement	Comprehension and Retention	Time and People Management	Training Techniques	Rewards and Recognition	Review of Knowledge and Skills	Closings	Change Management	Communication and Trust	Creativity	Customer Service	Organization Knowledge	Personal Development	Problem Solving	Process and Projects	Supervision, Management, and Leadership	Teamwork and Team Building
Acknowledging Our Team Resources	357		A	A									A				A				P
Alphabet Review	158									P											
Appraising Performance: A Home Building Challenge	324			A																P	A
Birthday Ball	133							P													
Brainstorming 101	218													P				A			
Brainstorming Boost	223			A										P				A			
Break Time—Roll the Dice!	102			A			P	A													
Bright Idea	306									P						A		A	P		A
Bull's Eye Bowl	172			A																	
By the Numbers	372												A					A			P
Call Me Princess Java	64			P																	A
Cat-A- Pult™ Challenge	281												A					P	A		A

Game	Page	1	2	3	4	5	6	7	8	9	10	11	12	13	14	15	16	17
Cell Phone Attack	113														P			
Certifying Your Self-Image	355	P				A			A		A							
Change That Tune	196	A							A	A		A					A	
Chicken, Salad, and Koosh® Ball Shuffle	317			P	A			A		A								
Constructive Feedback Key Pointers	206					A			P				A					
Content Relay	151											A	A					
Continuous Learning Review	93											A			A	P	A	
Crazy, Cool, Creative Closing	180										P			A			A	
Creative Idea Generation	221				A					A								
Customers—Up Close and Personal	232	A			A			P		A								
Dartboard Learning Review	166												A	P				
Developing Core Values	243	A	A				P		A				A					
Domino Effect	379	P							A									
Egg Drop Group	376	P			A				A									
Everybody Dance	68											A						
Express Expressions	273	A				P			A				A					
Fiddle While You Learn	127																	P

Activities P = Primary Use A = Alternative Use	Page	Openings	Icebreakers	Energizers	Participation Encouragement	Comprehension and Retention	Time and People Management	Training Techniques	Rewards and Recognition	Review of Knowledge and Skills	Closings	Change Management	Communication and Trust	Creativity	Customer Service	Organization Knowledge	Personal Development	Problem Solving	Process and Projects	Supervision, Management, and Leadership	Teamwork and Team Building
Fun Caps Versus Boring Table Tents	30	P	A															A		P	A
Getting Things in Focus: Koosh® Ball Mania	332			A	A								A								P
Getting to Know You	349																				A
Getting to Know You Differently	24	P	A																		A
Getting to Know You Feud	228			A										P			A	A			A
Goal Setter Game	155									P											
Go for the Goal: Influencing Performance to Reduce Shortage	296									A								P			
High Five	78				P	A		A	A												
I Appreciate My Job	270		A					A	A				A			A	P			A	A
I'm No Chicken Award	72			A	P				A												

Activity	Page															
If Life Gives You Lemons…	261	A					A	P	A							A
Is the Answer Correct?	175		A					P								
It's Your Choice	187		A				P									
Koosh® Ball Review	146		A	A			P									P
Koosh®—Koosh®	368		A											P		
Leadership Essentials	335		A													
Let's Return	104				P	A										
Magic Coloring Book	118					P	A									
Marble Run	352							A	A			A				P
Money for Trivia	96		A		P	A										
Monster MNEMONIC Maker	91			A	P	A	A			A						
More Than Meets the Eye	382	A														P
Music Makes the Training Go Round	130		A			P										
Name Tent Teams	121				A	P										
Non-Trash Trash Can	62		P	A		A	A	A		A						
Opposite Brains	226									A	P		A			
Organizational Lingo Crossword Puzzle	250						A	A		A		P				
"Peers Cheer Peers" Awards Ceremony	184		A	A		A	P	P	A	A					A	A
Pick It Up!	82		A	P		A	A									A

390

Activities P = Primary Use A = Alternative Use	Page	Openings	Icebreakers	Energizers	Participation Encouragement	Comprehension and Retention	Time and People Management	Training Techniques	Rewards and Recognition	Review of Knowledge and Skills	Closings	Change Management	Communication and Trust	Creativity	Customer Service	Organization Knowledge	Personal Development	Problem Solving	Process and Projects	Supervision, Management, and Leadership	Teamwork and Team Building
Pleasure Island Review	161			A	A					P			A								A
Press Conference	54		P	A																	
Prize Roulette	107			A			P														
Problem Solving Line Up	278				A			A					A					P			A
Project Change Challenge	313											A	A						P		A
Puzzling About Systems Thinking	308												A						P		A
Rapid-Fire Review	80				P	A			A	A											A
Red Light, Green Light	40	A	P																		A
"Role" of the Die	235														P						
See the Light to the Power of Positive Thinking	254	A		A	A			A				A	A	A	A	A	P	A			A
Shake It Icebreaker	38		P	A																	A
Shaping Our Fortune	198											P	A	A						A		
Share, Scratch, and Win	75				P	A		A	A	A											

Game	Page																				
Skills on a Stick	342	P																			A
SNAP	210		A	A			P	A		A			P				A		A	A	A
Spaghetti and Gum Drops	293																		P		A
Spinning Discovery	345			A				A													P
Spinning the Organizational Culture	246				A			A	A	A			P	A		P				A	A
Squeeze Play Course Review	164					P													A		
STAR Principle	288															P			P		
Stick 'em Up Review	148				A			A	P												A
Super Forts for Super Teams	213				A								P				A		A		A
Surprise Info	66				P																A
Team Challenge	136							P													
Tents Tell All—Myriad Uses for Table Tents	43	A	P	A					A												A
The Chicken Rules	110		A			P	A								P						
The Good Apple Award	178						A			P		A									A
The Good, the Bad, and the Ugly New Manager	240		A	A				A			A		A			P					A
The Hats We Wear	46		A										A								A
The Object of My Discusssion	265		A	A							A	A	A				P				A
The Organic Quiz Show	88			P		A		A													
The Power of Non-Verbals	204		A										P			A					
The Real Challenge	190			A		A	P	A								A					A

Activities P = Primary Use A = Alternative Use	Page	Openings	Icebreakers	Energizers	Participation Encouragement	Comprehension and Retention	Time and People Management	Training Techniques	Rewards and Recognition	Review of Knowledge and Skills	Closings	Change Management	Communication and Trust	Creativity	Customer Service	Organization Knowledge	Personal Development	Problem Solving	Process and Projects	Supervision, Management, and Leadership	Teamwork and Team Building
The Red and Black Game	360												A				A	A			P
This Treasure Is Me	58		P										A								A
Ticket Mixer to Assign Groups	124						A	P													
Topic Walk	33	P	A																		
Toys Are Us	48	A	P																		
True Colors	290			A	A			A					A					P			A
Truth or Chicken	267				A																A
Wanna Deal or Not?	142			A	A			A	P								P			A	A
Whaddaya Know?™	169						P			P											
Wheel of Consequences	99			A				A													A
Who's on My Team?	51		P	A	A																A
You're a Superhero	27	P	A	A					P												A
You're a Star!	140								P	A	A										A
Your Supervisor Hat	338									A	A									P	

Trainer's Warehouse Materials*

Answer Boards/Slim-Line Answer Boards
Continuous Learning Review
Customers—Up Close and Personal
Getting to Know You Feud
Puzzling About Systems Thinking
Surprise Info

Boomwhackers
Music Makes the Training Go Round

Call Bells
By the Numbers
Bull's Eye Bowl
The Power of Non-Verbals

*Note: Many Activities also require flip charts, Mr. Sketch markers, Dry Erase markers, specially shaped Post-it Notes, and prizes and awards. These are also available at Trainer's Warehouse.

Cartoons for Trainers
Getting to Know You Feud

Cat-A-Pult™
Cat-A-Pult™ Challenge

Certificate Paper
Certify Your Self-Image
"Peers Cheer Peers" Awards Ceremony

Chicken, Squawking or Rubber
Chicken, Salad, and Koosh® Ball Shuffle
I'm No Chicken Award
The Chicken Rules
Truth or Chicken

Classroom Cop
Red Light, Green Light

Colored Name Pins
True Colors

Dart Game
Dartboard Learning Review

Debrief Essentials Set
Acknowledging Our Team Resources
Brainstorming 101
Leadership Essentials
The Object of My Discussion

Dice/Dry Erase Cube

Alphabet Review
Break Time—Roll the Dice!
Pick It Up!
Pleasure Island Review
"Role" of the Die
The Good, the Bad, and the Ugly New Manager
The Real Challenge

Docu-Pockets

You're a Star!

Dominos, Jumbo Foam

Domino Effect

Easy-Snap™ Easel

Developing Core Values
Getting to Know You Differently
Project Change Challenge

Eggspert Selector & Buzzer
Squeeze Play Course Review

"Everybody Dance" CD
Everybody Dance
Music Makes the Training Go Round

Expression Cards
Express Expressions

Fiddle Assortment
Brainstorming Boost
Brainstorming 101
Fiddle While You Learn
"Peers Cheer Peers" Award Ceremony
The Object of My Discussion
This Treasure Is Me
Toys Are Us

Flashing Timer Ball
Birthday Ball

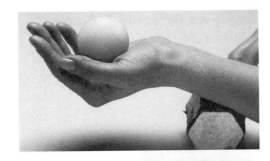

Fortune Cookie Debrief Set
Shaping Our Fortune

Goal Getter Thermometer
Goal Setter Game

Hand Shakers (see Shaker Collection)

Koosh® Ball
Bull's Eye Bowl
Chicken, Salad, and Koosh® Ball Shuffle
Getting Things in Focus: Koosh® Ball Mania
Getting to Know You Differently
Koosh® Ball Review
Koosh®—Koosh®

"Laughable Lyrics"
Cell Phone Attack
Music Makes the Training Go Round

Learn/Line Star
Egg Drop Group
STAR Principle

Lemon Trophy
If Life Gives You Lemons . . .

Lightbulb Shaped Post-its®
I Appreciate My Job
Bright Idea

Magic Coloring Book
It's Your Choice
Magic Coloring Book

Magic Light Bulb
See the Light to the Power of Positive Thinking

Marble Run Construction Set
Marble Run

Meeting Minder
Appraising Performance

Mini Oscars
The Good Apple Award

MNEMONIC Monsters
Monster MNEMONIC Maker

Painter's Hats
Fun Caps Versus Boring Table Tents
The Hats We Wear
Your Supervisor Hat

Pick Up Sticks, Jumbo
Pick It Up!

Pleasure Island Game Board
Pleasure Island Review

Prize Wheel

Team Challenge
Wheel of Consequences

Prizes, Classroom Prize Pack

Brainstorming 101
Crazy, Cool, Creative Closing
Creative Idea Generation
Goal-Setter Game
Money for Trivia
Non-Trash, Trash Can
Organizational Lingo Crossword Puzzle
Prize Roulette
Stick 'em Up Review
The Organic Quiz Show
Toys Are Us
Wanna Deal or Not?

Puzzle Power CD

Money for Trivia
Organizational Lingo Crossword Puzzle

Raffle Tickets

Ticket Mixer to Assign Groups

Reward Coins

High Five

Scratch and See Tickets

Is the Answer Correct?
Share, Scratch, and Win

Shaker Collection, Handshakers

Brainstorming 101
Change That Tune
Constructive Feedback Key Pointers
Shake It Icebreaker

Slim-line Answer Boards

(See Answer Boards)

Slinky Jrs

Opposite Brains

Stopwatch

Alphabet Review
Brainstorming Boost
Bull's Eye Bowl
By the Numbers
Chicken, Salad, and Koosh® Ball Shuffle
Organizational Lingo Crossword Puzzle
Press Conference
Spinning the Organizational Culture

Super Forts

Super Forts for Super Teams

Table Tents (Write-On, Wipe-Off)
Name Tents Teams
Tents Tell All—Myriad Uses for Table Tents
You're a Superhero

Thumball™
Alphabet Review
More Than Meets the Eye

Time Timer Clock
Alphabet Review
Bull's Eye Bowl
Contract Relay
Pleasure Island Review
Spaghetti and Gum Drops

TimerTools™
Appraising Performance: A Home Building Challenge
Contract Relay
Koosh®—Koosh®
Project Change Challenge
The Object of My Discussion

Time Tracker

Brainstorming Boost
Problem Solving Line Up
SNAP

Tingshas

Let's Return
Red Light, Green Light

Tip Taker/Suggestion Box

The Organic Quiz Show

Top Banana Trophy

Crazy, Cool, Creative Closing
The Good Apple Award

Treasure Chest
Share, Scratch, and Win
This Treasure is Me

"Tunes for Trainers"
Crazy, Cool, Creative Closing
Getting to Know You
Music Makes the Training Go Round
Skills on a Stick
Who's on My Team?

Turn 'n Learn Wheel
Press Conference
Prize Roulette
Spinning Discovery
Spinning the Organizational Culture
Wheel of Consequences

Vox Proxy Software
Cell Phone Attack

Whaddaya Know?™ Game Board
Waddaya Know?™

Whiteboard on a Stick
Continuous Learning Review
Getting to Know You Feud
I Appreciate My Job
Rapid-Fire Review
Stick 'em Up Review
Skills on a Stick
The Red and Black Game
Topic Walk
Wanna Deal or Not?
You're a Superhero

Who's First Gameshow Buzzer
Go for the Goal: Influencing Performance to
    Reduce Shortage
Squeeze Play Course Review
Whaddaya Know?

Write-on Wipe-off Name Cards (see Table Tents)

Contributors

Yara Almodovar
Two Men And A Truck
25 Van Zant Street
Norwalk, CT 06855
203-831-9300
Email: info0071@twomenandatruck.com
Email: yaraa0071@us.
    twomenandatruck.com
URL: www.twomenandatruck.com

Victoria Arellano
ESCO Corporation
Senior OD Specialist
Organizational Development
2141 NW 25th Avenue
Portland, OR 97210
503-778-6586
Email: victoria.arellano@escocorp.com

Kristin J. Arnold
Quality Process Consultants, Inc.
6589 Cypress Point Road
Alexandria, VA 22312
800-589-4733
Email: Kristin@ExtraordinaryTeam.com
URL: www.ExtraordinaryTeam.com

Halelly Azulay
TalentGrow
1719 Lorre Drive
Rockville, MD 20852
301-760-7179
Email: Halelly@talentgrow.com
URL: www.talentgrow.com

Elaine Biech
ebb associates inc
Box 8249
Norfolk, VA 23503
757-588-3939
Email: ebboffice@aol.com
URL: www.ebbweb.com

Ruby A. Bohannon
Learning and Development Consultant
860 Bitternut Drive
Coppell, TX 75019
972-870-6322
Email: bohannonR@hdvest.com
URL: www.hdvest.com

Sunny Bradford
Bradford Consulting Associates
PO Box 7132
Portland, ME 04112
207-878-2166
Email: sunford@earthlink.net

Dawn Brenner
Future Leaders Program Coordinator,
    Leadership York
39 East King Street
York, PA 17401
Email: dbrenner@leadershipyork.org
URL: www.leadershipyork.org

Kathy Cleveland Bull
N~Compass Consulting
919 Old Henderson Road
Columbus, OH 43220

614-324-5944
Email: kcb@ncompass-consulting.com
URL: www.ncompass-consulting.com

Patricia Burggraff
ADP
12250 E. Iliff Avenue
Aurora, CO 80011
303-369-1464
Email: patricia_burggraff@adp.com

Marcia A. Chambers, Ed.D.
Chambers Consulting Services, Inc.
3008 Leatherlips Trail
Dublin, OH 43017
614-798-1107
Email: drmaciii@aol.com

Carolyn E. Conway
Georgia Federal Credit Union
6705 Sugarloaf Parkway
Duluth, GA 30097
770-476-6415
Email: cconway@gfcuonline.org
URL: www.gfcuonline.org

Alexander W. Crispo
Purdue University
302 Wood Street
West Lafayette, IN 47909
765-494-5609
Email: alwc@purdue.edu

Carol A. Dawson, CIC, AIS, CISR
Personal Lines Learning and
    Performance Specialist
Nationwide Insurance
1100 Locust St DM 01 2026
Des Moines, IA 50391-2026
515-508-3158
Email: DAWSONC@nationwide.com

Amie Devero
The Devero Group
PO Box 320711
Tampa, FL 33679
813-835-0044
Email: Amie@TheDeveroGroup.com
URL: www.TheDeveroGroup.com

Lauri Devine
9855 S. 45th Place
Phoenix AZ 85044
602- 542-2419
Email: ldevine@azdes.gov

Mike Doctoroff
Trainer's Warehouse
89 Washington Avenue
Natick, MA 01760
800-299-3770
Email: Michael@trainerswarehouse
    .com
URL: www.trainerswarehouse.com

Amy Drennen
Yazaki North America
6300 Haggerty Road
Canton, MI 48239
734-983-1160
Email: amy.drennen@us.yazaki.com
URL: www.yazaki-na.com

Beth Ducker
National Education Manager
Hartford Steam Boiler Inspection &
    Insurance Company
820 Gessner, Suite 110
Houston, TX 77024
800-231-0907, ext. 43055
Email: Elizabeth_Ducker@HSB.com
URL: www.hsb.com

Jan Ferri-Reed, Ph.D.
KEYGroup®
1800 Sainte Claire Plaza
1121 Boyce Road
Pittsburgh, PA 15241
724-942-7900
Email: jferrireed@keygroupconsulting.com
URL: www.keygroupconsulting.com

Carrie Gendreau
The Training Connection
169 South Street
Littleton, NH 03561
603-444-0424
Email: trainconn@adelphia.net

Dennis E. Gilbert
Appreciative Strategies, LLC
2155 Warrensville Road
Montoursville, PA 17754
570-606-3780
Email: dennis@appreciativestrategies.com
URL: www.appreciativestrategies.com

Marci Goldshlack
Director of Corporate Training, OHRD
Philadelphia Workforce Development
    Corporation
1617 JFK Boulevard, Suite 1300
Philadelphia, PA 19102
215-963-3489
Email: mgoldshlack@pwdc.org
URL: www.pwdc.org

Leonard D. Goodstein, Ph.D.
Consulting Psychologist
4815 Foxhall Crescent, NW
Washington, DC 20007-1052
202-333-3134
Email: lendg@aol.com

Bruce Graham, CCDS
Vice President/Director-Career
    Development
Prudential New Jersey Properties
220 Davidson Avenue
Somerset, NJ 08873
732-627-8400, Ext. 338
Email: BruceGraham@PruNewJersey
    .com

Daniel Greene
ebb associates inc
1064 West Ocean View Avenue
Norfolk, VA 23503
757-588-3939
Email: danfgreene@aol.com

Cindy Lee Hall
CLI
722 West Ocean View Avenue
Norfolk, VA 23503
757-560-7400
Email: go2cli@yahoo.com
URL: cliadvantage.com

Diane Hamilton
Center for Organization Effectiveness
    and surveysbydesign.com
6515 Grand Teton Plaza, Suite 145
Madison, WI 53719
608-833-3332, ext. 22
Email: dhamilton@greatorganizations
    .com
URL: www.greatorganizations.com
URL: www.surveysbydesign.com

Dr. Lois B. Hart
Courageous Leadership Consortium
481 Claffey Drive
Polson, MT 59860

406-250-9860
Email: hart@montanasky.com
URL: www.courageousleadership.org

Amy Henderson
Henderson Training, Inc.
28770 Park Woodland Place
Santa Clarita, CA 91390
661-296-4490
Email: amy@hendersontraining.com
URL: www.hendersontraining.com

Cher Holton, Ph.D., CSP, CMC
The Holton Consulting Group, Inc.
1405 Autumn Ridge Drive
Durham. NC 27712
919-767-9620
Email: cher@holtonconsulting.com
URL: www.holtonconsulting.com

Cindy Huggett
128 Benedict Lane
Raleigh, NC 27614
919-349-4589
Email: chuggett@nc.rr.com
URL: www.home.nc.rr.com/chuggett

Sarah E. Hurst
Stewart & Stevenson LLC
581 Garden Oaks Boulevard
Houston. TX 77018
713-803-0716
Email: s.hurst@ssss.com

M.K. Key, Ph.D.
Key Associates
1857 Laurel Ridge
Nashville, TN 37215
615-665-1622 (phone/fax)
Email: keyassocs@mindspring.com
URL: http://www.mkkey.com

Lorraine Kohart
ebb associates inc
1064 West Ocean View Avenue
Norfolk, VA 23503
757-588-3939
Email: ebboffice@aol.com
URL: www.ebbweb.com

Michael Kroth
University of Idaho Boise
322 E. Front Street, Suite 440
Boise, ID 83702
208-364-9918
Email: mkroth@uidaho.edu

Susan Doctoroff Landay
Trainer's Warehouse
89 Washington Avenue
Natick, MA 01760
800-299-3770
Email: susan@trainerswarehouse
   .com
URL: www.trainerswarehouse.com

Karen Lawson
Lawson Consulting Group, Inc.
1365 Gwynedale Way
Lansdale, PA 19446
215-368-9465
Email: KLawson@LawsonCG.com
URL: www.LawsonCG.com

Stacy Lowman
SASA Partners
24140 Weldon Drive
Eustis, FL 32736
407-963-5536
Email: stacy.lowman@hughessupply
   .com
URL: www.sasapartners.com

Teri Lund
Strategic Assessment & Evaluation
   Associates
5015 SW Lodi Lane
Portland, OR 97221
503-244-3989
Email: Tlund_bls@msn.com

Linda S. Mills
Dynamic Communication Services
20 Worman Lane
Bernville, PA 19506
610-488-7010
Email: AhHaBook@aol.com
URL: www.theconsultantsforum.com/
   eckmills.htm

Ira J. Morrow
Lubin School of Business, Pace
   University
1 Pace Plaza
New York, NY 10038
212-618-6568
Email: imorrow@pace.edu

Edwin Mourino, Ph.D.
Lockheed Martin Corporation
12506 Lake Underhill Road, MP 143
Orlando, FL 32825
407-306-5218
Email: Edwin.l.mourino@lmco.com
Email: dredwinmourino@bellsouth
   .net

Terry Murray
Educational Studies Department
SUNY New Paltz
New Paltz, NY 12561
845-257-2828
Email: murrayt@newpaltz.edu

Mohandas Nair
A2 Kamdar Building
807, Gokhale Road (South)
Dadar, Mumbai – 400028
India
91-22-24226307
Email: mknair@vsnl.net
Email: nair_mohandas@hotmail.com

Niki Nichols
Stellar Associates
PO Box 628
Burnet, TX 78611
512-756-7065
Email: 8ganichols@earthlink.net

Holly M. O'Neill
Talking Business
620 Newport Center Drive,
   Suite 1100
Newport Beach, CA 92660
949-721-4160
Email: Holly@TalkingBusiness.net
URL: www.TalkingBusiness.net

David Piltz
The Learning Key®
1093 General Washington Memorial
   Boulevard
Washington Crossing, PA 18977
215-493-9641
Email: dpiltz@thelearningkey.com
URL: www.thelearningkey.com

Robert C. Preziosi
Preziosi Partners, Inc.
2259 South University Drive
Suite 244
Davie, FL 33314
954-915-0102

Kitty Preziosi
Preziosi Partners, Inc.
2259 South University Drive
Suite 244
Davie, FL 33314
954-915-0102

Dr. Linda M. Raudenbush
U.S. Department of Agriculture (NASS)
7201 Kindler Road
Columbia, MD 21046
410-381-2747
Email: lraudenbush@nass.usda.gov

Harriet Rifkin
Rifkin & Associates, LLC
17 Roosevelt Street
Albany, NY 12206
518-956-0511
Email: harriet@rifkin-associates.com
URL: www.rifkin-associates.com

Travis L. Russ, Ph.D.
Rutgers University
1718 P Street, NW, Suite L17
Washington, DC 20036
917-478-3572
Email: truss@scils.rutgers.edu

Jeffrey Russell
Russell Consulting, Inc.
1134 Winston Drive
Madison, WI 53711-3161
608-274-4482
Email: RCI@RussellConsultingInc.com
URL: www.RussellConsultingInc.com

Linda Russell
Russell Consulting, Inc.
1134 Winston Drive

Madison, WI 53711-3161
608-274-4482
Email: RCI@RussellConsultingInc.com
URL: www.RussellConsultingInc.com

Lou Russell
Russell Martin & Associates
6329 Rucker Road, Suite E
Indianapolis, IN 46220
317-475-9311
Email: lou@russellmartin.com
URL: www.russellmartin.com
URL: www.lourussell.com
URL: www.lplusearn.com

Jan M. Schmuckler, Ph.D.
3921 Burckhalter Avenue
Oakland, CA 94605
510-562-0626
Email: jan@lignumvitae.com
URL: www.janconsults.com

Sion Segal, Ph.D.
The Protea Group, LLC
PO Box 30029
Elkins Park, PA 19027
215-280-0588
Email: ssegal@theproteagroup.net
URL: www.theproteagroup.net

Elizabeth A. Smith, Ph.D.
Community Medical Foundation for
   Patient Safety
6800 West Loop South, Suite 190
Bellaire, TX 77401
832-778-7777
Fax: 281-920-1118
Email: smithce@flash.net
URL: www.communityofcompetence
   .com

Steve Sugar
The Game Group
10320 Kettledrum Court
Ellicott City, MD 21042
Email: info@thegamegroup.com
URL: www.thegamegroup.com

Marjorie Treu
Team Fusion LLC
3213 N. 104th Street
Wauwatosa, WI 53222
414-477-6655
Email: marjorie@teamfusion.net
URL: www.teamfusion.net

Rodney C. Vandeveer
Purdue University
302 Wood Street, Young Hall Room
  438
West Lafayette, IN 47909
765-494-6804
Email: vandeveer@purdue.edu
URL: vantechtraining.com

**Bruce G. Waguespack, Ph.D.,
  CPLP**
The University of Southern Mississippi
730 East Beach Boulevard
Long Beach, MS 39560
225-938-9143
Email: bruce.waguespack@usm.edu
URL: www.usm.edu/wlpi

Nicole Walton
Corporate Trainer III
University of Paychex
911 Panorama Trail South
Rochester, NY 14625
585-383-3104
Email: nwalton@paychex.com

Edie West
8611 Woodwren Lane
Fairfax Station, VA 22039
703-643-9816
Email: ediewest@erols.com
Email: ediewest@aol.com

Carson Key Whitehead
1857 Laurel Ridge
Nashville, TN 37215
615-218-6049

Cris Wildermuth
Diversity Effectiveness Group, LLC
311 Marcella Lane
Cridersville, OH 45806
419-645-6379
Email: cris@theeffectivenessgroup.com

Randy Woodward
Ho-Chunk Casino
S3214 Highway 12
Baraboo, WI 53913
608-356-6210 x 2457
Email: RWoodward@ho-chunk.com
URL: www.ho-chunk.com

Marty Yopp
University of Idaho Boise
322 E. Front Street, Suite 440
Boise, ID 83702
208-364-9918
Email: myopp@uidaho.edu

Devora Zack, MBA
Only Connect Consulting, Inc.
7806 Ivymount Terrace
Potomac, MD 20854
301-765-6262
Email: dzack@onlyconnectconsulting.com
URL: www.onlyconnectconsulting.com

Yvette Zgonc
Educational Consultant
2610 Manorwood Drive
Melbourne, FL 32901
301-725-6688
Email: yzgonc@aol.com

Johanna Zitto, CPT
JZ Consulting and Training Inc.
1243 Sequoia Road
Cherry Hill, NJ 08003-2652
856-428-0947
Email: jzcat@comcast.net
URL: www.jzcat.com

About the Editor

Elaine Biech is president and managing principal of ebb associates inc, a firm that helps organizations work through large-scale change. Elaine has been in the training and consulting field for twenty-five years and is the author or editor of dozens of books, including *Training for Dummies, The Business of Consulting* (2nd ed.), *Thriving Through Change,* and *90 World-Class Activities by 90 World-Class Trainers*. A long-time volunteer for ASTD, she has served on ASTD's National Board of Directors and was the recipient of the 1992 ASTD Torch Award, the 2004 ASTD Volunteer Staff Partnership Award, and the 2006 ASTD Gordon M. Bliss Memorial Award. Elaine was also the recipient of the 1995 Wisconsin Women Entrepreneur's Mentor of the year Award. She currently is the editor of the prestigious Pfeiffer Training and Consulting *Annuals*. You may reach her at ebboffice@aol.com or 757.588.3939.

Pfeiffer Publications Guide

This guide is designed to familiarize you with the various types of Pfeiffer publications. The formats section describes the various types of products that we publish; the methodologies section describes the many different ways that content might be provided within a product. We also provide a list of the topic areas in which we publish.

FORMATS

In addition to its extensive book-publishing program, Pfeiffer offers content in an array of formats, from fieldbooks for the practitioner to complete, ready-to-use training packages that support group learning.

FIELDBOOK Designed to provide information and guidance to practitioners in the midst of action. Most fieldbooks are companions to another, sometimes earlier, work, from which its ideas are derived; the fieldbook makes practical what was theoretical in the original text. Fieldbooks can certainly be read from cover to cover. More likely, though, you'll find yourself bouncing around following a particular theme, or dipping in as the mood, and the situation, dictate.

HANDBOOK A contributed volume of work on a single topic, comprising an eclectic mix of ideas, case studies, and best practices sourced by practitioners and experts in the field.

An editor or team of editors usually is appointed to seek out contributors and to evaluate content for relevance to the topic. Think of a handbook not as a ready-to-eat meal, but as a cookbook of ingredients that enables you to create the most fitting experience for the occasion.

RESOURCE Materials designed to support group learning. They come in many forms: a complete, ready-to-use exercise (such as a game); a comprehensive resource on one topic (such as conflict management) containing a variety of methods and approaches; or a collection of like-minded activities (such as icebreakers) on multiple subjects and situations.

TRAINING PACKAGE An entire, ready-to-use learning program that focuses on a particular topic or skill. All packages comprise a guide for the facilitator/trainer and a workbook for the participants. Some packages are supported with additional media—such as video—or learning aids, instruments, or other devices to help participants understand concepts or practice and develop skills.

- *Facilitator/trainer's guide* Contains an introduction to the program, advice on how to organize and facilitate the learning event, and step-by-step instructor notes. The guide also contains copies of presentation materials—handouts, presentations, and overhead designs, for example—used in the program.

- *Participant's workbook* Contains exercises and reading materials that support the learning goal and serves as a valuable reference and support guide for participants in the weeks and months that follow the learning event. Typically, each participant will require his or her own workbook.

ELECTRONIC CD-ROMs and web-based products transform static Pfeiffer content into dynamic, interactive experiences. Designed to take advantage of the searchability, automation, and ease-of-use that technology provides, our e-products bring convenience and immediate accessibility to your workspace.

METHODOLOGIES

CASE STUDY A presentation, in narrative form, of an actual event that has occurred inside an organization. Case studies are not prescriptive, nor are they used to prove a point; they are designed to develop critical analysis and decision-making skills. A case study has a specific time frame, specifies a sequence of events, is narrative in structure, and contains a plot structure—an issue (what should be/have been done?). Use case studies when the goal is to enable participants to apply previously learned theories to the circumstances in the case, decide what is pertinent, identify the real issues, decide what should have been done, and develop a plan of action.

ENERGIZER A short activity that develops readiness for the next session or learning event. Energizers are most commonly used after a break or lunch to stimulate or refocus the group. Many involve some form of physical activity, so they are a useful way to counter post-lunch lethargy. Other uses include transitioning from one topic to another, where "mental" distancing is important.

EXPERIENTIAL LEARNING ACTIVITY (ELA) A facilitator-led intervention that moves participants through the learning cycle from experience to application (also known as a Structured Experience). ELAs are carefully thought-out designs in which there is a definite learning purpose and intended outcome. Each step—everything that participants do during the activity—facilitates the accomplishment of the stated goal. Each ELA includes complete instructions for facilitating the intervention and a clear statement of goals, suggested group size and timing, materials required, an explanation of the process, and, where appropriate, possible variations to the activity. (For more detail on Experiential Learning Activities, see the Introduction to the *Reference Guide to Handbooks and Annuals*, 1999 edition, Pfeiffer, San Francisco.)

GAME A group activity that has the purpose of fostering team spirit and togetherness in addition to the achievement of a pre-stated goal. Usually contrived—undertaking a desert expedition, for example—this type of learning method offers an engaging means for participants to demonstrate and practice business and interpersonal skills. Games are effective for team building and personal development mainly because the goal is subordinate to the process—the means through which participants reach decisions, collaborate, communicate, and generate trust and understanding. Games often engage teams in "friendly" competition.

ICEBREAKER   A (usually) short activity designed to help participants overcome initial anxiety in a training session and/or to acquaint the participants with one another. An icebreaker can be a fun activity or can be tied to specific topics or training goals. While a useful tool in itself, the icebreaker comes into its own in situations where tension or resistance exists within a group.

INSTRUMENT   A device used to assess, appraise, evaluate, describe, classify, and summarize various aspects of human behavior. The term used to describe an instrument depends primarily on its format and purpose. These terms include survey, questionnaire, inventory, diagnostic, survey, and poll. Some uses of instruments include providing instrumental feedback to group members, studying here-and-now processes or functioning within a group, manipulating group composition, and evaluating outcomes of training and other interventions.

Instruments are popular in the training and HR field because, in general, more growth can occur if an individual is provided with a method for focusing specifically on his or her own behavior. Instruments also are used to obtain information that will serve as a basis for change and to assist in workforce planning efforts.

Paper-and-pencil tests still dominate the instrument landscape with a typical package comprising a facilitator's guide, which offers advice on administering the instrument and interpreting the collected data, and an initial set of instruments. Additional instruments are available separately. Pfeiffer, though, is investing heavily in e-instruments. Electronic instrumentation provides effortless distribution and, for larger groups particularly, offers advantages over paper-and-pencil tests in the time it takes to analyze data and provide feedback.

LECTURETTE   A short talk that provides an explanation of a principle, model, or process that is pertinent to the participants' current learning needs. A lecturette is intended to establish a common language bond between the trainer and the participants by providing a mutual frame of reference. Use a lecturette as an introduction to a group activity or event, as an interjection during an event, or as a handout.

MODEL   A graphic depiction of a system or process and the relationship among its elements. Models provide a frame of reference and something more tangible, and more easily remembered, than a verbal explanation. They also give participants something to "go on," enabling them to track their own progress as they experience the dynamics, processes, and relationships being depicted in the model.

ROLE PLAY A technique in which people assume a role in a situation/ scenario: a customer service rep in an angry-customer exchange, for example. The way in which the role is approached is then discussed and feedback is offered. The role play is often repeated using a different approach and/or incorporating changes made based on feedback received. In other words, role playing is a spontaneous interaction involving realistic behavior under artificial (and safe) conditions.

SIMULATION A methodology for understanding the interrelationships among components of a system or process. Simulations differ from games in that they test or use a model that depicts or mirrors some aspect of reality in form, if not necessarily in content. Learning occurs by studying the effects of change on one or more factors of the model. Simulations are commonly used to test hypotheses about what happens in a system—often referred to as "what if?" analysis—or to examine best-case/worst-case scenarios.

THEORY A presentation of an idea from a conjectural perspective. Theories are useful because they encourage us to examine behavior and phenomena through a different lens.

TOPICS

The twin goals of providing effective and practical solutions for workforce training and organization development and meeting the educational needs of training and human resource professionals shape Pfeiffer's publishing program. Core topics include the following:

Leadership & Management

Communication & Presentation

Coaching & Mentoring

Training & Development

e-Learning

Teams & Collaboration

OD & Strategic Planning

Human Resources

Consulting